Programming
in
BASIC-PLUS

315-2
2

Programming in BASIC-PLUS

Jasper J. Sawatzky
Professor, Business Information Systems
Humboldt State University

Shu-Jen Chen
Associate Professor, Management Science
California State University, Fullerton

John Wiley & Sons
New York · Chichester · Brisbane · Toronto

Library of Congress Cataloging in Publication Data:

Sawatzky, Jasper J
    Programming in BASIC-PLUS.

Includes index.
    1. BASIC-PLUS (Computer program language) I. Chen,
Shu-Jen, II. Title.
QA76.73.B3S3   001.64′24   80-27869
ISBN 0-471-07729-1

Printed in the United States of America
10 9 8 7 6 5 4 3 2 1

Preface

This text was written to enable students to experience the excitement of using a computer. More specifically it is designed to introduce students to computers by learning the BASIC language; it is also designed to provide the essentials for students interested in developing sound programming skills. The text is arranged so that it can be used for a general introductory course or for a more technical applications-oriented program.

Learning the BASIC language is important to the understanding of the logic of computers—a necessity in this computer age. BASIC is used in many practical applications, particularly in small organizations. BASIC has become the most widely used teaching language because it is easy to learn; yet, it is a powerful language. Most of today's low-cost microcomputers use the BASIC language.

This text reflects an effort to provide a serious treatment of a popular version of BASIC—BASIC-PLUS. Sound structured programming principles are stressed so that students planning to continue their study of languages and computer systems will have the background to develop well-organized software.

We have used Digital Equipment's version of BASIC-PLUS and BASIC-PLUS-2 exclusively. BASIC-PLUS is one of the most widely used versions of BASIC in the educational environment. BASIC-PLUS is similar to other versions of BASIC; thus, this text can be used with systems supporting different versions of the language. We have deliberately avoided the approach commonly used in texts which attempt to describe several different versions of BASIC when programs are explained. We have found that students become confused when studying materials that attempt to explain more than one version of a computer language.

The text includes more content than can be covered in a normal term. Thus it provides flexibility to the instructor in selecting topics appropriate for a specific course. Some instructors will find that the first 10 chapters will provide adequate treatment for a course. For courses of a technical nature, Section III, File Editing and Processing, provides content specifically designed to cover these topics in the PDP-11 environment. For the general education or introductory course, Chapter 9, Functions and Subroutines, may be omitted and Chapter 10, Character Strings, can be included since the content of these chapters is independent.

The pedagogical objective of this text is to develop students' programming proficiency in a progressive manner. A minimal mathematical background is assumed. We believe the student should interact with the computer with the first assignment.

Each chapter begins with summary statements of the content to be covered. The format of each statement introduced is listed, followed by a series of examples that illustrate how the statement can be used. A summary program incorporating the features of the statements presented is listed and explained. Terms introduced in the chapter are defined at the end of each chapter. A large selection of problems of varying difficulty are included.

The text is organized into three sections:

Section I provides coverage of a minimum set of BASIC-PLUS instructions. Chapter 1 includes a short introduction to the language and the PRINT, END, and REMARK statements. A special assignment at the end of this chapter provides the necessary practice in logging on and off the system, coding simple PRINT statements, listing and running a program, and saving programs on disk. Students begin the course using the computer terminal immediately.

Chapter 2 explains variables and constants, the assignment statement, and introduces students to loops and counters. Our experience in teaching BASIC is that including simple conditional statements early in the course, as we do in this chapter, is highly motivating to students. Problem assignments can be more realistic when simple conditional statements are included.

Chapter 3 covers the READ, DATA, INPUT, and RESTORE statements. Also included are additional concepts related to conditional statements. Chapter 4 introduces flowchart symbols and flowcharting as a logical toolinproblem solving. Conditional statements are explored in greater depth. The FOR. . .NEXT loop structure is introduced.

Section II, Structured Programming and Applications in BASIC-PLUS, covers a broad range of topics but focuses on the importance of structured program design. Chapter 5 provides logical problem-solving approaches to debugging programs so that students understand methods of locating errors, particularly logic errors.

Formatting output approaches in BASIC-PLUS are explained in Chapter 6. Some differences between BASIC-PLUS and other language versions appear in this chapter. Single and double subscripts are explained through numerous examples in Chapter 7. The use of the EXTEND mode for creating meaningful variable names is introduced.

The essentials of structured programming with emphasis on program documentation are thoroughly explained in Chapter 8. Chapter 9 covers both the standard built-in BASIC functions, explains user-defined functions, and develops approaches for using subroutines. Character strings and various built-in functions for manipulating strings are explained in Chapter 10.

Chapters 11 and 12 are technical chapters that presume additional mathematical background and cover topics on matrix manipulation, multiple line functions, subprograms, and error-handling routines.

Section III covers file editing and processing in the BASIC-PLUS environment. This is a particularly valuable section in the text since students are given clear examples on using the Text Editor, file processing, and batch processing.

We thank our teaching colleagues who have provided ideas for improving the content of the manuscript and who have tested some of the teaching approaches in their own classes. Particular appreciation goes to our spouses, Rose and Kang-Shen, for their encouragement and sympathy during the development of this text.

Jasper J. Sawatzky
Shu-Jen Chen

Contents

SECTION III FILE EDITING AND PROCESSING IN BASIC-PLUS

Appendixes

I
Introduction to BASIC-PLUS

Chapter 1
Introduction to Programming

Objectives   You will learn:

The meaning of programming.

About the BASIC-PLUS language.

To read a BASIC program using PRINT and END statements.

To use a computer terminal.

To use the REMARK statement.

Computers are information processing machines. Computers can be programmed to do mathematical computations, control a flight to the moon, compute your income tax, and perform a wide variety of other tasks. Since the computer is a machine, it must be given detailed instructions in order to perform an information processing task.

1.1 PROGRAMMING

Programming is the process of preparing instructions that can be "understood" by a computer. In other words, a BASIC program is a series of instructions written by humans that can be translated into machine language. These instructions to the computer must be placed in a logical order, since the computer is designed to follow instructions step by step. Instructions to the computer in a program are usually given in the form of statements. These statements must conform to the rules of the computer language that is being used.

1.2 THE BASIC-PLUS LANGUAGE

There are many computer languages that have been developed since computers were invented. These languages have evolved over the years because computer technology has advanced so rapidly that more sophisticated instructions are possible.

BASIC is an acronym for "Beginners All-purpose Symbolic Instruction Code." BASIC was developed to make computer programming easier to learn. It is considered to be a high-level language, since it does not require technical knowledge about computers. The BASIC-PLUS version evolved from standard Dartmouth BASIC. This book uses a version of BASIC-PLUS introduced in 1971 specifically for the PDP-11 series of computers manufactured by Digital Equipment Corporation. BASIC-PLUS is a powerful version of the BASIC language; yet, even though there are differences in the many forms of BASIC, learning BASIC-PLUS is valuable for using other computers including microcomputers, such as the TRS-80, PET, and APPLE.

You can enter BASIC statements on a terminal connected to a computer where your instructions will be interpreted, and your program will produce the answers you need. The results of your BASIC instructions, called output, will appear on the same terminal on which you entered your program. Two common types of terminals, called I/O devices, are a video-type terminal, the CRT—cathode ray tube, and a typewriter-type device which has paper inserted in it. A common typewriter-type terminal is the DECwriter shown in Figure 1-1. The CRT is more commonly used because it has fewer moving parts and a picture screen where all input and output appears (See Figure 1-2).

Figure 1-1 A Printing Terminal

Figure 1-2 A CRT Terminal

As you key in your instructions to the computer on the terminal, your instructions will appear on the screen or paper precisely as you entered them. This enables you, the programmer, to edit and make corrections in the event they are needed. Interaction using a terminal connected to a computer also allows special computer program instructions to signal you when you key in statements that are not "understood" by the computer. Used in this way, BASIC-PLUS is operating in a timesharing mode—that is, you are using the computer to solve problems together with other users. There may be 40 or more other users also using the same computer to solve problems for them at the same time that you are entering instructions on your terminal. The term, timesharing, is used to describe multiple use of a computer designed for this purpose. Special operating and hardware systems handle many users so that one has the illusion that they are the only person using the computer. A timesharing computer can perform operations so rapidly that the user may not experience noticeable pauses or delays in obtaining responses to instructions. When the computer system is being used by large numbers of programmers, however, there may be delays and pauses due to the load placed on the system. Figure 1-3 shows a sketch of an interactive computer system.

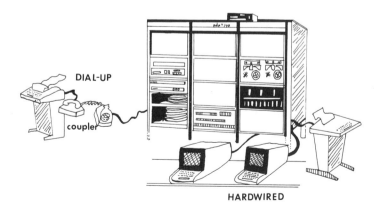

Figure 1-3 An Interactive Timesharing Computer System

1.3 A BASIC PROGRAM USING PRINT AND END STATEMENTS

Let's take a look at a short BASIC program and see what it does.

Example 1.1

```
10      PRINT 'A PROGRAM TO COMPUTE 3 VALUES'
20      PRINT 10 + 20, 8 * 9, 100/25
30      PRINT 'PROGRAM BY JOHN K. HENRY'
40      END

A PROGRAM TO COMPUTE 3 VALUES
  30          72              4
PROGRAM BY JOHN K. HENRY
```

The numbers for each of the BASIC instructions in Example 1.1 are used to ensure that a logical sequence is followed by the computer when this program is run. Note that there is room for additional statements to be inserted between each statement since statement numbers (commonly called line numbers) are assigned in increments of ten. Line numbers can be assigned any integer between 1 and 32767. The word PRINT is a special word that must be used whenever we wish to have words, numbers, or other symbols printed or appear on the terminal. The use of quotation marks, either single (') or double ("), signals the computer that we want the symbols appearing between the quotes to appear in output exactly as we have arranged that line. Statement 10

> 10   PRINT 'A PROGRAM TO COMPUTE 3 VALUES'

produces the output line

> A PROGRAM TO COMPUTE 3 VALUES

Note that the quotes do not appear in output, but they are needed as part of statement 10 in order to have the line printed as it was keyed.

Statement 20 instructs the computer to print the results of the arithmetic operations specified after the word, PRINT,

> 20   PRINT 10 + 20, 8 * 9, 100/25

The second line of output in example 1.1 is printed as

> 30   72   4

The computer performs the arithmetic operation in statement 20 until it detects a comma; then it combines 10 and 20 for the sum of 30. The second operation results in the multiplication of 8 times 9 (the asterisk is the signal to multiply). The third operation results in 100 being divided by 25 with only the quotient printed. Note that in statement 20 no quotes were placed around the numbers and symbols following PRINT. Had quotes been placed before and after these symbols, they would have appeared exactly as keyed, and no computation would have occurred. Statement 30 functions in the same way as statement 10. Statement 40 is an END statement that terminates further execution of the program; thus, it should be the last statement in the program.

1.4 USING A COMPUTER TERMINAL

Procedures for using computer terminals vary depending on the types of hardware and supporting programs used. The following example illustrates a log-in procedure, a short program, and log-out procedures. The system used is Digital Equipment Corporation's PDP 11/70 (RSTS).[1] After switching on the CRT power switch, press the return key (CR) and type HELLO. Now let's examine the following printout of the steps involved in using a computer terminal and running a program:

Example 1.2

```
HELLO

RSTS V06C-03 CSU Fullerton   Job 11   KB54   11-Jul-80   09:12 AM
#90,199
Password: _____


        Summer weekend hours for the Computer Center
                are from 10:00am to 6:00pm.




Ready

NEW
New file name--PROB2

Ready

10        REM SAMPLE PROBLEM 2
20        PRINT 'THE VALUE OF 16 CUBED IS'; 16**3
90        END
RUN
PROB2    09:13 AM        11-Jul-80
THE VALUE OF 16 CUBED IS 4096

Ready

BYE
Confirm? E
```

The underlined words and numbers are keyed in by the user. Note that a # sign appears, and the user is required to supply an account number that has been assigned to him by the instructor. The word PASSWORD appears on the screen, and the user usually is required to furnish a six-character password that has also been assigned to him. Note that when the password is keyed in by the user that it does not appear. This is for the user's security so that other individuals cannot use the password and thereby gain access to another user's programs. The next series of statements shown on the CRT (if any appear) merely are informative and will vary with each installation. When the word READY appears, the user who is creating a new program usually wishes to identify it in some way so the word NEW is keyed in by the user. The user then keys in a file name of up to six characters in length that describes the program in some meaningful way. In this example, the file name is PROB2. After the word READY appears, the user can begin keying in statements.

---

[1] Log-in procedures vary with installation. Some installations have dial-up terminals which require dialing a number, placing a coupler on the modem, and responding to an inquiry with an account number and a password.

1.5 THE REMARK STATEMENT

Statement 10 is a REMARK statement that can be used by the programmer to make explanatory statements in the program that will not appear in the printed output. REMARK is abbreviated by REM. In statement 20, a PRINT statement, a descriptive statement enclosed by quotes is inserted before an arithmetic operation is performed. Once the END statement is keyed in, the program is ready to RUN. The word RUN is keyed in by the user. The computer prints out a header line, indicating the name of the program, the time it was run, and the current date followed by the output generated by statement 20. If the user does not wish to continue use of the terminal, he may log-off by keying in BYE. The word CONFIRM will appear on the screen, and the user can respond by keying in an "F" (Note that there are other responses to CONFIRM that also can be used, such as N. Logoff is terminated, but the user is not logged off, and the system replies READY).

1.6 HOW TO SAVE YOUR PROGRAM

In order to retain your program for future use or revisions, it is necessary to have identified a program with a specific name no longer than six characters. Once you have keyed in a program on a terminal, it is necessary to type the word, SAVE, following the END statement of the program.[2] In the event you make changes in your program at a later time, be sure to save the revised program statements by typing the word, REPLACE; otherwise, the changes you have made will not be stored on the disk file. Once you have saved a program, it can be retrieved later by typing OLD following log-in procedures.

Word List

BASIC. A programming language that allows the user to give instructions in the form of statements which are executed by the computer.

CRT. An I/O device using a typewriter form of keyboard with a video screen to display data that is keyed into the computer.

I/O. A device that handles both input and output of data.

Interactive system. A computer system connected to some I/O device that provides immediate response when interrogated by a user.

Operating system. Computer programs that control computer hardware and take care of the many details required to run and store programs.

Programming. The process of preparing a logical sequence of instructions that can be followed by a computer.

Statements. Numbered instructions that follow specific requirements of a computer language.

Timesharing. A computer system that handles multiple users on an interactive basis.

INTRODUCTORY ASSIGNMENT

Objectives   To become familiar with a CRT Terminal and RSTS/E system commands—NEW, OLD, LIST, RUN, SAVE, CAT, REPLACE, UNSAVE.

---

[2] Procedures for saving programs will vary with different systems.

Instructions   Following are instructions that will provide you with practice in using some system commands on the RSTS/E system. Print out those statements that have instructions for producing a hard copy.

> CR stands for
> carriage return

1. LOG ON to the system — Use Local Procedures

2. Type NEW XXX   CR   (XXX are your initials)

3. Type the following BASIC program:
    10 PRINT "THIS IS MY FIRST BASIC PROGRAM"
    100 END

4. Type LIST   CR   (what is the purpose of LIST?)

5. Type RUN   CR   (what is the purpose of RUN?)

6. Type RUNNH   CR   (what is different about this command?)

7. Type SAVE   CR   (note that this saves your program for later use)

8. Type CAT   CR   (what is the purpose of CAT?)

9. Type NEW TEST   CR   (TEST is the name of a program)

10. Type LIST   CR   (Explain why the response to LIST is different from #4 above)

11. Type LISTNH   CR   (what is the function of NH?)

12. Type OLD XXX   CR   (remember XXX are your initials used in #2 above)

13. Type LIST   CR   (explain why the response is different than #10 above)

14. Type 20   PRINT "ZZZZZZ"   CR   (where the Z's stand for your name)

15. Type LIST   CR   (has the program changed?)

16. Type 20   PRINT "LLLLL"   CR   (where the L's stand for only your last name)

17. Type LIST   CR   (explain the change in your program)

18. Type SAVE   CR   (do you get an error message? Why?)

19. Type REPLACE   CR   (this command stores and saves statement 20)

20. Type CAT   CR   (notice what appears)

21. Print your revised program XXX on the printer by switching on the print key on your terminal and the power on switch on the slave printer.
    Type LIST   CR
          RUN   CR
    Now switch off the terminal print key by depressing it; remove your output from the printer.

22. Type UNSAVE XXX   CR   (this erases your program from storage)

23. Type CAT   CR   (explain what happens)

24. Log off system using BYE Y option. Notice how little CPU time you have used as opposed to how much elapsed time (wall clock time) you have used.

Note: See Appendix H for more details on using the RSTS SYSTEM.

PROBLEMS

1. Explain the purpose of statements in the BASIC language.

2. What is the purpose of statement numbers? How should statement numbers be organized?

3. Why is BASIC used as a computer language?

4. What is the key difference between a CRT and a printing terminal?

5. What is the purpose of having a timesharing system?

6. Determine specific procedures you will need to follow to use the computer terminals available to you.

7. Write (code) a program in BASIC that will compute and print the sum of the following values:

$$10 + 15 + 20$$

8. Write additional statements for the program in problem 7 above that will produce output as follows:

PROGRAM BY (your name)

TOTAL IS 45

9. If a terminal is available, try keying in and running the program you coded in problem 8.

10. Write a BASIC program to print a short autobiography; limit the length to no more than 20 statements.

Chapter 2
Your First Program in BASIC

Objectives You will learn:

Methods of correcting keying errors.

Types of variables and constants.

The assignment statement—LET.

The output statement—PRINT.

The purpose of loops and counters.

To write you own BASIC program using conditional statements.

You have been exposed to the PRINT statement in BASIC which is used to produce different types of output. You also have had some experience in using a computer terminal. With that background, we can proceed to learn more about the language, BASIC. First, let's look at some problems relating to keying in incorrect characters or instructions.

2.1 CORRECTING INPUT ERRORS

Typing errors invariably cause serious problems when they are made on the computer terminal. When the number 10 is typed on the terminal and the letter "O" is typed instead of the zero, the computer will print an error message. For example:

$$10 \quad PRINT \ 2O * 2.66$$

This statement will produce the error message, SYNTAX ERROR AT LINE 10, due to the fact that the zero in the number 20 was typed as a capital "O." To correct this error, the user needs to retype the statement making sure that the same statement number is used. In this way, the incorrect statement will be replaced with the revised statement. If the error is detected before the return key is typed while typing a statement, the rub-out key[1] can be used to backspace to the character where the error was made, and the correct character can be typed. To eliminate a statement from a program, just type the statement number that is to be deleted and hit the carriage return key. This procedure effectively eliminates that statement from the program. In the event that a statement is accidentally left out of a program, that statement can be typed at the end of the program. It is important to have a statement number that will place the statement in the proper location in the program. For example, if you wanted an additional PRINT statement following statement 40 but before statement 50, then the added statement should be given a number, such as 42, so that it would be executed after statement 40.

2.2 VARIABLES AND CONSTANTS

A constant is a value. For example, the number, 10, is a '10' and does not change to another value. Constants may be integers (whole numbers) or reals (fractional numbers). Examples of integers are:

---

[1] Some CRTs have a DEL key. Do not use the BACKSPACE key to erase characters.

$$25 \qquad -400 \qquad 0 \qquad 1224$$

Examples of reals in decimal fractions are:

$$-22.667 \qquad 0.09 \qquad 19.80 \qquad 1.59$$

Examples of illegal reals are:

$$1,000.99 \qquad \$25.20 \qquad 1/4 \qquad 17\%$$

Presently, most BASIC versions print out six significant digits in output. When the results of an arithmetic operation are greater than six significant digits, the output is printed in scientific notation. For example, if you accumulate a total of 1234567890, the printed output from a BASIC program would probably appear as .123457E 10. The ten-digit number of 1234567890 is shown in six significant digits rounded, and the location of the decimal point is considered to be 10 places to the right of the printed decimal. Other examples of scientific notation are:

$$.123456E - 3 = .000123456 \quad - .999999E \ 7 = -9999990 \quad - .123456E - 3 = -.000123456$$

Note that a value is negative only when the minus sign appears *before* the value. The minus sign following the E indicates the decimal point is located three places to the left of the printed decimal point.

Variables are symbols that hold values. Variables are locations or addresses in the memory of the computer. Since variables represent locations, different values can be stored at these locations. For example, the values of $10 * 20$ can be stored in a location called T. T, which can represent some total, is a location where the sum of 10 added to 20 can be kept. In the BASIC language, numeric variables can be designated by any one of the 26 letters of the alphabet or by a letter with any one of the 10 decimal digits placed immediately following the letter. Examples of variables[2] in BASIC are:

$$A \qquad B1 \qquad A4 \qquad X \qquad Y2$$

It is possible to use longer and more meaningful variable names in BASIC by using the EX-TEND statement, which is explained in Chapter 7. Special integer variable names also can be used; examples of these will be given later.

You have already used some of the math symbols for computational purposes. Following is a summary of math symbols used in BASIC:

Addition   +

Subtraction   −

Multiplication   *

Division   /

Raising to a power ** or $^\wedge$ or ↑

The precedence of operations is (1) raising to a power; (2) division and/or multiplication working from left to right; (3) addition and/or subtraction working left to right. When parentheses are used, calculations of the values within the parentheses are made first.[3]

---

[2] Variables and constants are stored internally as floating point numbers. It is possible to store numbers in integer variable or constant form by placing a % following the variable name or constant which saves space in memory and results in faster computations as: A%   B1%

[3] $5 + 4 + 4/2 = 11$ (division has precedence)
   $(5 + 3 + 4)/2 = 6$ (parentheses have precedence)
   $(5 + 3 + 4)/2**2 = 3$ (raising to a power precedes division)

Following is a program that illustrates the sequence of arithmetic computations performed on a computer:

Example 2.1

```
10       REM EVALUATION OF ARITHMETIC EXPRESSIONS
20       PRINT 'MULTIPLICATION/DIVISION HAVE PRECEDENCE OVER + AND _'
30       PRINT '5 + 3 + 4/2 ='; 5 + 3 + 4/2
40       PRINT '5 + 3 * 4/2 ='; 5 + 3 * 4/2
50       PRINT '5 + 3/6 * 4 =' 5 + 3/6 * 4
60       PRINT 'VALUES WITHIN PARENTHESES HAVE PRECEDENCE
70       PRINT '(5 + 3 + 4) / 2 ='; (5 + 3 + 4 ) / 2
80       PRINT 'RAISING TO A POWER PRECEDES DIVISION/MULTIPLICATION'
90       PRINT '(5 + 3 + 4) / 2**2 ='; ( 5 + 3 + 4) / 2**2
100      PRINT ' 5 * 3 + 2**2 ='; 5 * 3 + 2**2
110      PRINT '((5 - 3) * 4) **2 ='; ((5 - 3) * 4) **2
190      END

Ready

RUN
EX21    10:56           15-Aug-80
MULTIPLICATION/DIVISION HAVE PRECEDENCE OVER + AND —
5 + 3 + 4/2 = 10
5 + 3 * 4/2 = 11
5 + 3/6 * 4 = 7
VALUES WITHIN PARENTHESES HAVE PRECEDENCE
(5 + 3 + 4) / 2 = 6
RAISING TO A POWER PRECEDES DIVISION/MULTIPLICATION
(5 + 3 + 4) / 2**2 = 3
 5 * 3 + 2**2 = 19
((5 - 3) * 4) **2 = 64

Ready
```

Verify that you understand the sequence of arithmetic computations by mentally computing the expressions and comparing the results with those shown in the output section shown in Example 2.1.

In the section which follows you will learn that a programmer usually stores the results of a computation in a location for further processing. Instead of storing the results to the right side of an equal (=) sign, results are stored in some location that you will place to the left of the equal sign in your program.

2.3 THE ASSIGNMENT STATEMENT—LET

One of the most useful statements in BASIC is the assignment statement. The LET statement performs calculations and stores the results in a variable location in memory. The format of the assignment statement is:

Line number   LET variable = expression, constant, or variable

---

Following are examples of the assignment statement:

10 LET K = 5

20 LET M = M + 1

30 LET T = M + K

40 LET P1 = P * (1 + I/12) ** M

The assignment (LET) statement:

1. Performs the calculation to the *right* of the equal sign

2. Stores the resulting value in the variable to the *left* of the equal sign

For example:

10 LET K = 5   stores a 5 in location K

20 LET M = M + 1   assuming M has a zero, 1 is added to M to equal 1

30 LET T = M + K   adds the 5 in K to 1 in M and stores 6 in location T

Statement 40 would store in location P1 the results of the expression computed based on the values stored in locations P, I, and M. The function of the LET statement is to evaluate the expression to the *right* of the equal sign and store the result in the location placed to the *left* of the equal sign. Note that variables to the *left* of the equal sign *lose* whatever values were previously stored while variables used to the *right* of the equal sign are not changed.

BASIC-PLUS is flexible when it comes to spacing since the spacing between constants and/or variables and arithmetic operators are not important. For example:

10LET A=(X+Y)*Z

20LET A=   (X+Y)*Z

Both statements 10 and 20 are acceptable in BASIC-PLUS; however, from the user's standpoint, normal spacing permits easier editing. One caution, don't leave out any arithmetic operator in the assignment statement as

20 LET A = (X + Y) Z

since an error message will be printed due to the omission of the asterisk (*) which is required for multiplication. It is important to write expressions acceptable in BASIC since the algebraic format is different. Note the following examples corresponding BASIC forms:

Algebraic

1. $\dfrac{A}{BC}$

2. $A^2 + B^2$

3. $\dfrac{A^2 + B^2}{1 - C^2}$

Example 2.2 illustrates the use of the assignment stateme triangle:

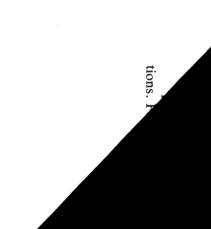

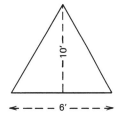

$$\text{area} = \frac{\text{height} * \text{base}}{2}$$

Example 2.2

```
10      REM THIS PROGRAM CALCULATES THE AREA OF A TRIANGLE
20      LET H = 10
30      LET B = 6
40      LET A = B * H / 2
900     END
```

Example 2.2 shows that location H is assigned a value of 10; location B is assigned a value of 6. Statement 40 stores the area of the triangle, 30 in location A. Notice that the sequence of statements is important. If we had assigned values to H and B *after* we computed the area, H and B would be zero and our program would be inaccurate.

2.4 ASSIGNING STRINGS USING LET

In BASIC, one or more alphanumeric symbols are called strings. Alphanumeric symbols include alphabetic characters, numbers, and other commonly used symbols. The following statement illustrates the assignment of a string constant to a string variable location:

100   LET A$ =   'JESSE JAMES'

Either single or double quotation marks can be used before and after the string, JESSE JAMES. A$ is a string variable location that has been assigned the string, JESSE JAMES. Note that variable locations that store alphanumeric symbols are identified with a $ sign following the alphabetic character so that the computer can distinguish between numbers and words. Valid variable string names are:

A1$ Z$ C9$

Invalid string names are:

A1 $A   9A

VARIATIONS IN THE ASSIGNMENT STATEMENT

Since the LET statement is used so frequently, BASIC-PLUS does not require the key word, LET, in an assignment statement. The following are legal assignment statements in BASIC-PLUS:

10   X = 5
20   A$ = 'JIMMY CARTER'

There are times when we will want to assign the same value to different variable loca-
or example:

10   X = 1
20   Y = 1
30   Z = 1

BASIC-PLUS allows us to use one multiple assignment statement instead of three single assignments statements.

$$10 \quad X, Y, Z = 1$$

Thus, X, Y, and Z all have a 1 stored in their locations.

2.6 THE OUTPUT STATEMENT—PRINT

The assignment statement assigned a value, numeric or string, to a location in memory. In order to display information stored in the computer memory, it is necessary to have an output statement. The PRINT statement which you have already used signals the computer to produce output in a form that humans can understand. The general format of the PRINT statement is:

| Line number | PRINT | variables; constants; expressions |

Both numeric items and strings can be a part of the PRINT statement. The following table illustrates three types of numeric output:

Type	Example		Effect
CONSTANT	10	PRINT 100	The constant is printed
VARIABLE	20	PRINT X	The content of X is printed
EXPRESSION	30	PRINT 10 + 2 * X	Value of expression is printed

Example 2.3 is a short program which illustrates the output of three PRINT statements.

Example 2.3

```
10        REM USING PRINT STATEMENTS
20        X = 10
30        PRINT 100
40        PRINT X
50        PRINT 10 + 2 * X
900       END

Ready

RUN
EX23      11:08          15-Aug-80
 100
 10
 30
```

Let's complete the program that was described in Example 2.2 where we wrote statements to compute the area of a triangle. The statements needed to calculate the area of a triangle were:

$$20 \quad H = 10$$
$$30 \quad B = 6$$
$$40 \quad A = B * H / 2$$

When we add the instruction

$$50 \quad PRINT \ A$$

the result, 30 in the example, will be displayed on the terminal. We can combine statements 40 and 50 into one PRINT statement that will produce the same output.

$$40 \quad PRINT \qquad B * H \, / \, 2$$

Thus, we instructed the computer to perform a series of computations and print the result in one statement. There will be times, however, when we will want to store the results of a computation in computer memory for later use. In that event, we would not use the PRINT statement; rather, we would store the results in some variable location in memory.

Strings can also be printed in several ways. The following table shows three types of string output:

Type	Example	Effect
CONSTANT	10 PRINT 'COMPUTER'	The constant is printed
VARIABLE	20 PRINT A$	The content of A$ is printed
BLANK	30 PRINT	Output is a blank line

Example 2.4 illustrates three different types of string output using the PRINT statement:

Example 2.4

```
10        A$ = "PROGRAM"
20        PRINT ' COMPUTER'
30        PRINT
40        PRINT A$
900       END

RUNNH
COMPUTER
                        blanks are printed (appear) caused by statement 30
PROGRAM
```

The following two examples illustrate the differences between numeric and string output:

Example 2.5

```
10        PRINT 007          numeric constant
20        PRINT '007'        string constant

Ready

RUNNH
 7
007
```

Example 2.6

```
5         X$ = 'PDP-11'
10        X = 5
20        PRINT X            numeric variable
30        PRINT 'X'          string constant
40        PRINT X$           string variable
900       END


RUNNH
 5
X
PDP-11
```

Whenever quotes (either single or double) are placed around alphanumeric characters, they are strings and cannot be used for computational purposes. Any combination of the PRINT items in Examples 2.5 and 2.6 can be placed following the key word, PRINT, on one line, but either commas or semicolons must be used between each item. When commas are used to separate output items, BASIC-PLUS divides the output line into five zones of 14 spaces each.[4] Each item appears in a new zone. If more than five items are listed in a PRINT statement with commas used as separators, items will be printed on the next line(s). Example 2.7 illustrates how the print zones function:

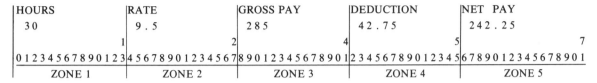

HOURS	RATE	GROSS PAY	DEDUCTION	NET PAY
3 0	9 . 5	2 8 5	4 2 . 7 5	2 4 2 . 2 5

```
                    1                 2               4               5                       7
0 1 2 3 4 5 6 7 8 9 0 1 2 3 4 5 6 7 8 9 0 1 2 3 4 5 6 7 8 9 0 1 2 3 4 5 6 7 8 9 0 1 2 3 4 5 6 7 8 9 0 1 2 3 4 5 6 7 8 9 0 1
```

ZONE 1	ZONE 2	ZONE 3	ZONE 4	ZONE 5

PRINTING ZONE FORMAT

Example 2.7

```
10        REM THIS IS A SIMPLE PAYROLL PROGRAM
20        H = 30
30        R = 9.5
40        G = H * R
50        D = .15 * G
60        N = G - D
70        PRINT 'HOURS','RATE','GROSS PAY','DEDUCTION','NET PAY'
80        PRINT H,R,G,D,N
900       END

Ready

RUNNH
HOURS           RATE            GROSS PAY       DEDUCTION       NET PAY
  30            9.5               285             42.75          242.25

Ready
```

Note that the zones act like tabulator stops on a typewriter. Occasionally, you will print a string that is longer than the 14-space print zone. When that occurs, the next field printed skips to the next zone. When you wish to print your output with two spaces between numeric fields, use semicolons between numeric values. BASIC-PLUS provides a space before a numeric field for a negative sign and a space following the field. No spaces are provided for string fields in output before and after each field, but spaces can be included within the quotes as illustrated in the following statement:

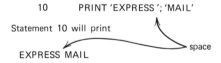

```
10        PRINT 'EXPRESS '; 'MAIL'
```

Statement 10 will print

EXPRESS MAIL → space

with one blank space between the two words in output because a blank was inserted after EXPRESS in statement 10. Chapter 6 covers output formatting in more detail.

---

[4] The DECwriter can be set to print a 132 character line. Following log-in, type SET WIDTH 132. Additional 14-unit print zones will be provided.

2.7 AN APPLICATION USING THE ASSIGNMENT AND PRINT STATEMENTS

The program listed and RUN in example 2.8 illustrates the use of the assignment and PRINT statements to produce meaningful information. In this example, Linda is considering buying a new sports car. The monthly payment for an installment purchase is calculated using the formula:

$$P = \frac{(T - D)(1 - R)}{1 - R^M}$$

where

P is the monthly payment

T is the purchase price

D is the down payment in dollar amount

R is an intermediate value computed as $\frac{12}{12 + I}$

I is the annual interest rate

Linda writes a program in BASIC-PLUS and stores data in variable locations in memory so that she can determine her monthly payments. Note that the price of the car is listed at $10,000 is to be paid for within a five-year period at 15 per cent interest and 10 per cent as a downpayment.

Example 2.8

```
10      REM THIS PROGRAM WILL CALCULATE A MONTHLY PAYMENT
20      REM T IS THE PURCHASE PRICE
30      REM D IS THE DOWNPAYMENT IN DOLLAR AMOUNTS
40      REM M IS THE NUMBER OF INSTALLMENTS
50      REM I IS THE INTEREST RATE
60      N$ = 'LINDA'
70      C$ = 'DATSUN 280ZX'
80      T = 10000
90      D = .1 * T
100     M = 12 * 5
110     I = .15
120     R = 12/(12+I)
130     P = (T-D) * (1-R) / (1-R**M)
140     PRINT "BUYER'S NAME:",,N$
150     PRINT "CAR MODEL:",,C$
160     PRINT "MONTHLY PAYMENT:",P
170     END

Ready

RUNNH
BUYER'S NAME:            LINDA
CAR MODEL:              DATSUN 280ZX
MONTHLY PAYMENT:         211.466
```

2.8 LOOPS AND COUNTERS

There are times when you will want to repeat statements several times. For example, if you want to say I LOVE YOU one hundred times to a friend by using the computer, you could write 100 PRINT statements as:

```
10    PRINT 'I LOVE YOU'
20    PRINT 'I LOVE YOU'
30    . . . . .
.     . . . . .
1000  PRINT 'I LOVE YOU'
```

Since this a rather tedious way of writing the same statement, let's print our sentiments by including one simple statement.

```
10    PRINT 'I LOVE YOU'
20    GO TO 10
```

Statement 20 is an unconditional branch statement that tells the computer to branch to statement 10. Each time statement 20 is executed, the computer jumps to statement 10 and follows the instruction to print I LOVE YOU. This unconditional branching is a form of looping which can be illustrated as follows:

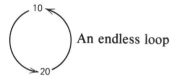 An endless loop

The format of the GO TO statement is simple:

```
Line number    GO TO    line number
```

Once GO TO is encountered, the computer will transfer control to the line specified following GO TO. GO TO allows us to jump to any location that we wish in the program as long as we branch to a statement number that exists in our program. If we state GO TO 200 and line 200 does not appear in our program, an error message will be displayed.

The capacity to branch to any place in a program makes the computer a very powerful tool. But there is one problem that occurs when our short, repetitive program is run. Note what happens:

```
10     REM USING GO TO——AN UNCONDITIONAL BRANCH
20     PRINT 'I LOVE YOU'
30     GOTO 20
900    END

RUNNH
I LOVE YOU
I LOVE YOU
I LOVE YOU
I L^C
```

We are caught in an endless loop. We stopped the computer from printing by pressing the control key and C simultaneously. It is necessary to include an instruction that will tell the computer to stop after printing 100 lines of the PRINT statement. Most of us subconsciously keep track of the number of times we perform a repetitive task, like counting the number of stairs up a stairway. We have a counter built into part of our memory system. All we need to do is set up a counter in computer memory and have the computer do the counting; then, we can have the computer test to determine if the program has completed the proper number of loops. The simple conditional statement that we will use appears as follows:

```
Line number    IF   condition    THEN   line number
```

Example 2.9 illustrates the use of a simple conditional statement to control the number of times the program loops:

Example 2.9

```
10      REM THIS PROGRAM ILLUSTRATES A LOOP AND COUNTER
20      C = 0
30      PRINT 'I LOVE YOU'
40      C = C + 1
50      IF C= 100 THEN 900
60      GO TO 30
900     END
```

First we set C equal to zero; then, after printing our first line of output, we add 1 to C. So, C is our counter and keeps a tally on the number of times that we loop through the program. Statement 50 checks to see if our counter, C, has reached 100. If C doesn't equal 100, statement 60 is executed jumping back to statement 30 and printing another line. Finally, when 100 lines of output have been printed, C will equal 100 and will cause a branch to statement 900, END. We will be using simple conditional statements to control loops throughout Chapter 3, and include a thorough discussion on variations of conditional statements in Chapter 4.

Now let's go over an example that further illustrates using a counter, looping, and accumulating a total.

Example 2.10

```
10      REM LOOPING, COUNTING AND ACCUMULATING TOTALS
20      PRINT 'WEEK', 'WEEKLY PAY', 'TOTAL PAY'
30      REM W = WEEK; T = TOTAL PAY; P = WEEKLY PAY
40      W,T = 0
50      P = 250
60      T = T + P
70      W = W + 1
80      PRINT W, P, T
90      IF W = 4 THEN 900
100     GO TO 60
900     END

Ready


RUNNH
WEEK          WEEKLY PAY    TOTAL PAY
  1              250           250
  2              250           500
  3              250           750
  4              250          1000
```

Example 2.10 shows how you can use a location in memory to accumulate totals. Location T is used to accumulate weekly pay beginning with the first week and continuing through four pay periods. W acts as a counter to count the weeks. Note that locations W and T are both set to zero in line 40. The weekly pay of 250 is stored in location P at line 50. Statement 80 produces the numeric output for this program with the counter, W, printing the week, and location, T, printing the accumulated pay for each successive week. Location P produces the same output with each PRINT, since no change is made to the variable P any place in the program. The program in Example 2.10 was terminated in statement 90 when W equalled 4, and a branch was made to the END statement.

Conditional branching. Statements that test numbers or strings; branching to other locations in the program will occur when the conditions of the test are met.

Constants. Numeric or alphanumeric values that do not change.

Counters. Variable locations that are used to count the number of times a loop is completed.

Integers. A whole number

Looping. The process of repeating a series of statements in a program.

Reals. Numeric values that can be expressed in decimal form or in scientific notation.

String. One or more alphanumeric characters treated as a unit.

Unconditional branching. Statements that instruct the computer to branch to a specific statement number.

Variables. Locations or addresses in the memory of the computer that allow different values to be stored through the course of completing a program.

PROBLEMS

1. Explain the reason for having a counter in a program.

2. Which of the following are defined as integers? Which are reals?
   (a) 12   (b) 3.4   (c) −5   (d) −9.1   (e) 5000

3. Why is looping important in programming?

4. How can one control the number of times statements are executed in a program?

5. Which of the following are defined as variables in BASIC? Which are constants?
   (a) A   (b) Z5   (c) 1   (d) 99   (e) AB   (f) B$ (g) 'JOHN'

6. Correct any errors you detect in the following BASIC statements:

   (a) Let A10 = 5   (d) PRINT X = 24 * 3 − 5
   (b) PRINT TOTAL = M   (e) LET X = Y = Z = 10
   (c) LET 25 = Z

7. Code a program that will set location A to zero and add 10 to that location until A = 50. The output of the program should appear as follows:

   10
   20
   30
   40
   50

8. Include a counter in the program you coded in problem 7 above so that the output would appear as follows:

LOOP	AMOUNTS
1	10
2	20
3	30
4	40
5	50

9. Include statements in the program you revised in problem 8 that will sum the amounts and produce output as follows:

LOOP	AMOUNTS	TOTALS
1	10	10
2	20	30
3	30	60
4	40	100
5	50	150

10. Write statements that will set location A = 5 and location B = 10; then write PRINT statements that will compute the following expressions:

    (a) $\dfrac{5A + 2B}{A^2}$

    (b) $A + B + 10 - (A * B)$

    (c) $A - B^2$

    (d) $\dfrac{10A}{B}$

    (e) $\dfrac{A + B^3}{A}$

    (f) $4A^2 + 2B - A$

    (g) $\dfrac{A + B}{B} + \dfrac{3A}{B} - 2B^3$

11. Write statements that will
    (a) store the following strings in three string variable locations:

    JAMES J. SMITH
    1500 S. STREET
    SAN FRANCISCO, CALIFORNIA

    (b) print these strings using string variable names on three separate lines as shown in the above format.

12. Write a program to produce the following:

```
* * * * * * * * * * * * * *
*                         *
*    WE'RE NUMBER 1       *
* * * * * * * * * * * * * *
```

13. Write BASIC statements to exchange the values stored in X and Y. Assume values of X and Y are assigned.

14. Which one of the following statement is not legal? Why?

    10 LET A = -A
    20 LET -A = A

15. Write a BASIC program to produce the following list of names. Arrange the layout so that your output is neatly arranged.

NAME	AGE	PARTY
BROWN	42	DEMOCRAT
BUSH	55	REPUBLICAN
CARTER	55	DEMOCRAT
KENNEDY	49	DEMOCRAT
REAGAN	69	REPUBLICAN

16. Write a BASIC statement to print the following sentence:

HE SAID: "I'LL GO"

17. Express the following mathematical statements in BASIC:

(a) $Y = \sqrt[3]{27} + A^2$

(b) $X = \dfrac{-B + \sqrt{B^2 - 4AC}}{2A}$

(c) $V = \sqrt{2GH}$

(d) $P = \dfrac{T \cdot \dfrac{I}{12}}{1 - \left(1 + \dfrac{I}{12}\right)^{-12 \cdot N}}$

18. Assume that the population of Eureka is 25,000 and that the annual population rate is increasing at 1.2%. Write a program to calculate the population 5, 20, and 80 years in the future.

Chapter 3
Data Entry

Objectives
You will learn:

To input numbers and strings with READ and DATA statements.

More about looping and conditional statements.

How to reuse data previously processed.

Methods of inputting data during a RUN.

We have already used data in our programs through the use of the PRINT and LET statements. Only a limited amount of data can be entered efficiently with these statements. To enter large amounts of data into a program, the READ/DATA or INPUT statements are preferable.

3.1 READ AND DATA STATEMENTS

The READ statement requires that there be a DATA statement in the program. When you instruct the computer to READ something, it is logical to assume that you will provide the computer with numbers, symbols, or words to READ so that processing can occur. The general format of the READ and DATA statements appear as follows:

line number	READ	variable list	place commas between variables

line number	DATA	constant list	place commas between constants

Here's an example of a simple program to read a number and a name and print them:

Example 3.1

```
10      REM READIN AND PRINTOUT OF A NAME AND NUMBER
20      READ A1, B$
30      PRINT A1, B$
90      DATA 24947, 'JANE MORGAN'
900     END

Ready

RUNNH
 24947      JANE MORGAN
```

Example 3.1 instructed the computer to read into variable locations called A1 and B$ the two fields in the DATA statement, 24947 and 'JANE MORGAN'. If the DATA statement had been omitted from this program, an error message would have been printed. Any number of DATA statements can be included in a program; one DATA statement can include up to 255 characters. The actual length of a single DATA statement will vary with the computer system being used. DATA statements are non executable; therefore, they can be placed anywhere in the program *before* the END statement. A common practice is to place DATA statements at the end of the program.

The following short program illustrates reading two numeric variables:

Example 3.2

```
Ready

10      REM READIN AND PRINTOUT OF TWO NUMERIC VARIABLES
20      READ A1, B
30      PRINT A1,B
90      DATA 99,79
900     END

Ready

RUNNH
 99              79
```

Note that commas are required between variable names as well as between values placed in the DATA statement. Example 3.2 illustrates how the computer follows the READ statement by placing the first value in the DATA statement in location A1 and the second value of 79 in location B. The printout verifies that the values of 99 and 79 were stored in A1 and B, respectively. Example 3.3 shows that there must be at least as many values stored in DATA statements as there are variables in READ statements.

Example 3.3

```
10      REM TOO FEW VALUES STORED IN DATA STATEMENT
20      READ A1, B, B2
30      PRINT A1, B
90      DATA 99, 79
900     END

Ready

RUN
EX33    11:46           15-Aug-80
?Out of data at line 20
```

Note that in Example 3.3 there were three variables placed in the READ statement—A1, B, B2. Yet, there were only two numeric values available to be read in the DATA statement—99, 79. The output from this run produced the line, "Out of data at line 20." Since line 20 was our READ statement, the computer was telling us that there were too few values in the DATA statement to match the number of variables in the READ statement. The response of the computer was quite logical. We had asked the computer to read a value that didn't exist. Thus, our program did not work.

In the following program, Example 3.4, the number of values in the DATA statement are increased to four.

Example 3.4

```
10      REM DATA STATEMENT WITH 4 VALUES
20      READ A1, B, B2
30      PRINT A1, B
90      DATA 99, 79, -20, 49
900     END

Ready

RUN
EX34    11:47           15-Aug-80
 99              79
```

In the above program, we tell the computer to read three values and place them in the three variable locations shown in statement 20. The computer will store 99, 79, and −20 in A1, B, and B2, respectively. However, since the PRINT statement requested a printout of only A1 and B locations, our RUN produced only two values, 99 and 79. Note that no error message occurred in Example 3.4 even though the number of constants in the DATA statement was greater than the number of variables in the READ statement.

Example 3.5

```
10        REM VARIABLE WITH UNASSIGNED VALUE
20        READ A1, B, B2
30        PRINT A1, B, B2, C
90        DATA 99, 79, -20, 49
900       END

Ready

RUN
EX35      11:50               15-Aug-80
  99               79              -20                 0
```

Example 3.5 shows that we can include variables in our PRINT statement that have not been assigned values. The results are just what we would predict, a zero. We included the variable, C, in statement 30 which was not in the READ statement; thus a zero was printed in the fourth print position of our output line. The first three values of our output were the first three constants appearing in our DATA statement, line 90.

Example 3.6

```
10        REM USE OF TWO DATA STATEMENTS
15        REM PRINTOUT ORDER OF VARIABLES CHANGED
20        READ A1, B, B2, C
30        PRINT B, C, B2, A1
90        DATA 99, 79, -20
100       DATA 49, 59, 69, 79, 89
900       END

Ready

RUN
EX36      11:54               15-Aug-80
  79               49              -20                99
```

Example 3.6 shows that data are read in order by statement number. Although there are three values stored in statement 90, the fourth value is read from statement 100 and stored in location C. Note that the variables can be arranged in any order desired in the PRINT statement. For example, 79, which was stored in location B, is the first number printed in output.

Example 3.7

```
10        REM UNCONDITIONAL BRANCH TO THE READ STATEMENT
20        READ A1, B, B2, C
30        PRINT B, A1, C, B2
40        GO TO 20
90        DATA 99, 79, -20
100       DATA 49, 59, 69, 79, 89
900       END

Ready

RUN
EX37      11:57          15-Aug-80
  79               99              49              -20
  69               59              89               79
?Out of data at line 20

Ready
```

Example 3.7 above illustrates the use of an unconditional branch using four variable locations and eight numeric constants in two DATA statements. Since we have instructed the computer in statement 40 to continue to branch back to statement 20, the READ statement, an error message is generated, indicating that there were no additional data elements to read.

3.2 TESTING DATA WITH A CONDITIONAL STATEMENT

One way to solve the problem of the OUT OF DATA diagnostic message is to place a value at the end of the DATA statement that acts as a flag or signal to inform the computer that no more data fields are to be processed. Thus, it is necessary to use a conditional statement to test each value that is read. Recall that the general format of a simple conditional statement is:

```
LINE number     IF   condition       THEN   line number or statement
```

For example, the statement

$$150 \text{ IF A } = 100 \text{ THEN } 900$$

instructs the computer to compare the value stored in location A with the constant, 100. If A = 100, the computer branches to statement 900. If A is some other value than 100, the computer executes the next statement in the program following this conditional statement. Chapter 4 includes a more detailed discussion of conditional statements.

Example 3.8 shows how a conditional statement can be used to test each data value that is read. This early test of each data field allows the programmer to determine whether or not this data element should be processed as valid data. Note that, in statement 90, the last data element is −999. The last value acts as a flag to signal that all valid data has been read and processed. When A1 has stored −999, statement 30 will cause the computer to branch to statement 900, and the program will be terminated. A programmer can select any number for a flag that is not a valid value to be processed. Statement 40 illustrates a method for printing more than one value per line of output by inserting a comma *following* the variable, A1. Note that five values are printed in output in five print zones available on a terminal handling 72 characters per line.

Example 3.8

```
10        REM USING A CONDITIONAL STATEMENT TO TEST
                    FOR VALID DATA
20        READ A1
30        IF A1 = -999 THEN 900
40        PRINT A1,
50        GO TO 20
90        DATA 99, 79, -20, 49, 59, 69, 790, -999
900       END

Ready

RUN
EX38      12:02           15-Aug-80
   99            79            -20           49            59
   69            790
Ready
```

3.3　THE RESTORE STATEMENT

There may be occasions when it is desirable to reuse data fields that previously have been processed in a program. The RESTORE statement resets the data pointer so that READ statements will begin at the first DATA statement and continue to read values in all of the DATA statements in the program unless some condition terminates execution of the program. Following is an example of the RESTORE statement:

Example 3.9

```
10      REM REUSE OF DATA VALUES WITH THE RESTORE STATEMENT
20      READ A
30      IF A = -1 THEN 60
40      PRINT A, A**2
50      GO TO 20
60      RESTORE
70      READ A
80      IF A = -1 THEN 900
90      LET A = A + 1
100     PRINT A, A**2
110     GO TO 70
120     DATA 2, 4, 6, 8, -1
900     END

Ready

RUN
EX39    12:08           15-Aug-80
  2             4  ⎤
  4            16  ⎬  ←——— GENERATED BY 1ST LOOP (20–50)
  6            36  ⎪
  8            64  ⎦
  3             9  ⎤
  5            25  ⎬  ←——— GENERATED BY 2ND LOOP (70–110)
  7            49  ⎪
  9            81  ⎦

Ready
```

Example 3.9 includes a conditional branch in statement 30 which requires a branch to statement 60. This branch is made when the four data values to be squared have been computed and printed as illustrated in the printout above.

Statement 60 instructs the computer to RESTORE all data included in the program which are part of DATA statements. Thus, when statement 70 is executed, the first data item in the DATA statement is stored in location A. The last part of Example 3.9 increments each data item by one before that value is squared resulting in odd values and squares of 3, 5, 7, and 9 computed and printed. Note that the flag, -1, is used to end processing for each part of the program.

3.4　THE INPUT STATEMENT

Another method to record data for use in a program is with an INPUT statement. This INPUT statement is particularly useful when the programmer wishes to supply data at his own choosing during the execution of a program. Through the use of an INPUT statement it is not necessary to provide data in the program itself. It allows the user to interact with the program and to try different data. The general format of the INPUT statement is

LINE number	INPUT	list of variables

Example 3.10 illustrates the use of the INPUT statement with one variable.

Example 3.10

```
10       REM USING THE INPUT STATEMENT INSTEAD OF
                 THE READ STATEMENT
20       INPUT X
30       PRINT X
900      END

Ready

RUN
EX310    12:10             15-Aug-80
? 998
 998

Ready
```

Note that no data is in the program itself. When the user types RUN, the INPUT command causes the computer to print a question mark and wait until the user types in a value. In this example, the user types 998. Once this value has been inserted, the computer responds by printing the value. It is a good practice to have a message printed that acts as a cue to the user so that there is no question about what type of data is to be entered. Example 3.11 shows how descriptive words can be included in the INPUT statement itself to aid the user.

Example 3.11

```
10       REM USE OF DESCRIPTIVE WORDS TO TELL
                 THE USER WHAT DATA TO INPUT
20       INPUT 'AMOUNT OF PRINCIPAL ='; P
30       PRINT P
900      END

Ready

RUN
EX311    12:11             15-Aug-80
AMOUNT OF PRINCIPAL =? 25000
 25000
```

Example 3.12 illustrates a more practical approach to using the INPUT statement.

Example 3.12

```
10       REM USE OF THE INPUT STATEMENT TO COMPUTE
                 INTEREST  COMPOUNDED ANNUALLY
20       INPUT 'AMOUNT OF PRINCIPAL ='; P
30       INPUT 'INTEREST RATE ='; R
40       I = R * P               !ANNUAL INTEREST IS COMPUTED
50       PRINT 'INTEREST=';I, 'PRINCIPAL ='; P, 'RATE =';R
900      END

Ready

RUN
EX312    12:18             15-Aug-80
AMOUNT OF PRINCIPAL =? 10000
INTEREST RATE =? .12
INTEREST= 1200            PRINCIPAL = 10000        RATE = .12

Ready
```

Example 3.12 illustrates a program for computing annual interest and allows the user to input varying interest rates as well as different principals. Example 3.12 illustrates several features of the BASIC PLUS language. One unique feature is that the programmer can include explanatory statements following a statement if an ! symbol is used to separate the BASIC statement from the explanatory statement that follows. Statement number 40 illustrates the use of explanatory statements. The second feature mentioned in Chapter 1 is also shown in statement 40:

$$40 \quad I = R * X \quad \text{(the explanatory statement is omitted here)}$$

Note that the word, LET, is not required in BASIC-PLUS, so the computation in statement 40 is reduced to a simple formula. The variable location, I, stores the results of the computation made to the *right* of the equal sign.

```
AMOUNT OF PRINCIPAL =? 500000
INTEREST RATE =? 1O
%Data format error at line 30
INTEREST RATE =? 10
INTEREST= .5E 7              PRINCIPAL = 500000           RATE = 10

Ready
```

A second RUN was made using Example 3.12, and the output is shown above. An error was made in typing the interest rate since the letter 'O' was typed rather than a numeric zero. An error message was immediately generated informing the user that this item was not acceptable. The computer then requested another value for interest rate. The user typed in 10 rather than .10 (10 %). Even though the decimal was omitted by the user, the computer accepted this illogical number and computed interest at 1000 per cent. The interest generated is stated in scientific notation which is equivalent to 5,000,000 (.5E 7). This type of error is easily resolved with an INPUT oriented program since the user merely retypes RUN and keys in values that are to be computed.

Word List

Flag. A number or string placed at the end of a DATA statement to signal the end of data.

INPUT. A BASIC command which requires data to be input during the program RUN.

RESTORE. A BASIC command used to reset the pointer to the first data item.

PROBLEMS

1. Indicate the output that the following program will produce:

   ```
   10   READ A, B, C
   20   PRINT C, A, B
   30   DATA 15, 30, 45, 22, −10, 49
   40   END
   ```

2. Change the program in problem 1 so that all six values will be printed in output. Do not add additional variables.

3. Change the program in problem 1 so that no "Out of data at line 10" error message will be printed.

4. What output will the following program produce?

   ```
   10   READ X
   20   X = X + 1
   30   GO TO 10
   40   PRINT X
   50   DATA 10, 20, 30, 40
   60   DATA 50, 60, 70, 80
   70   END
   ```

5. What changes need to be made in problem 4 in order to print all eight values in output?

6. Assume you wish to reuse the data in problem 4 and add 10 to each data item. Write BASIC statements that will print out the original eight values, as well as the original data values that are to be increased by ten.

7. Explain what the following program will do:

```
10   READ A1
20   PRINT A1,
30   IF A1 = −1 THEN 100
40   GO TO 10
50   DATA 1,2,3,4,5,6,7,8,9,−10, −1
100  END
```

8. How many values are printed on the first line of output in problem 7? Why?

9. Write a BASIC statement that will allow the insertion of three data items in a program *during* its RUN.

10. Rewrite the statement for problem 9 and include a descriptive statement to aid the user in inserting data during its RUN.

11. Write a program that will compute the floor space for five different rooms and show the cumulative area totals of these rooms. The data which indicate the length and width of these five rooms is:

10, 15, 12, 12, 14, 10, 10, 12, 10, 13

Output for your program should appear as follows:

BASIC PROBLEM #12

ROOM NUMBER	FLOOR AREA	CUM TOTAL
1	150	150
2	144	294

(continue until all five computations are made)

Use a counter to provide the data for the first column which indicates the room number. (Do not place these values—1 to 5—in a DATA statement. Do not use an INPUT statement with this program.)

12. Revise the program written for problem 11 to compute the cost of carpeting the floors in each of the five rooms, assuming that materials and labor will be $15.95 per square yard. Add a fourth column to the output with the heading, CUM COST. Note that the figures in problem 11 are in square feet.

13. Write a program that will read the figures listed with the DATA statement below and PRINT these figures on one line. Then, PRINT another line that doubles the values of each of these figures as illustrated below. Hint: Use a flag and the RESTORE statement.

DATA   25, 50, 75, 100, 200

BASIC PROBLEM #14

25	50	75	100	200
50	100	150	200	400

14. The formula for converting fahrenheit to celsius is

$$C = 5/9 * (F - 32)$$

Write a program using the INPUT statement to compute and print the following fahrenheit temperatures converted to celsius:

32   40   60   72   80   95   102

Your output should appear as follows: _____ CELSIUS IS EQUAL TO _____ FAHRENHEIT

15. Write a program to convert height measured in feet and inches to centimeters. Your output should appear as follows:

PLEASE ENTER YOUR HEIGHT IN FEET AND INCHES; I'LL CONVERT IT TO METRIC MEASUREMENT!

HOW TALL ARE YOU IN FEET? 5
HOW MANY INCHES DO YOU EXCEED YOUR HEIGHT IN FEET? 6

YOUR HEIGHT 5 FEET 6 INCHES CONVERTS TO 165 CENTIMETERS

Chapter 4
Multiple Decisions and Looping

Objectives   You will learn:

Flowchart symbols and flowcharting procedures.

More about conditional statements.

About logical operators and compound conditions.

About multiple-level decisions.

Applications of conditional statements.

The basic structure of the FOR. . .NEXT loop.

Nested loops.

You have learned that you can write instructions in BASIC to repeat sections of a program through loops as well as to test how to branch out of a program loop to end a program. One of the most important capabilities of computers is the ability to test conditions, and then, based on instructions, to perform a variety of arithmetic operations or respond to the user in different ways. Computer capabilities can be viewed as an extension of the human mind. The computer makes decisions based on facts or conditions that reflect the logic of the individual writing the instructions.

4.1 PROGRAM FLOWCHARTING

As instructions to the computer become more involved, it is necessary to think through the sequence of these instructions before typing them on a terminal. Otherwise, programs become inefficient and more complicated than necessary, and a great deal of time will be spent correcting them.

One approach used to plan a computer program is the use of flowchart symbols. Flowcharting is a kind of shorthand using symbols to represent the major functions that a computer performs. The following symbols are commonly used in program flowcharting.

START/END — This symbol is used at the beginning and end of each program that is flowcharted.
Example: END statement

INPUT/OUTPUT — This symbol is used to show any type of data entry as well as printouts.
Examples: READ, INPUT, PRINT statements

PROCESSING — This symbol is used to indicate any type of operation(s) resulting in a change in one or more variables
Examples: Assignment (LET) statement
    RESTORE statement

DECISION — This symbol shows that some condition is to be tested.
Example: IF - THEN statement

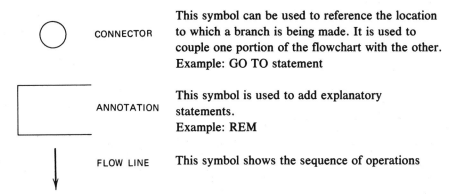

CONNECTOR   This symbol can be used to reference the location to which a branch is being made. It is used to couple one portion of the flowchart with the other.
Example: GO TO statement

ANNOTATION   This symbol is used to add explanatory statements.
Example: REM

FLOW LINE   This symbol shows the sequence of operations

Figure 4-1. Flowchart symbols.

Figure 4-2 illustrates the use of flowchart symbols. This flowchart shows the steps needed to compute the average quiz score for a student who has two or more quizzes during

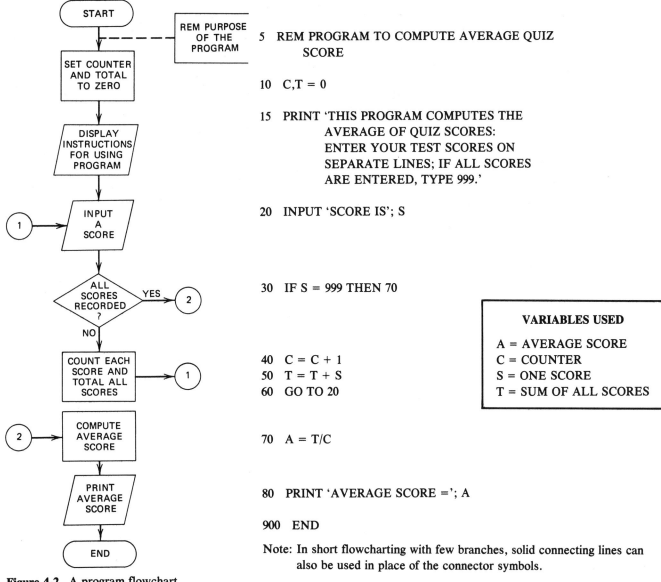

```
 5   REM PROGRAM TO COMPUTE AVERAGE QUIZ
       SCORE

10   C,T = 0

15   PRINT 'THIS PROGRAM COMPUTES THE
       AVERAGE OF QUIZ SCORES:
       ENTER YOUR TEST SCORES ON
       SEPARATE LINES; IF ALL SCORES
       ARE ENTERED, TYPE 999.'

20   INPUT 'SCORE IS'; S

30   IF S = 999 THEN 70

40   C = C + 1
50   T = T + S
60   GO TO 20

70   A = T/C

80   PRINT 'AVERAGE SCORE ='; A

900  END
```

VARIABLES USED

A = AVERAGE SCORE
C = COUNTER
S = ONE SCORE
T = SUM OF ALL SCORES

Note: In short flowcharting with few branches, solid connecting lines can also be used in place of the connector symbols.

Figure 4-2. A program flowchart.

a term for a class. After this program has been coded, the student can run this program by typing in a quiz score each time the computer requests a score. When all scores are recorded, a number used as a flag, 999, signals the computer to compute and print the average score.

Figure 4-2 shows that the sequence of arranging flowchart symbols is from top to bottom. Had this program been longer and more involved, the symbols would have been placed in sequence top to bottom, then left to right. Note that the flowchart symbols are large enough to enable you to print a short description of each step in the program. Templates are available to enable you to sketch an attractive program flowchart. Once a flowchart has been completed, coding can be done directly on a terminal from the flowchart. The flowchart acts as an outline of the program and enables you to think through each step in the program before you attempt to code your instructions.

A listing and run of the program shown in Figure 4-2 are shown in Example 4.1.

Example 4.1

```
10       C, T = 0
15       PRINT 'THIS PROGRAM COMPUTES THE AVERAGE OF QUIZ SCORES;'
16       PRINT 'ENTER YOUR TEST SCORES ON SEPARATE LINES;'
17       PRINT 'IF ALL SCORES ARE ENTERED, TYPE 999.'
20       INPUT 'SCORE IS'; S
30           IF S = 999 THEN 70
40           C = C + 1
50           T = T + S
60           GO TO 20
70       A = T/C
80       PRINT 'AVERAGE SCORE ='; A
900      END

Ready

RUN
EX42    12:22            15-Aug-80
THIS PROGRAM COMPUTES THE AVERAGE OF QUIZ SCORES;
ENTER YOUR TEST SCORES ON SEPARATE LINES;
IF ALL SCORES ARE ENTERED, TYPE 999.
SCORE IS? 78
SCORE IS? 65
SCORE IS? 89
SCORE IS? 90
SCORE IS? 72
SCORE IS? 999
AVERAGE SCORE = 78.8
```

4.2 MORE ABOUT CONDITIONAL STATEMENTS

We have previously used conditional statements to branch to different parts of a program. Recall that the general format of a conditional statement is:

LINE number　　IF　condition　　THEN　statements

The function of the above statement is straightforward. First, the computer will evaluate the condition. If the condition is true, the statement(s) following the key word, THEN, will be performed. For example:

```
10  IF A = 10 THEN B = B + 1 \  GO TO 30
20  PRINT 'A IS NOT EQUAL TO 10'
30  . . . . . . . . . .
```

When A = 10, B will be increased by 1 and a branch to 30 will be made. When A ≠ 10, none of the instructions following the key word, THEN, will be executed; and the instruction immediately following will be executed—line 20 in the example. BASIC-PLUS allows us to place more than one statement on one line—a multiple statement. For example:

```
100  B = B + 1
105  GO TO 30
```

is identical to

```
100  B = B + 1 \  GO TO 30
```

OR

```
100  B = B + 1: GO TO 30
```

Either the backslash or colon can be used to separate multiple statements. Care is required in using multiple statements following the key word, THEN. Note what occurs in the following statements:

```
10  IF A = 10 THEN GO TO 30 \  B = B + 1
20  PRINT 'A IS NOT EQUAL TO 10'
30  . . . . . . . . . .
```

Statement 10 requires a branch to statement 30 when A = 10, but B = B + 1 never occurs since it is placed *after* the unconditional branch, GO TO 30.

One important point needs to be made. Since

IF condition   THEN   GO TO line number

is a commonly used conditional statement, it is also used in the following two formats:

```
1)  IF   condition       THEN    line number
2)  IF   condition       GO TO   line number
```

The first format is preferred and is most commonly used by programmers, and one that has been used in previous chapters.

The condition in an IF statement can be simple or compound. Let's discuss the simple condition first. A simple condition is two expressions connected with a relational operator. Recall (chapter 2) that an expression is made up of constants and/or variables used with arithmetic operators. For example:

$$A + 1$$
$$B * 2$$

Relational operators that can be used in conditional statements are:

= equal to

< less than

<= less than or equal to

== approximately equal

<> not equal to

> greater than

>= greater than or equal to

Hence,

$$A + 1 = B * 2$$

is a legal simple condition. The arithmetic expressions in the following statement will be evaluated and then compared

$$40 \quad \text{IF } A + 1 = B * 2 \text{ THEN PRINT A}$$

If A = 5 and B = 3, the condition would be true and the value of A would be printed.

Now let's take a look at a program that illustrates simple conditions. Example 4.2 illustrates the use of relational operators with simple conditional statements.

Example 4.2

```
5       REM USE OF RELATIONAL OPERATORS
10      INPUT 'A =';A, 'B =';B
20      IF A >= B THEN PRINT 'A IS GREATER THAN OR EQUAL TO B'
30      IF A = B THEN PRINT 'A IS EQUAL TO B'
40      IF A <= B THEN PRINT 'A IS LESS THAN OR EQUAL TO B'
50      IF A <> B THEN PRINT 'A IS NOT EQUAL TO B'
60      IF A == B THEN PRINT 'A IS APPROXIMATELY EQUAL TO B'
900     END

Ready

RUNNH
A =? 29.5
B =? 29.555
A IS LESS THAN OR EQUAL TO B
A IS NOT EQUAL TO B

Ready

RUNNH
A =? 29.5555
B =? 29.55
A IS GREATER THAN OR EQUAL TO B
A IS NOT EQUAL TO B

Ready

RUNNH
A =? 29.5556
B =? 29.5555
A IS GREATER THAN OR EQUAL TO B
A IS NOT EQUAL TO B

Ready

RUNNH
A =? 29.55559
B =? 29.55558
A IS GREATER THAN OR EQUAL TO B
A IS NOT EQUAL TO B
A IS APPROXIMATELY EQUAL TO B

Ready
```

Example 4.2 demonstrates an inefficient program because it requires that all conditional statements be tested for each value of A and B; however, this program shows how relational operators test values. Note that the last run in Ex. 4.2 resulted in A approximately equal to B where A = 29.55559 and B = 29.55558; however, A is not approximately equal to B when A = 29.5556 and B = 29.5555. Relational operators enable the programmer to utilize one of the most powerful capabilities of computers—the ability to test conditions followed by implementing action prescribed by the programmer.

4.3 LOGICAL OPERATORS AND, OR and COMPOUND CONDITIONS

There are times when we may wish to test two conditions in one conditional statement. Let's assume we want to determine the number of students in the freshman class who are either 18 or 19 years old. The following conditional statement using the AND operator would enable us to tally the number of students in these two age groups:

        40   IF S > 17 and S < 20 THEN T = T + 1   (T acts as a counter)
        50   . . .

Assume that we have INPUT S as the age of any student. Statement 40 tests to determine if S is greater than 17 *and* less than 20. If both conditions are met, the variable T is incremented by one to tally a student who is either 18 or 19 years old. If either condition is false, T is not incremented and control passes to the next statement in the program.

The same goal can be achieved by the following conditional statement:

        40   IF S = 18 OR S = 19 THEN T = T + 1

The above statement requires that only one of the two conditions be true in order to increment T. It is obvious that a student either 18 or 19 years of age will meet the condition. This is an example of a compound condition. A compound condition is more than one simple condition coupled with the logical operators, AND, OR. One caution! The following compound condition is not legal and will result in an error message:

        40   IF S = 18 OR = 19 THEN T = T + 1

While S = 18 is a legal simple condition; = 19 is not. You must include S = 19 following OR.

In summary, a compound condition will be evaluated by the following hierarchy:

1. Arithmetic operators (+, −, *, /, **)

2. Relational operators (=, >, <, >=, <=, <>, ==)

3. Logical operators (AND, OR)[1]

---

[1] The computer evaluates a compound condition according to the following truth tables:

AND operation				OR operation		
Condition A	**AND**	**Condition B**		**Condition A**	**OR**	**Condition B**
T	T	T		T	T	T
T	F	F		T	T	F
F	F	T		F	T	T
F	F	F		F	F	F

For instance, the conditions at line 30 will be evaluated as follows:

5 A$ = 'YES'

10 X = 1

20 Y = 4

30 IF X + 1 = 4 OR Y − 1 = 3 AND A$ = 'YES' THEN PRINT 'EUREKA'

Step 1: Evaluate expressions (arithmetic operators)

$$X + 1 = 2$$
$$Y - 1 = 3$$

Step 2: Compare the expressions at both sides of relational operators

$$2 = 4 \;?\quad \text{false}$$
$$3 = 3 \;?\quad \text{true}$$
$$A\$ = \text{'YES'} \;?\quad \text{true}$$

Step 3: Logical evaluation of three simple conditions

false OR true AND true yields true

hence, EUREKA will be printed.

Following is a program that illustrates the use of compound conditional statements.

Example 4.3

Mr. McCarthy, computer center director, is considering selection of one female programmer from his programming staff to be his assistant. The person to be selected must be 18 or younger or have five or more years of experience. The following program has been written to produce a list of persons that meet the above specifications:

```
10      REM USING COMPOUND CONDITIONAL STATEMENTS TO
                SELECT A COMPUTER PROGRAMMER
20      PRINT 'NAME', 'SEX', 'AGE', 'EXPERIENCE'
30      READ N$
40      IF N$ = 'DUMMY' THEN 900
50      READ S$, A, E
60      IF S$ = 'F' AND (A<=18 OR E>=5)
                THEN PRINT N$,S$, A, E
70      GO TO 30
80      DATA 'FRED', 'M', 18, 2, 'JOHN', 'M', 24, 5
90      DATA 'JUDY', 'F', 21, 5, 'DALE', 'M', 18, 2
100     DATA 'MARY', 'F', 25, 3, 'JULIE', 'F', 18, 2
110     DATA 'ANDY', 'M', 28, 1, 'ANNIE', 'F', 17, 10
120     DATA 'DUMMY'
900     END

Ready

RUNNH
NAME          SEX          AGE          EXPERIENCE
JUDY          F            21           5
JULIE         F            18           2
ANNIE         F            17           10

Ready
```

Each programmer's data consists of name, sex, age, and experience. You can see the data of eight programmers at lines 80 through 110. The program started by printing the heading. Line 30 read the programmer's name, storing it in location N$. The name, DUMMY, acts as a flag and results in termination of the program. Line 40 tests to determine whether the name read in is the flag, DUMMY. If N$ = DUMMY, the program branches to END and stops. Statement 60 is the key compound conditional statement in this program since it tests for sex, age, and experience.

$$60 \quad \text{IF S\$} = \text{'F' AND (A} <= 18 \text{ OR E} >= 5)$$
$$\text{THEN PRINT N\$, S\$, A, E}$$

Note that statement 60 is placed on two lines. It is necessary to press the LINE FEED key instead of the RETURN key. You may use additional lines for one statement provided you do not separate keywords, a string, or a variable name. Check the output of Example 4.3 to see if all specifications have been met for the three women whose names and characteristics are listed. Note that the IF statement consists of three simple conditions:

condition 1   S$ = 'F'

condition 2   A $<= 18$

condition 3   E $>= 5$

Normally, a compound condition will be evaluated from left to right. AND has precedence over OR. Since conditions 2 and 3 are enclosed in parentheses, they will be evaluated first. If either condition 2 or condition 3 is true, and condition 1 is true (the programmer is a female), that person's name and characteristics will be printed; otherwise no output will occur and another person's data will be read and checked.

4.4 MULTIPLE-LEVEL DECISIONS AND NESTED IF STATEMENTS

Any legal statement(s) can be placed after the key word, THEN, as part of an IF statement. In other words, we can place another IF statement following the word, THEN. For example, instead of testing a compound condition:

$$10 \quad \text{IF S} >= 17 \text{ AND S} <= 20$$
$$\text{THEN T} = \text{T} + 1$$

we can break the decision into two levels:

$$10 \quad \text{IF S} >= 17$$
$$\text{THEN IF S} <= 20$$
$$\text{THEN T} = \text{T} + 1$$

Statement 10 tests the variable S against two constants, 17 and 20, by using two successive IF statements. If both tests are true, T is incremented. If either test is false or both are false, control passes to the next statement. BASIC-PLUS allows multiple use of IF/THEN statements to substitute for the AND operator. Whether you use AND to make a compound statement or nest several simple conditions is a matter of choice.

Following is a program to illustrate the use of nested IF statements:

Example 4.4

```
10      REM USE OF NESTED CONDITIONAL STATEMENTS
20      INPUT 'A,B,C,D'; A,B,C,D
30      IF A > B THEN IF A > C
            THEN IF A > D THEN PRINT 'A IS THE LARGEST VALUE'
40      IF B > A THEN IF B > C
            THEN IF B > D THEN PRINT 'B IS THE LARGEST VALUE'
50      IF C > A THEN IF C > B
            THEN IF C > D THEN PRINT 'C IS THE LARGEST VALUE'
999     END

Ready

RUNNH
A,B,C,D? 40,30,20,10
A IS THE LARGEST VALUE

Ready

RUNNH
A,B,C,D? 30,40,50,35
C IS THE LARGEST VALUE

Ready

RUNNH
A,B,C,D? 10,10,30,40

Ready
```

Example 4.4 calls for four values in the INPUT statement and tests for the largest of three of these variables. In statement 30, the variable A is tested against B, C, and D to determine whether A was the largest value. Since no test was made to determine when the variable D was the largest value, no printout occurs in the last run where the variable D was assigned 40, the largest of the four values used in that run. Example 4.4 is not an efficient program because all tests must be made by the computer even though one test would be sufficient to isolate the largest value. Later, you will have the chance to improve the structure and logic of finding the largest value.

4.5 FURTHER APPLICATIONS OF CONDITIONAL STATEMENTS

Now let's review some of the features of the conditional statement by working a problem that selects a few scores from a list of ten scores and computes the average of these scores. Figure 4.3 outlines the problem in flowchart form.

Example 4.5 is a program that is designed to read and process ten scores but is selective since it computes the average of scores in the 30 to 50 range. Statement 60 is the key conditional statement that determines whether or not a score falls within the 30 to 50 range. If these conditions are found to be true, then the score is counted and totaled so that the average of these selected scores can be computed when all ten scores have been processed. Note that in Figure 4-3, the flowchart of this problem, only one flowchart symbol is used to show the computation of the average and the printout of the average score in the 30 to 50 range.

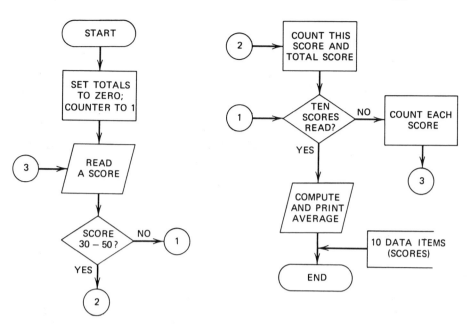

Figure 4-3. Flowchart of program to print average of selected scores.

Of course, a separate process symbol could have been included along with the output symbol.

In designing your flowchart of a problem where you are processing a specific number of data elements, it is important that you count all of the data elements in order to process the correct number as well as to avoid the OUT OF DATA error message.[2] Figure 4-3 shows that all data elements are read and counted. Even though selected scores were used to compute an average, all scores that were read were tested to determine if all ten scores had been processed.

Example 4.5

```
10      REM COMPUTING THE AVERAGE OF SCORES WHICH RANGE
                   FROM 30 TO 50
20      REM N = THE NUMBER OF SCORES IN THE 30 TO 50 RANGE
30      REM T = THE TOTAL OF SCORES IN THE 30 TO 50 RANGE
40      N, T = 0 \  C = 1          ! C COUNTS ALL SCORES
50      READ X                     ! X = INDIVIDUAL SCORE
60      IF X >= 30 AND X <= 50
                   THEN N = N + 1\  T = T + X
70      IF C < 10 THEN C = C + 1\  GO TO 50
80      PRINT 'AVERAGE ='; T/N
90      DATA 29,40,51,30,50,45,52,25,32, 49
900     END

Ready

RUNNH
AVERAGE = 41
```

---

[2] If using a counter is not practical, use a flag.

4.6 PROGRAM LOOPS USING FOR. . .NEXT STATEMENTS

Since data that is used to produce information requires counting and a variety of other arithmetic operations, most computer programs repeat sections many times. We have performed this looping process through the use of the GO TO statement and the IF. . . THEN conditional statement. Of course, we had to have some way of stopping the looping process through the use of a counter or a flag. The FOR. . .NEXT statements are designed to combine the counting and testing process. First, let's review the key elements in program loops. The four distinct parts of program loops are:

1. The loop must be initialized in order to get it started.

2. The statements included in the loop must be located in a logical order.

3. The loop should include a value which controls the number of loops.

4. Some method of terminating the loop should be included.

One of the most powerful statements in BASIC-PLUS for looping are the FOR. . .NEXT statements. The format of these statements is:

```
LINE number      FOR    variable = expression  TO expression   STEP expression
LINE number      NEXT   variable
```

For example:

```
10      For I = 2 TO 10 STEP 2
  •
  •     (body of the loop)
  •
50      NEXT I
```

The FOR statement at line 10 sets the loop control variable, I, to its initial value, 2. The FOR statement also keeps track of the ending value, 10, and the STEP value, 2. Then, the body of the loop is executed. Once the NEXT statement is encountered, the control variable will be compared with the ending value. As long as it is less than the ending value, the control variable will be incremented by step values and the computer passes the control to the top of the body of the loop (the statement immediately following the FOR statement). Thus, I = 4 for the second loop; I = 6 for the third, and so on. This process continues until I = 10 when the last loop occurs through statement 50. The following example illustrates this process:

Example 4.6

```
10        REM USING THE FOR. . .NEXT LOOP TO COMPUTE AN AVERAGE
20        N, T = 0
30        REM C IS THE CONTROL VARIABLE
40        FOR C = 1 TO 10      ! THE LOOP WILL BE MADE 10 TIMES
50              READ X
60              IF X >= 30 AND X <= 50
                      THEN N = N + 1\ T = T + X
70        NEXT C
80        PRINT 'AVERAGE ='; T/N
90        DATA 29,40,51,30,50,45,52,25,32,49
900       END

Ready

RUNNH
AVERAGE = 41
```

Example 4.6 is essentially the same program as Example 4.5. The two statements that are different are lines 40 and 70. In Example 4.6, statement 40 sets the counter, C, to 1 and increments C by one each time the loop is completed at statement 70. Once C = 10, control passes to statement 80. Since the variable, C, was incremented by 1 for each pass, it was unnecessary to include STEP 1 as part of the FOR statement. Omitting the word, STEP, in statement 40 resulted in C being incremented by 1. Each time the loop body (statements 40 to 70) was executed, a score was tested to see if it fell within the appropriate range.

Variables can be used as part of the FOR statement provided they are identified prior to entering the FOR loop. For example:

$$90 \quad FOR \quad J = I \quad TO \quad L \quad STEP \quad Y$$

The variables, I, L, and Y should have preassigned values so that the proper looping and incrementing as well as loop termination will occur. The number of times a FOR loop is executed can be calculated by the formula:

$$\text{Integer part of } \left(\frac{L - I}{Y}\right) + 1$$

Example 4.7

```
10        REM FOR. . .NEXT LOOP USING FRACTIONAL VALUES
20        FOR J = 0.5 TO 2.5 STEP 0.5
30              PRINT 'I LOVE THE MINI'
40        NEXT J
900       END

Ready

RUNNH
I LOVE THE MINI
I LOVE THE MINI
I LOVE THE MINI
I LOVE THE MINI
I LOVE THE MINI
```

Example 4.7 begins the FOR loop with the control variable, J, set to 0.5 and incremented by 0.5 for each loop resulting in five lines of output.

Both positive and negative values can be used as STEP values.

$$120 \quad FOR \quad K = 100 \quad to \quad 10 \quad STEP \quad -5$$

Statement 120 sets K = 100 for the first loop; then K is decremented to 95 for the second loop since STEP is set to a −5. Statement 120 would be processed until K = 10 before control would pass to statements following the loop.

4.7 NESTED LOOPS

FOR loops can be used to control other FOR loops—that is, they can be nested. Example 4.8 shows how the FOR I. . .NEXT I loop controls the FOR J. . .NEXT J loop. The FOR J loop is executed six times since the J loop is set to repeat three times, and the controlling FOR I loop repeats twice. Note that the second line of output that prints all values for I and J within the FOR J loop, prints I = 2 and the three values of J which range from one to three.

Example 4.8

```
5        REM NESTING FOR. . .NEXT LOOPS
10       FOR I = 1 TO 2
20               FOR J = 1 TO 3
30                       PRINT 'I=';I;'J=';J,  !ENDING COMMA
                                         PREVENTS SPACING
40               NEXT J
50       PRINT                       !FORCES PRINTER TO SPACE TO THE
                                         NEXT LINE
60       NEXT I
900      END

Ready

RUNNH
I= 1 J= 1     I= 1 J= 2     I= 1 J= 3
I= 2 J= 1     I= 2 J= 2     I= 2 J= 3
```

Figure 4-4 illustrates that FOR loops can be nested to more than two levels, but care is required to ensure that the loops do not overlap.

It is acceptable to transfer out of a FOR loop to another point in the program provided the transfer is logical. It is also acceptable to transfer or branch around some statements within a specific FOR loop. Figure 4-5 shows some examples of acceptable and unacceptable approaches in transferring within and outside FOR loops:

Flowcharting programs containing FOR loops present a problem, since the FOR statement sets values to several variables and tests to determine whether or not looping should continue. One approach to identifying FOR loops in a flowchart is illustrated in Figure 4-6.

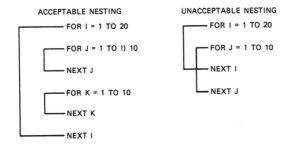

Figure 4-4. Nesting FOR loops.

ACCEPTABLE FOR LOOP TRANSFERS	UNACCEPTABLE FOR LOOP TRANSFERS

```
10   FOR K = 1 TO N
20      IF A1 = K THEN 40
30   NEXT K
40   ...
```
(K holds it incremented value in
   subsequent processing)[3]

```
10   IF A1 = A2 THEN 30
20   FOR K = 1 TO N
30      IF A1 = K THEN 40
40   NEXT K
```
(transfer into a FOR loop must be to
   the FOR statement line number)

* * *

```
10   FOR K = 1 TO N
20      IF A1 = K THEN 40
30      B = B + T
40   NEXT K
```
(statement 30 is not executed when
   A1 = K, yet the loop continues)

* * *

```
10   FOR K = 1 TO N
20      IF A1 = K THEN 10
30      B = B + T
40   NEXT K
```
(transfer must be either out of the
   FOR loop or to statement 40)

Figure 4-5. Acceptable and unacceptable transfers in the FOR. . .loop.

The processing and decision symbols are combined into one symbol to identify the beginning of the FOR loop.
The end of the FOR loop is identified by placing the control variable for the loop within a connector symbol. Finally, a solid line is drawn to bracket the entire FOR loop.

Example 4.9 shows the coded program and run of the problem flowcharted in Figure 4-6. Note that the program is much easier to read, and the nested FOR S loop's relationship

Example 4.9

```
5          PRINT '              THIS PROGRAM SHOWS THE NEW SALARY SCHEDULE'
10         PRINT, 'STEP 1', 'STEP 2', 'STEP 3'   \   PRINT
20         FOR R = 1 TO 4
30              READ R$
40              PRINT R$,
50              FOR S = 1 TO 3
60                   READ M
70                   M1 = M*(1+0.135)
80                   PRINT M1,
90              NEXT S
100             PRINT
110        NEXT R
120        DATA 'INSTRUCTOR', 13200, 14460, 15850
130        DATA 'ASST PROF', 14460, 15850, 17385
140        DATA 'ASSO PROF', 18200, 19982, 21930
150        DATA 'PROFESSOR', 23000, 25250, 27750
900        END
Ready

RUNNH
           THIS PROGRAM SHOWS THE NEW SALARY SCHEDULE
                STEP 1          STEP 2          STEP 3

INSTRUCTOR      14982           16412.1         17989.8
ASST PROF       16412.1         17989.8         19732
ASSO PROF       20657           22679.6         24890.6
PROFESSOR       26105           28658.8         31496.2

Ready
```

---

[3] While it is acceptable to transfer out of a FOR loop, from the standpoint of structured programming, the loop should have one entry and one exit. See Chapter 8 for more on this topic.

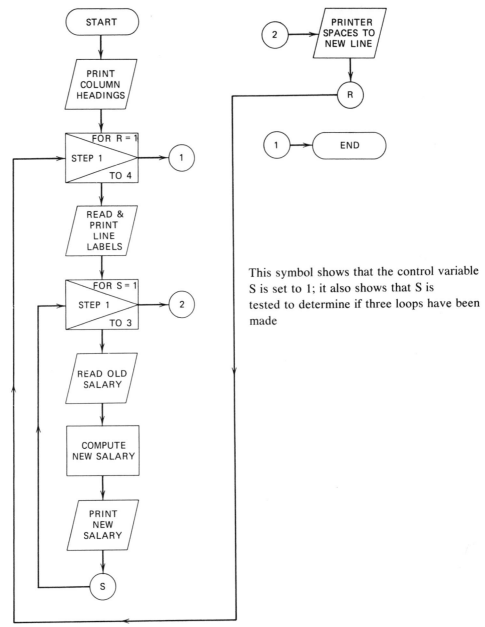

Figure 4-6 Flowchart of Nested FOR Loops

This symbol shows that the control variable S is set to 1; it also shows that S is tested to determine if three loops have been made

to the outer FOR R loop is clearer because the lines of the inner loop are indented further than the outer loop's lines.

Example 4.9 uses data taken from an existing salary schedule from a fictitious Fullboldt State University where faculty are classified into four ranks. Within each rank there are three steps. The current salary schedule follows:

	Step 1	Step 2	Step 3
Instructor	13200	14460	15850
Assistant Professor	14460	15850	17385
Associate Professor	18200	19982	21930
Professor	23000	25250	27750

Example 4.9 produces a new salary schedule based on an increase of 13.5 percent that has just been approved.

Compound Conditions. Two or more conditions included as part of a conditional statement.

Flowchart. An outline of a program using special symbols to represent the functions and logical sequence.

Initialized. Setting a variable to a specific value such as A = 0.

Logical Operators. AND, OR as used in a compound condition.

Loop Control Variable. The variable used with the FOR. . .NEXT statements to control the number of loops through a series of statements.

Multiple Statements. When more than one statement is placed after a single statement number. Statements are separated by a colon (:) or backslash (\ ).

Nested Loops. The placement of a FOR. . .NEXT loop inside one or more additional FOR. . .NEXT loops.

Relational Operators. Symbols used to test relationships in conditional statements, such as equal to (=), and so on.

Truth Tables. Tables that show how the computer evaluates the AND, OR compound conditions.

PROBLEMS

1. Determine the output for each of the following programs:

(a)
```
10  A=1\  B=2
20  IF A+B=3 THEN PRINT 'YES'\  GO TO 99
30  PRINT 'NO'
99  END
```

(b)
```
10  A=1\  B=2\  C=3
20  IF A+B=C THEN PRINT 'YES'
30  PRINT 'NO'
99  END
```

(c)
```
10  X=5\  Y=3
20  IF X**2=25 AND Y-1<0 THEN PRINT 'JACK'\  GO TO 99
30  PRINT 'JILL'
99  END
```

(d)
```
10  A=1\  B=3\  C=5
20  IF A+B<C**2 AND A<=1 OR B**2+1=10 THEN PRINT 'JA'
30  GO TO 99
40  PRINT 'NEIN'
99  END
```

(e)
```
10  FOR X=1 TO 5
20  IF X=3 THEN PRINT 'PLUS'\  GO TO 40
30  PRINT 'BASIC'
40  NEXT X
99  END
```

(f) 10   A=1 \   B=5 \   C=−2
   20   IF A<3
         THEN IF A+B>4
           THEN IF C**2>=100
             THEN PRINT 'ALL RIGHT' \   GO TO 99
   30   PRINT "SOMETHING'S WRONG"
   99   END

2. What output will be produced by the following program segments?

(a) FOR I=3 TO 12 STEP 2
     PRINT I+1
   NEXT I

(b) I=2 \   S=10 \   L=.5
   FOR K=I TO S STEP L
     PRINT K
   NEXT K

(c) 10   N=10
   20   FOR J=1 TO N
   30   FOR I=1 TO N
   40   K=I+J
   50   IF I=5 AND J=5 THEN 80
   60   NEXT I
   70   NEXT J
   80   PRINT I,J,K

3. How many times will K be printed in the following program segments?

(a) FOR I=1 TO 10
     FOR J=1 TO 20
       K=J+I
     NEXT J
     PRINT K
   NEXT I

(b) FOR I=1 TO 10
     FOR J=1 TO 20
       K=J+I
       PRINT K
     NEXT J
   NEXT I

4. Write a BASIC program to sum the first 100 even integers.

$$(2 + 4 + 6 + \ldots \ldots \ldots + 100)$$

5. Write a program to compute the product of first N integers, your program should allow you to INPUT N. For example, if you input 5 for N, then compute $1 \times 2 \times 3 \times 4 \times 5$.

6. Write a program to calculate the following expression:

$$1/2 + 2/3 + 3/4 + \ldots \ldots + 98/99 + 99/100$$

7. Flowchart and code a program to select and print the largest of four numbers that are to INPUT into a program. Your program should not use the inefficient, brute force approach used in Example 4.4

8. Flowchart, code and run a program to analyze test scores. Assume that:
(a) 100 is the highest possible test score
(b) 70 is the minimum passing score
(c) the last data value acts as a flag

Use the following data: 75, 80, 69, 70, 49, 95, 85, 100, 45, 86, 71, 101

You are to compute and print out the following information:

       NUMBER FAILING TEST = ?
       NUMBER PASSING TEST = ?
       AVERAGE TEST SCORE   = ?
       LOWEST TEST SCORE   = ?
       HIGHEST TEST SCORE   = ?

9. The ages of residents in the Paradise Community are: 11, 45, 56, 87, 98, 23, 75, 77, 54, 33, 65, 90, 51, 38, 88, 101, 44, 23. Write a program to count the total number of senior citizens (65 or older) and their average age. (Note: Use a flag at the end of the data block.)

10. Mrs. Lucey will rent a car to drive from Los Angeles to San Francisco. (400 miles) Due to the gas crunch, she doesn't want to fill her tank on the way. In addition to that, she needs air-conditioning. The total travel cost shouldn't exceed $200. If the gas is $2 per gallon, help her to write a program to pick car(s) from the following list, which suit her needs:

Maker	Model	Tank Size	Miles/gallon	Charge/day	Rate/mile	Air
Ford	Escort	12	35	20	.25	N
Chevy	Citation	15	28	22	.27	Y
Audi	5000	20	22	50	.30	Y
Honda	Accord	15	28	22	.29	Y
Fiat	Strada	20	33	30	.18	N
Cadl	Seville	25	18	50	.20	Y
Chevy	Impala	25	16	33	.25	Y
Datsun	210	15	27	20	.15	N

11. Tabulate the function value of $f(x) = X^5 - 3X + 1$ in the interval of $(-2, 2)$ at step of 0.5.

12. It is assumed that there is a relationship between a husband's and wife's education. A statistical correlation coefficient can be calculated to verify the assumption. The correlation coefficient is a number between -1 and 1. If it's close to one, the husband's and wife's education are highly correlated. If it's close to 0, there's no relationship existing. A negative correlation coefficient means that they are correlated in the opposite direction. The formula to calculate correlation coefficient is:

$$R = \frac{\Sigma(x - X)(y - Y)}{\sqrt{\Sigma(x - X)^2 \, \Sigma(y - Y)^2}}$$

where x: husband's years of education
      X: husband's average years of education
      y: wife's years of education
      Y: wife's average years of education

Make up data of five couples you know about and write a BASIC program to calculate the correlation coefficient.

13. Flowchart, code, and run a program to compute accumulated earnings (principal invested plus interest) on an investment of $5,000 for a five-year period with an interest rate of 12 percent. Design the program so that you can compare the accumulated earnings when interest is compounded annually, monthly, and daily (360-day period). Your INPUT statement should allow varying amounts of investments to be recorded, inclusion of a shorter or longer investment period, different interest rates, and three possible methods for computing interest (annually, monthly, or daily). Output should appear:

```
INITIAL INVESTMENT = 5000
INTEREST RATE = .12
COMPOUNDED ANNUALLY
YEAR      AMOUNT
  1       9999.99
  2       9999.99
  .
  5       9999.99
```

Your output should include at least three runs which compare computations for the three methods for compounding interest.

14. (Amortization Schedule)
A mortgage is the most common loan payment form in the United States, in which each installment is used both to pay interest and to reduce the principal. For a loan of R dollars installed over M months at an annual interest rate of I%, the monthly payment will be:

$$R \times \frac{I/12}{1 - (1 + I/12)^{-M}}$$

The amount applied toward the interest charge is:

$$\text{Previous Balance} \times (I/12)$$

The amount credited to the principal is:

$$\text{Monthly Installment} - \text{Interest Charge}$$

While the monthly payment remains the same from month to month, the portion for interest charge decreases and that for the principal increases. Write a program that will produce an amortization table for any loan amount, period of installments and interest rate. For instance, for a loan of $1,000 amortized over one year at 5% interest rate, the amortization schedule table will look as follows:

```
LOAN AMOUNT? 1000
PERIOD OF INSTALLMENTS IN MONTHS? 12
INTEREST RATE?   0.05
PERIOD  INSTALLMENT    INTEREST    PRINCIPAL    BALANCE
  1       85.6065      4.16667     81.4399      918.56
  2       85.6065      3.82733     81.7792      836.781
  3       85.6065      3.48659     82.1199      754.661
  .
  .
  .
 12       85.6065       .355264    85.2513       .012001
```

Note: Due to rounding error, the last balance does not exactly equal zero.

15. (Date matching game)
(a) Flowchart, code, and run a program to search a file to find a match with a person of the opposite sex whose characteristics are similar to yours. Data are coded as follows:

Sex: Male = 1   Age: < 21 = 1
     Female = 2   ≥ 21 = 2

Interests: Sports = 1   Height: < 5'9" = 1
           Art, music = 2   ≥ 5'9" = 2

You will need to code your own data in order to match it with the data fields of the file that are to be read in. Your data field could appear as follows:

200   DATA 1,1,1,2

The interpretation of statement 200 would be sequentially: male, less than 21, key interest is sports, over 5'9".

Use the following DATA statement for the 12-record file you are to search:

    300   DATA 1,1,1,1, 2,1,1,1, 1,2,1,1, 2,2,1,1, 1,1,2,1, 2,1,2,1
    400   DATA 1,1,1,2, 2,1,1,2, 1,1,2,2, 2,1,2,2, 2,2,2,1, 1,2,2,1

A sample printout could appear as follows:

> I AM (USE YOUR NAME) CODED 1,1,1,2
> MY MOST COMPATIBLE MATCH IS RECORD NUMBER 8

In the event no compatible match is found, print NO DATE TONIGHT.

(b) Modify your program to make a second search of the file to find someone of the opposite sex who is shorter and/or younger than you are if such characteristics exist. If such a match is found, print out this record number. If no match is found, print I'M A BORN LOSER.

16. Following is a fibonacci series:

$$1, 1, 2, 3, 5, 8, 13, 21 \ldots$$

Each fibonacci number is the sum of the previous fibonacci numbers (except the first two). Write a program to determine the 30th fibonacci number.

17. Modify the program in #16 so that fibonacci series of various lengths (e.g., 1 to 12) will be printed. Your output should appear as follows:

LENGTH OF SERIES	FIBONACCI NUMBERS
1	1
2	1 1
3	1 1 2
4	1 1 2 3
....	
12	1 1 2 3 5 8 13 21 34 55 89 144

18. A department store determines whether or not an individual is granted credit based on the following policy:

(a) The customer must have opened a credit account
(b) Credit limit without managerial approval is $100

Write a program and make a flowchart to determine whether or not a request for credit will be approved. Write the program so that the computer can be used to evaluate the credit request. The suggested dialogue is:

```
RUNNH
WHAT IS YOUR NAME?  HENRY JOHNSON
DO YOU HAVE AN ACCOUNT WITH US?  YES
HOW MUCH IS YOUR CREDIT PURCHASE?  150
DO YOU HAVE THE MANAGER'S APPROVAL?  I'M NOT SURE
PLEASE ANSWER WITH YES OR NO
DO YOU HAVE THE MANAGER'S APPROVAL?  NO
 WE CAN'T APPROVE YOUR PURCHASE, HENRY JOHNSON, UNLESS YOU
GET THE APPROVAL FROM THE MANAGER
```

II
Structured Programming
and Applications in BASIC-PLUS

Chapter 5
Debugging Programs

Objectives   You will learn:

More about syntax and runtime errors.

To use simulation techniques to find errors.

The value of inserted PRINT statements.

To use the immediate mode.

The STOP statement and CONTINUE command.

In the previous four chapters, you have acquired a solid background in the BASIC language. You should be able to write programs to solve a variety of problems, although your programs may be inefficient. Before more powerful BASIC statements are studied, let's examine approaches to finding errors in our programs.

Errors occur rather frequently in about everything that we do. By now you have learned that it is unusual if your program produces accurate output on the first run. You have also found that fewer errors occur when you plan your program by sketching a flowchart before you code a program. Program assignments to this point have not been complex, and, usually, if you could not locate an error, someone was able to help you debug your program. There are some valuable techniques as well as some special features of BASIC-PLUS that are helpful in program debugging. We will explore some of these techniques in this chapter.

5.1 MORE ABOUT SYNTAX ERRORS

There are three types of errors in a BASIC program:

Syntax errors

Runtime errors

Logic errors

Syntax errors violate language format. Frequently, a syntax error is a typo, or the error may be due to lack of knowledge about correct format arrangement. For example:

10   PRNIT 'BUG'

will cause the error message

?ILLEGAL VERB AT LINE 10

because PRINT is misspelled.

20   X = 3Y

will cause an error message

?ILLEGAL EXPRESSION AT LINE 20

because 3 times Y should be expressed as 3*Y in BASIC. The timesharing mode lists a syntax error immediately; so, you should have your BASIC textbook with you as an aid to debug your syntax error.

Another syntax error that may be difficult to find follows:

```
10     A = 5

2O     PRINT A
```

?Illegal verb at line 2

At first glance it appears that you have no line 2 in these two statements. If you examine line 20 carefully, however, you will notice that the letter 'O' was typed instead of a zero. So, the computer read line 20 as 2 OPRINT A; since OPRINT is not a legal keyword, an error message occurred. (See Appendix A for a list of error messages.)

5.2 RUNTIME ERRORS AND EXPLANATION OF ERROR MESSAGES

Situations may arise where there is no syntax error in your program, but error messages are still generated at the time the program is running. This is a runtime error which is usually caused by improper composition of statements. READ/DATA and FOR/NEXT are two pairs of statements which commonly cause errors. For example:

FORMAT

neither	10 READ N$, A	line number READ variable list
nor	20 DATA 55, 'CARTER'	line number DATA constant list

violate format. When line 10 is encountered, the computer tries to fetch a character string for N$ and a numerical value for A. However, according to the way data items are arranged in the DATA statement, 55 is assigned to N$ and CARTER is assigned to A which causes

?DATA FORMAT ERROR AT LINE 10

In using FOR loops, it is not uncommon to make errors by leaving out the NEXT statement or by identifying the wrong control variables, particularly when several loops are nested. Example 5.1 illustrates a common error made in identifying the control variable, I.

Example 5.1

```
10         REM EXAMPLE OF A RUNTIME ERROR
20         FOR I = 1 TO 10
30             A = I ** 2
40             PRINT A
50         NEXT J
900        END

Ready

RUNNH

?NEXT without FOR at line 50
?FOR without NEXT at line 20

Ready
```

The two error messages generated are not made until RUN is typed; then, the error messages state quite clearly that the computer cannot process FOR loops or NEXT statements that do not have similar control variables at lines 50 and 20. Thus, line 50 should be corrected to read

50   NEXT I

5.3 SIMULATION TECHNIQUES TO LOCATE ERRORS

The most difficult errors to find are errors in logic—that is, no error message occurs, yet the output is either nonexistent or inaccurate. Errors of this type are particularly hard to find for the person who coded the program since even simple errors can be overlooked. Example 5.2 illustrates common errors that are made. This program also illustrates that a variety of test data should be used before concluding that a program will produce consistent, accurate results. Example 5.2 is designed to square three numbers in sequence; then, to print the three squared values and their sum. The first number used to test the program was INPUT as 2. The output shows that three values to be squared as 3, 4, and 5 rather than as 2, 3, and 4, as it should. Before locating and correcting this error, however, let's try another run even though the values squared of 4, 9, and 16 total 29 which is the correct sum. The second value INPUT is 3, and the output generated is shown below in example 5.2. Now a serious error appears. The sum of the squared values of 3, 4, and 5 (9 + 16 + 25) is printed as 79 when it should be 50. Note that we terminated the continuation of this program by typing in 'NO' when the computer asked, 'DO YOU WANT TO TRY AGAIN?' Now we need to determine why the sum of the first three numbers squared was accurate while the squared values of the second value INPUT was inaccurate. The identical program processed both of these runs, except that the second INPUT value was a continuation of the program, not a separate run.

One method of locating errors is to simulate or hand trace each variable as it is being processed by the program. Figure 5-1 illustrates a method to hand trace a computer pro-

Example 5.2

```
10      REM PROGRAM TO SQUARE THREE SUCCESSIVE VALUES
20      PRINT 'SQUARING THREE SUCCESSIVE VALUES'
30      INPUT 'WHAT IS THE FIRST VALUE';S
35      T = 0            !T SET TO ZERO TO CORRECT SUMMING ERROR
40      PRINT 'VALUE', 'VALUE SQUARED'
50      FOR I = 1 TO 3
60          N = S ** 2
65          PRINT S,N  !S SHOULD BE PRINTED BEFORE IT IS
                           INCREMENTED
70          T = T + N
80          S = S + 1
100     NEXT I
110     PRINT 'TOTAL OF SQUARED VALUES IS'; T
120     INPUT 'DO YOU WANT TO TRY AGAIN'; A$
130     IF A$ = 'YES' THEN 30
900     END

Ready

RUNNH
SQUARING THREE SUCCESSIVE VALUES
WHAT IS THE FIRST VALUE? 2
VALUE            VALUE SQUARED
  2                    4
  3                    9
  4                    16
TOTAL OF SQUARED VALUES IS 29
DO YOU WANT TO TRY AGAIN? YES
WHAT IS THE FIRST VALUE? 3
VALUE            VALUE SQUARED
  3                    9
  4                    16
  5                    25
TOTAL OF SQUARED VALUES IS 50
DO YOU WANT TO TRY AGAIN? NO
```

	Variables in Memory				Variables Output		
	S	N	I	T	S	N	T
INPUT? 2	2						
1st loop			1				
	3	4		4	3*	4	
2nd loop			2				
	4	9		13	4*	9	
3d loop			3				
	5	16		29	5*	16	29
INPUT? 3	3						
1st loop			1				
	4	9		38	4*	9	
2nd loop			2				
	5	16		54	5*	16	
3d loop			3				
	6	25		79	6*	25	79*

*errors in output

Figure 5-1. Simulation trace table of Example 5.2.

gram. The variables to be traced are placed in columns and the values assigned to each variable are written in as they are processed and printed out on a line by line basis. Since we INPUT the number 2 and stored it in location S, we can easily trace what happens to variable S in this table. Note that S is increased to 3 in our first loop and thus is printed out as 3. Obviously, we should print out the value of S before it is incremented. The most serious error, the sum of the values squared, however, has not been located, so it is necessary to continue the simulation of the program. Eventually, the error in variable T (total of squared numbers) becomes apparent when we note that T has not been reset to zero prior to summing the squared values. In coding this program we made a serious programming error—we failed to set location T = 0. The error had not appeared in the first run because the BASIC compiler sets values of zero for all undefined variables. However, when we INPUT the value of three in the second run, T had accumulated the sum of the first three values squared—29. Thus, it is necessary to insert the expression, T = 0, into the proper location in our program. Example 5.3 shows the corrected version of Example 5.2 with two sample runs to verify that our errors in logic have been corrected. Simulation of a program by tracing values stored in each variable may be tedious, but it is effective!

5.4 USE OF ADDITIONAL PRINT STATEMENTS

Another effective way of debugging programs is to place additional PRINT statements in locations where errors appear to occur in order to find out what specific values are stored in variables. Once errors are detected and corrected, these extra PRINT statements can be removed. For example, we can add the following PRINT statement to Example 5.2 to get more information about the variables, I and T:

$$85 \quad \text{PRINT, , 'I = '; I; 'T = '; T}$$

Example 5.3

```
10        REM PROGRAM TO SQUARE THREE SUCCESSIVE VALUES
20        PRINT 'SQUARING THREE SUCCESSIVE VALUES'
30        INPUT 'WHAT IS THE FIRST VALUE';S
35        T = 0            !T SET TO ZERO TO CORRECT SUMMING ERROR
40        PRINT 'VALUE', 'VALUE SQUARED'
50        FOR I = 1 TO 3
60             N = S ** 2
65             PRINT S,N !S SHOULD BE PRINTED BEFORE IT IS
                                     INCREMENTED
70             T = T + N
80             S = S + 1
100       NEXT I
110       PRINT 'TOTAL OF SQUARED VALUES IS'; T
120       INPUT 'DO YOU WANT TO TRY AGAIN'; A$
130       IF A$ = 'YES' THEN 30
900       END

Ready

RUNNH
SQUARING THREE SUCCESSIVE VALUES
WHAT IS THE FIRST VALUE? 2
VALUE          VALUE SQUARED
 2                4
 3                9
 4                16
TOTAL OF SQUARED VALUES IS 29
DO YOU WANT TO TRY AGAIN? YES
WHAT IS THE FIRST VALUE? 3
VALUE          VALUE SQUARED
 3                9
 4                16
 5                25
TOTAL OF SQUARED VALUES IS 50
DO YOU WANT TO TRY AGAIN? NO
```

A rerun of Example 5.2 with this new statement would produce the output shown in Figure 5-2 which is essentially the same information generated by hand simulation shown in Figure 5-1. The errors in this program are now much easier to find when more information about variables is in hard copy form.

Figure 5-2. Inserted PRINT statements to debug programs.

```
85                  PRINT,,'I=';I; 'T= ';T
RUNNH
SQUARING THREE SUCCESSIVE VALUES
WHAT IS THE FIRST VALUE? 2
VALUE          VALUE SQUARED
                          I= 1 T=  4
 3                4
                          I= 2 T=  13
 4                9
                          I= 3 T=  29
 5                16
TOTAL OF SQUARED VALUES IS 29
DO YOU WANT TO TRY AGAIN? YES
WHAT IS THE FIRST VALUE? 3
VALUE          VALUE SQUARED
                          I= 1 T=  38
 4                9
                          I= 2 T=  54
 5                16
                          I= 3 T=  79
 6                25
TOTAL OF SQUARED VALUES IS 79
DO YOU WANT TO TRY AGAIN? NO
```

5.5 USING IMMEDIATE MODE

In BASIC-PLUS one can execute a statement immediately without running a complete program by omitting the statement line number. For example:

PRINT 'IMMEDIATE MODE IS USEFUL IN PROGRAM DEBUGGING'

results in the following immediate output:

IMMEDIATE MODE IS USEFUL IN PROGRAM DEBUGGING

Ready

The Ready message is printed to show that the computer is ready for more input. Statements which start with line numbers are stored as part of a program, while statements without line numbers are compiled and executed immediately. The immediate mode is useful in computing formulas or arithmetic statements that you may wish to check without running a program; or, by stopping a program (depress CONTROL and C keys simultaneously), you can check the accuracy of a statement while coding a program by typing it in immediate mode.

Example 5.4

```
5         REM USE OF IMMEDIATE MODE TO CHECK ACCURACY OF AN EXPRESSION
10        PRINT 'COMPUTATION OF PRINCIPAL + INTEREST BEGINNING IN 1980'
15        INPUT 'PRINCIPAL=';P;'RATE=';I;'PERIOD =';J;'YEARS =';N
20        FOR Y = 1985 TO 2000 STEP N
30            P = P * (1 + I/J) ** J * N
40            PRINT '   YEAR IS';Y;'         TOTAL IS ';P
50        NEXT Y
900       END

Ready

RUNNH
COMPUTATION OF PRINCIPAL + INTEREST BEGINNING IN 1980
PRINCIPAL=? 1000
RATE=? .1
PERIOD =? 12
YEARS =? 5
    YEAR IS 1985        TOTAL IS  5523.57
    YEAR IS 1990        TOTAL IS  30509.8
    YEAR IS 1995        TOTAL IS  168523
    YEAR IS 2000        TOTAL IS  930848

Ready

P = 1000 * (1 + .1/12) ** (12 * 5)←!IMMEDIATE MODE CHECKS FORMULA

Ready

PRINT P
  1645.31 ←─────────── IMMEDIATE MODE PRINTOUT SHOWS CORRECT OUTPUT

Ready

30                P = P * (1 + I/J) ** (J *N) !STATEMENT 30 CORRECTED
RUNNH
COMPUTATION OF PRINCIPAL + INTEREST BEGINNING IN 1980
PRINCIPAL=? 1000
RATE=? .1
PERIOD =? 12
YEARS =? 5
    YEAR IS 1985        TOTAL IS  1645.31
    YEAR IS 1990        TOTAL IS  2707.05
    YEAR IS 1995        TOTAL IS  4453.93
    YEAR IS 2000        TOTAL IS  7328.1

Ready
```

Example 5.4 illustrates a method for using the immediate mode to check the accuracy of a formula used to compute compounded interest. The formula is:

$$T = P\left(1 + \frac{I}{J}\right)^{J*N}$$

T = accumulated principal & interest; P = principal; I = interest rate;

J = number of times interest compounded annually; N = number of years

This compounded interest formula is placed in statement 30 of Example 5.4. The accuracy of statement 30 is suspect because the first line of output of $5,523.57 appears unreasonably large for the $1,000 principal that is being computed in five-year increments. Since we are computing interest at 10 percent, we know that in five years the principal and interest must be less than $2,000; therefore, some error in computation is occuring. Using the immediate mode, we type in actual values into the formula. We also note that we had not placed the exponent in parentheses which we are quite sure resulted in output errors in Example 5.4. We typed

P = 1000 * (1 + .1/12) ** (12 * 5)

Ready (computer response)

PRINT P
1645.31 (immediate output)

The output produced by this immediate mode statement verifies that statement 30 requires parentheses around the exponent (J * N). The final step is to type in a corrected statement 30 which appears prior to the final printout in Example 5.4.

5.6 THE STOP AND CONTINUE COMMANDS

Another approach in debugging programs is to place STOP statements at points in the program where errors are suspect. The STOP statement is a standalone statement. Its general format is:

line number   STOP

When this statement is encountered, the execution of the program is terminated and a message is printed. Only one END statement is permitted in a program, while any number of STOP statements can be placed in a program as they are needed. For example:

35   IF K = 0 THEN STOP

causes the program to halt when K = 0 at statement 35 and prints the message

STOP AT LINE 35

This allows you to use the immediate mode to check the values of variables and/or to correct the logic of statements you find in error. Once your corrections are made, type CONT (continue), and the program should resume execution. If you make a typing or logical error in the immediate mode, the error message

?CAN'T CONTINUE

will appear after you have typed CONT.

There will be programs that are difficult to debug regardless of how carefully they are studied. In that event, it is wise to list the program in hard copy form and wait several hours before you restudy the program and attempt to debug it. You may find that "sleeping" on the program is all that you need to get that bit of inspiration that will help you find that elusive error.

Debugging. Locating and correcting programming errors.

Immediate Mode. Immediate execution of a BASIC statement through omission of a statement number.

Logic Error. Inaccurate or nonexistent output due to illogical instructions in the program.

Runtime Error. Errors in statements which are detected during the RUN of a program.

Syntax Error. An error in the grammar or format of BASIC.

Trace Table. Placing variables into a table so that values can be hand traced as the program is followed manually, step by step.

PROBLEMS

Find and correct the errors in the following programs:

1.
```
10 FOR K = 1 TO N
20     T = K * 10
30     PRINT T
40  NEXT K
```

2.
```
10  READ A,B,C
20  PRING A * B * C
90  END
```

3.
```
10  READ A,B,C
20  PRINT (A + B + C)/D
30  DATA 2, 4, 6
90  END
```

4.
```
10  READ C D
20  IF C = D OR C > D THEN 10
30  PRINT 'C IS LESS THAN D'; D   C
40  DATA 5,5,5,4,8,5
50  END
```

5.
```
10  READ X, Y
20  IF X > Y AND X < 10 THEN 40
30  PRINT 'Y IS GREATER THAN X'
40  PRINT 'X IS GREATER THAN Y' \ GO TO 10
50  DATA 10, 9, 20, 21, 17
90  END
```

6.
```
10  J = 1, K = 20, L = 3
20  FOR I = J TO K STEP L
30     FOR J = 1 TO K
40        T = J + L
50     NEXT I
```

```
         60    PRINT 'TOTAL ='; T
         70  NEXT I
         90  END

7.  10  FOR I = 1 TO 10
    20     FOR J = 1 TO 20
    30        T = T + J/K
    40     NEXT J
    50     PRINT T
    60  NEXT I
    70  DATA 1,2,3,4,5,6,99
    90  END

8.  10  REM PROGRAM DESIGNED TO PRINT EVEN INTEGERS SQUARED
              UNTIL I = 256
    20  I = 2
    30  I = I ** 2
    40  IF I = 256 THEN 900
    50  PRINT I
    60  I = I + 2 \ GO TO 20
    900  END
```

(Suggestion: Hand simulate values stored in I in each statement; your output should PRINT I as 4, 16, 36 . . .

9. Rewrite the program listed in problem 8 using a FOR. . .NEXT loop.

```
10.  10  FOR I = 1 TO 20
     20     IF X > 10 THEN 10
     30     IF X < 11 THEN PRINT X
     40     X = X + 2
     50  NEXT I
     90  END

11.  10  READ A, N$
     20  IF N$ = 'DUMMY' THEN GO TO END
     30  PRINT N$, A
     90  DATA 'HEIDEN', 'JOHNSON', 'DUMMY', 25,21
     99  END

12.  10  INPUT A, B
     20  T = T * (A + B)
     30  PRINT 'T = '; T
     40  IF T = 0 THEN STOP \ GO TO 10
     50  IF T > 100 THEN PRINT 'T IS GREATER THAN 100'
     90  END
```

After debugging this program, indicate procedures to follow to continue execution following a STOP statement.

13. (a) Hand simulate the following program by tracing values stored in the variables I, J, and X and show the values as they are printed.
    (b) Using additional PRINT statements, reproduce a trace table that is similar to the simulation you made in part (a) of this problem.

```
10  K, M = 2 \ L = 10
20  FOR I = K to L-2 STEP M
30     FOR J = M TO L STEP M + 2
```

```
40      X = J + I
50       IF X > 16 THEN 80
60    NEXT J
70    PRINT X;
80  NEXT I
90  PRINT X + I + J
99  END
```

Chapter 6
Formatting Output

Objectives   You will learn:

Output rules for PRINT statements.

The PRINT TAB function.

The PRINT USING statement.

To use separate format statements.

We have been rather limited in the way in which output has been printed. We have been able to produce readable output through the use of string constants in headings, such as

> 10   PRINT '   THE AVERAGE SCORE IS'; A

which produces

> THE AVERAGE SCORE IS 30.1

assuming the value stored in the variable A is 30.1. In this example, we had the printer begin printing at the eighth print position on the line by leaving seven blank spaces after the beginning quote mark. Before we introduce new methods of formatting output, let's review the rules for using the PRINT statement with commas and semicolons.

6.1 REVIEW OF OUTPUT FORMAT

Recall that there are normally five print zones on each line of output when commas are used following constants or variables as part of the PRINT statement. Most terminals have 14 spaces for each of the first four print positions; 16 spaces are available for the fifth print zone. Example 6.1 shows the typical arrangement of output with the five print zones:

Example 6.1

```
10      REM REVIEW OF PRINTING ZONES
20      READ A,B,C,D,E
30      PRINT A,B,C,D,E
40      DATA 1,2,3,4,5
900     END

Ready

RUNNH
 1              2              3              4              5

Ready
```

When a semicolon is used after numeric variables or constants in a PRINT statement, the semicolons cause an override of the print zones, and spacing is reduced to two spaces between positive numbers as illustrated in Example 6.2.

Example 6.2

```
10      REM SEMICOLONS OVERRIDE PRINT ZONES
20      READ A,B,C,D
30      PRINT A;B;C;D
40      DATA 1,2,3,4
900     END

Ready

RUNNH
 1  2   3   4
```

It is possible to position values in different printing zones through the use of leading commas in the PRINT statement, as the following immediate mode statement shows:

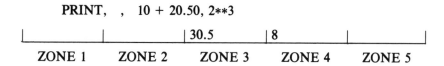

PRINT, ,   10 + 20.50, 2**3

The two commas following PRINT causes a skip to the third and fourth print zones where output is printed. The preceding example in immediate mode illustrates that trailing zeros to the right of a decimal point are not printed; this results in inadequate output especially when you wish to show dollar amounts accurate to two decimal places. Ideally, the sum of

$$10 + 20.50$$

should produce output of 30.50. We'll solve this problem by using a special form of the PRINT statement called PRINT USING later in this chapter.

6.2 THE PRINT TAB FUNCTION

The PRINT statement with the TAB function allows you to tabulate to the exact column of a line much like you do with a typewriter. For example:

PRINT   TAB(5);1;TAB(10);2;TAB(15);3
                    1   2   3

where these three numbers are printed 5, 10, and 15 spaces in from the left margin. So the TAB function acts as a tabulator and makes it easy to create neatly arranged tables and other data. Let's make a list of names and arrange them in columns with the last name first.

Example 6.3

```
10      REM ARRANGING OUTPUT WITH THE TAB FUNCTION
20      PRINT TAB(12);'BIS 55 CLASS LIST'  \   PRINT
30      FOR I = 1 TO 30        !WE EXPECT NO  MORE THAN 30 STUDENTS
40           READ F$, L$
50           IF F$ = 'LAST' THEN 900
60           PRINT TAB(12);L$;',';TAB(22);F$  \ PRINT
70      NEXT I
80      DATA SUSNA, BLACK, JANICE, GOODRICH, HARRY, JONES, HAROLD,
             MARTINS, JON, SMITH, LAST, NAME
900     END

Ready

RUNNH
            BIS 55 CLASS LIST

            BLACK,      SUSNA

            GOODRICH, JANICE

            JONES,     HARRY

            MARTINS,   HAROLD

            SMITH,     JON
```

Example 6.3 shows how easy it is to arrange a list of names under a heading by using the TAB function as part of the PRINT statement. Each first name and last name is READ and stored in F$ and L$, respectively. In printing the last name first, we TAB 12 spaces before typing L$ for the last name. Then, we TAB 22 spaces from the left margin and type F$ for the first name. Note that we inserted a comma between quotes to get the conventional printout to separate the last name from the first name. We also used an extra PRINT statement to double space. The flag used to end the program was 'LAST.' Quotes around 'LAST' are required in a conditional statement as shown in statement 50. When strings that include imbedded spaces are read, it is necessary to place quote marks around string fields in the DATA statement; otherwise, the space between words will be lost (e.g.,

Example 6.4

```
10      REM USING THE TAB FUNCTION TO PRINT A DESIGN
20      REM B = CONTROL VARIABLE TO CONTROL TAB
30      REM N = VALUE TO INCREMENT OR DECREMENT B
40      B, N = 1  \  Z = 10  \  S$ = 'O'
50      FOR J = 1 TO 2
60           FOR I = B TO Z STEP N
70                PRINT TAB(10-I);S$; TAB(10+I); S$
80           NEXT I
90           B = 10\  N = -1\  Z = 1
100     NEXT J
900     END

Ready

RUNNH
                O O
              O   O
            O     O
           O       O
          O         O
         O           O
        O             O
       O               O
      O                 O
     O                   O
    O                     O
    O                     O
     O                   O
      O                 O
       O               O
        O             O
         O           O
          O         O
           O       O
            O     O
              O   O
                O O
```

JOHN SMITH would appear as JOHNSMITH). It is acceptable to include both numeric and string data within the DATA statement as long as the variables fit the data field that is read. Additional ways of handling strings will be explained in Chapter 10.

The TAB function can also be used in more creative ways. Example 6.4 illustrates its use to print a design. By using an expression within the parentheses following TAB, the number of spaces a character is placed in relationship to the left margin changes for each line of output. In Example 6.4, we TAB(10–I) for the first character printed; then TAB(10 + I) for the print location of the second character. The letter 'O' is printed at the 9th and 11th print positions on the first output line. The FOR loop changes these print positions in a linear pattern each time as the output illustrates.

6.3 THE PRINT USING STATEMENT

One of the most valuable of all variations of the PRINT statement for producing edited output is the PRINT USING statement. The general format of this statement is:

> LINE number   PRINT USING string, list

The string can be either a string constant or variable; the string may also be an expression which shows the format of the line to be printed. The list refers to variables or constants that are to be printed. Following are several examples to illustrate the PRINT USING statement:

```
10      REM FORMATTING WITH THE PRINT USING STATEMENT
20      A = 20.90\  B = 197.965
30      PRINT USING '      ###.##       ###.##'A,B
900     END

Ready

RUNNH
     20.90       197.97
```

The first part of the PRINT USING statement placed within quotes shows the format of the two fields that are to be printed; the last part of this statement includes the two variables, A and B, whose values are to be printed according to the format preceding them. Note that the value of A is printed as 20.90 with a trailing zero. The field size of each variable is designated through the use of # symbols with a decimal point appropriately placed. The format for variable B, ###.##, results in the rounding of variable B accurate to two decimal places. Thus, 197.965 is printed as 197.97.

When the format for a field is too small for a numeric value, the following occurs:

```
10      REM ANOTHER EXAMPLE OF THE PRINT USING STATEMENT
20      A = 569.12\  B = 129.55
30      PRINT USING '    ##.##      ####'A,B
900     END

Ready

RUNNH
     % 569.12       130
```

Even though the format for variable A was smaller than the value stored in A, the significant digits of A were retained and a % sign was printed before 569.12 in output. The % sign signaled that a field format size error exists in the PRINT USING statement. The printout of the value stored in variable B is printed as an integer rounded since the format of #### did not include a decimal point.

Some editing symbols can be placed in the format part of the PRINT USING statement. For example:

Example 6.5

```
10      REM USE OF $ SIGN AND COMMAS WITH PRINT USING
20      A = 1234.567\  B = 300000000
30      PRINT USING '     $$#,###.##      ###,###,###'A,B
900     END

Ready

RUNNH
        $1,234.57      300,000,000
```

Example 6.5 shows how $ signs and commas can be included in the FORMAT portion of the PRINT USING statement. Even though two $ signs are used in the first formatted field, only one $ sign is printed since $ signs "float" to the proper position when two $ signs are used. Note also that rounding occurs for the value of A, since our format specified only two digits were to appear to the right of the decimal point. The use of commas aids in reading large numbers.

In addition to the comma and $ sign, we can include the editing symbols of a minus sign and the asterisk (*).

When a numeric field is followed by a minus sign, the sign of the output number is printed following the number, rather than preceding it. Example 6.6 illustrates the use of the trailing minus sign for editing purposes:

Example 6.6

```
10      REM USING MINUS SIGNS WITH PRINT USING
20      FOR X = 1 TO 3
30          READ A
40          PRINT USING '###-',A
45      NEXT X
50      DATA 100, -12, -123
900     END

Ready

RUNNH
100
 12-
123-

Ready

40              PRINT USING '###',A
RUNNH
100
-12
%-123
```

The second run shown in Example 6.6 shows that the changed format of statement 40 which eliminated the trailing minus sign in the PRINT USING statement resulted in a field too small to accommodate the negative value of -123. As a result, the computer signalled this overflow by printing

$$\%-123$$

where the % sign indicated an inadequate format in the PRINT USING statement.

Asterisks (*) can also be used in editing a numeric field. If we place two asterisks immediately preceding the # signs, unused spaces will be filled with asterisks instead of spaces. Example 6.7 shows the uses of the editing asterisk:

Example 6.7

```
10      REM USING ASTERISKS WITH PRINT USING
20      FOR X = 1 TO 3
30              READ A
40              PRINT USING '$**#,###,###.##',A
50      NEXT X
60      DATA 123456.789, 500, 100000000
900     END

RUNNH
$****123,457.00
$********500.00
$100,000,000.00
```

Note how the asterisks float to eliminate spaces between the $ sign and the number. Asterisks are commonly used to protect amounts written on checks.

6.4 STRING EDITING

Strings can be edited as part of the format in the PRINT USING statement. A pair of backslashes with blanks between these symbols determine the position of a string field. Example 6.8 illustrates how strings are edited.

Example 6.8

```
10      REM PLACING STRINGS IN THE PRINT USING STATEMENT
20      FOR X = 1 TO 5
30              READ F$, L$
40              PRINT USING '\         \ \           \',L$,F$
50      NEXT X
90      DATA 'JOHN','KENNEDY','LYNDON','JOHNSON','RICHARD','NIXON',
                'GERALD','FORD','JIMMY','CARTER'
900     END

Ready

RUNNH
KENNEDY    JOHN
JOHNSON    LYNDON
NIXON      RICHARD
FORD       GERALD
CARTER     JIMMY
```

The program in Example 6.8 reads in two string locations, the first and last names of recent presidents. The PRINT USING statement includes two pairs of backslashes that control the format for the two names that are printed. Note that strings are left justified in each of the formatted fields.[1] We allowed eight spaces between slashes to accommodate the longest name we anticipated printing. Actually, the formatted backslash accommodates up to ten characters, since these backslashes themselves reserve space for characters. For example:

```
      \               \ \               \
      1 2 3 4 5 6 7 8 9 0   1 2 3 4 5 6 7 8 9 0
      K E N N E D Y         J OHN
```

The two formatted fields actually place the first string character where the backslash was placed in the PRINT USING statement. As a result, there are four spaces between KENNEDY and JOHN. If the format in the PRINT USING statement is too small for the string, the excess characters in the string will be truncated.

---

[1] BASIC-PLUS-2 allows right justification for string fields.

Selected characters can be extracted from string fields by placing exclamation points within quotes as part of the PRINT USING statement.

Example 6.9

```
10      REM ABBREVIATING WORDS WITH PRINT USING
20      PRINT USING '!!!!','CALIFORNIA','STATE','UNIVERSITY','SYSTEM'

Ready

RUNNH
CSUS
```

Example 6.9 illustrates how the four exclamation points placed within quotes control the output format so that the first character in each of the four string fields are printed. Characters following the first character in each string field are omitted.

BASIC-PLUS allows other symbols to be inserted in the format portion of the PRINT USING statement. Example 6.10 illustrates this feature:

Example 6.10

```
10      REM ALPHANUMERICS AS PART OF THE PRINT USING STATEMENT
20      PRINT 'THIS PROGRAM PRINTS NAMES OF FIVE PROFESSORS'
30      FOR X = 1 TO 5
40          READ N$
50          PRINT USING '     PROF. \            \',N$
60      NEXT X
90      DATA 'BARID', 'CHU', 'MELENDY', 'HARPER', 'DERKSON'
900     END

Ready

RUNNH
THIS PROGRAM PRINTS NAMES OF FIVE PROFESSORS
     PROF. BARID
     PROF. CHU
     PROF. MELENDY
     PROF. HARPER
     PROF. DERKSON
```

Statement 50 includes the string constant, PROF., within the format part of this statement placed outside the backslashes. Thus, PROF. is printed each time statement 50 is executed as the output reflects in Example 6.10.

There are other editing features of the PRINT USING statement. You can refer to the BASIC-PLUS manual for your computer system.

6.5 USING SEPARATE FORMAT STATEMENTS

Output sometimes requires lengthy formatting which results in a PRINT USING statement that requires several lines for a single statement. These long statements are difficult to type, and errors in typing require repeated typing of these long statements. BASIC-PLUS provides for a separate format statement which is referenced through a string name identified in the PRINT USING statement. The structure of these two related statements is:

Line number   string name = 'format description'

Line number   PRINT USING string name, list of variables

The string name used in the PRINT USING statement is also used in the format statement which describes the arrangement of the variables listed in the PRINT USING statement. The PRINT USING statement should follow the format statement. If the PRINT USING statement is executed before the format statement is reached in the program, an error message occurs. It is a good programming practice to place the format statement early in the program. Example 6.11 illustrates the use of the PRINT USING statement with a separate format statement:

Example 6.11

```
10      REM PRINT USING WITH A SEPARATE FORMAT STATEMENT
20      PRINT USING F$, 'NAME',50
30      F$ =' \          \   ###'
900     END
RUNNH
?PRINT-USING format error at line 20

Ready

20
40      PRINT USING F$, 'NAME',50
LISTNH
10      REM PRINT USING WITH A SEPARATE FORMAT STATEMENT
30      F$ =' \          \   ###'
40      PRINT USING F$, 'NAME',50
900     END

Ready

RUNNH
NAME         50
```

The PRINT USING statement references the format portion of the separate statement number with the string variable name, F$. Statement 30 specifies the format for the PRINT USING statement, that is, space for 'NAME' and the numeric constant, 50. Example 6.11 also illustrates that the PRINT USING should be executed *after* the format portion that is referenced; otherwise an error message is generated.

Example 6.12 shows a program using the PRINT USING statement with a separate format statement. Statement 40 sets the format arrangement for the body of the table that is printed. By placing the format arrangement in statement 40 below the PRINT statement which outputs the columnar headings (line 20), alignment of the body of the output is facilitated, and less time is spent in determining spacing between fields. Statement 80, the PRINT USING statement, references statement 40 through the use of the string variable F$.

In summary, these two related statements have specialized functions, statement 40 specifies the format and statement 80 specifies the variables that are to be formatted.

Example 6.12

```
10      REM PROGRAM SHOWING A SEPARATE FORMAT STATEMENT WITH
                 PRINT USING
20      PRINT'DEPARTMENT       SALESMAN       GROSS SALES   COMMISSION'
30      PRINT
40      F$ = '\          \      \          \   $##,###.##   $#,###.##'
50      FOR I = 1 TO 50
60          READ D$,S$,G \  IF D$ = 'FLAG' THEN 900
70          C = G * .2
80          PRINT USING F$,D$,S$,G,C
90      NEXT I
100     DATA 'AUTOMOTIVE','FRANK KAY',15000,'APPLIANCE','KAY HOLLY',
             18500,'FOOTWEAR','KENT DOUGLAS',12200,'FLOORING',
             'TRESA DOUGLAS', 19950,'FLAG',X,0
900     END

Ready

RUNNH
DEPARTMENT        SALESMAN        GROSS SALES   COMMISSION

AUTOMOTIVE        FRANK KAY       $15,000.00    $3,000.00
APPLIANCE         KAY HOLLY       $18,500.00    $3,700.00
FOOTWEAR          KENT DOUGLAS    $12,200.00    $2,440.00
FLOORING          TRESA DOUGLAS   $19,950.00    $3,990.00
```

The output editing capabilities of BASIC-PLUS, which many versions of BASIC do not provide, makes BASIC-PLUS highly competitive with other commonly used computer languages.

Word List

Format statement. A statement that describes the arrangement used for a PRINT USING statement.

PRINT USING. A special form of PRINT statement that includes special output editing features.

Printing Zones. Sections of 14 spaces each on a print line; most terminals provide five zones for each line of output.

TAB Function. A function which is used with the PRINT statement to tabulate to specific column positions.

PROBLEMS

1. Correct errors you find in the following statements. Show the output that is produced in valid statements. Assume X = 1; Y = 3; X$ = 'XXX'; Y$ = 'YYY.'

   (a) PRINT X =, X, Y = ,Y
   (b) PRINT X + Y * Y
   (c) PRINT X$;Y$
   (d) PRINT X;X$,Y;Y$
   (e) PRINT   TAB(10),X, TAB(10) Y
   (f) PRINT ,,X$,,Y$
   (g) PRINT USING ' ###   .##' X, Y
   (h) PRINT USING '$$#.##   −#.##' Y, X
   (i) PRINT USING ' / / # / / #'X,X$,Y$,Y
   (j) PRINT USING '###,###   ##' 10,000,   X

2. What output will be generated from the following statements? Assume that A = 5; B = 10; A$ = 'AAA'; B$ = 'BB'

   (a) PRINT A, B, A + B, A * B
   (b) PRINT 100, 'A ='; A, 'B =', B
   (c) PRINT 'THE AVERAGE OF A + B = '; (A + B)/2
   (d) PRINT A$;B$, A, B;
       PRINT A + 5
   (e) PRINT ,,A$,,B$
   (f) PRINT ,,,A,,B
   (g) PRINT "THE NUMBER '20' IS TOO LARGE"
   (h) PRINT A, \ PRINT A$, \ PRINT B
   (i) PRINT TAB(A);A;TAB(B);B
   (j) 10   N = 1
       20   FOR I = 1 TO N
       30   FOR K = 1 TO N
       40   PRINT"X";
       50   NEXT K
       60   PRINT \ N = N + 1
       70   IF N > 10 THEN 99
       80   NEXT I
       99   END

3. Write PRINT or PRINT USING statements that will produce the output requested below using the following variables and values:
   A = 1, B = 2, C = 3, D = −4, E = 5, F = −6, A$ = 'JOHN ADAMS', B$ = 'ALICE JONES.'

   (a) Print the numeric values stored in variables A through F on one line as close together as possible.
   (b) Print the six numeric values on one line with 10 spaces between each number.
   (c) Print the six numeric values on one line edited as follows:
       $1.00 $2.00 $3.00 $4.00− $5.00 $6.00−
   (d) Print the following output by using the variable string names, A$, B$:

   JOHN ADAMS LOVES ALICE JONES

   (e) PRINT THE FOLLOWING OUTPUT Using the variable string names and the numeric value stored in E:

   JOHN ADAMS OWES ALICE JONES $5.00

   (f) Print the following output using the variable string names with the variable numeric values stored in A and B:

   ALICE JONES CODED AS 1; JOHN ADAMS CODED AS 2

4. Use the PRINT statement with the TAB function to create a square or a rectangle using the letter 'X' as the string. Do not use more than two PRINT statements. Use FOR loops as part of this program.

5. Code a program using READ and DATA statements to print output as described below utilizing the PRINT USING statement with the separate format statement:

Phone number	Name	Street	City	State	Zip
8229941	Henry James	196 Jane Street	Arcata	Calif.	95521
4421213	Mary Stennis	1004 4th Street	Eureka	Calif.	95501
6682234	Tresa Biehn	123 Railroad Ave	Blue Lake	Calif.	95525

6. Write a program that will print out the ACE of diamonds in the form shown. Keep PRINT statements to a minimum.

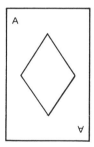

7. Write a program to print the following letters:

8. Write a program to plot a linear function F(X) = X + 10 within the range of −5 and 5. Your output should appear as follows:

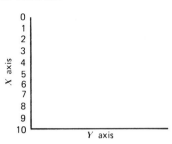

9. Write a program to plot the quadratic function F(X) = X² + 4 in the range of −5 ⩽ × ⩽ 5.

10. Using the functions described in questions 8 and 9, write a BASIC program to plot these two functions on the same surface. Make sure that the two functions intersect at X = −2 and X = 3.

11. A balance sheet is an important financial statement which has the following format:

Balance sheet—Parkside Development
December 30, 1980

Assets		Liabilities and Equity	
Cash	$45,000	Accounts Payable	$21,000
Supplies	3,000	**Stockholder's equity**	
Land	34,000	Capital Stock	68,000
Equipment	7,000		
	$89,000		$89,000

11. Continued:
Write a program that will generate a balance sheet as described. The program should compute the stockholder's equity which is the difference between total assets and liabilities. Enter data of a company by using INPUT statements such as:

NAME OF COMPANY

DATE

CASH

SUPPLIES

LAND

EQUIPMENT

ACCOUNTS PAYABLE

12. Your employer, a TV manufacturer called the Sharpe Company, has just received some important data from a market research organization regarding the trends in TV buying. Your company wishes to analyze this data to help them decide whether they should continue to manufacture black and white TV sets.

Write a program that uses a FOR–NEXT loop and the PRINT USING command to compute and print out the following:

The average income of households having no color TVs, but one or more black and white TVs.

The average number of children in households having no color TVs, but one or more black and white TVs.

The average income and average number of children in households where the newest TV is a black and white set purchased from your firm.

The average income and average number of children in households where the newest TV is a black and white set purchased from one of your three major competitors, Brand X, Brand Y, or Brand Z.

Design your PRINT USING statements so that all average incomes will be rounded to two decimal places, and the average number of children will be rounded to the nearest whole.

Hand in a listing and a run of your program as well as a flowchart.

Household code	No. of color TVs	No. of b&w TVs	Brand of last b&w TV	No. of children	Annual income
21020	0	1	SHARPE	2	$14500
25792	1	1	SHARPE	3	$15000
20419	0	1	X	4	$ 9500
51200	1	1	Y	1	$10000
13491	1	1	Z	2	$13000
24150	0	1	Y	0	$ 9500
17914	2	1	SHARPE	2	$18500
25933	0	1	Z	2	$14500
15006	0	2	X	5	$13000
97500	0	1	Z	1	$ 8000
10056	1	1	SHARPE	2	$16000
76590	1	1	X	1	$21000
15841	1	1	Y	3	$15500
12084	0	1	Z	1	$10000

Chapter 7
Arrays and Tables

Objectives   You will learn:

The use of subscripted variables.

To search arrays.

About the EXTEND mode.

Methods for sorting arrays.

Table organization.

To store data in tables.

To retrieve data from tables.

There are times when we will want to store lists of related information in the computer's memory so that we can select certain information for quick retrieval. Up to this point, we have stored information in numeric and string variables where one location could contain one data field at any point in time. So, if we wanted to store 100 data fields, we would need 100 variables to hold these values for processing. Imagine writing a BASIC program which reads into memory 100 integers and prints them out in reverse order. Obviously, this process is too cumbersome; fortunately, it is a problem that is easily resolved in BASIC-PLUS.

7.1 USE OF SINGLE SUBSCRIPTS TO STORE ARRAYS

An array is a list of related numeric or string fields that uses the same variable name. The same variable name can be used with a list of values if a subscript is used following the variable name. For example:

$$A(1), A(2), A(3), A(4), A(5)$$

are five different locations in memory that use the same variable name, A; the numbers in the parentheses following A, uniquely identify each of the five locations. These can be viewed as follows:

Locations	Storage
A(1)	0
A(2)	0
A(3)	0
A(4)	0
A(5)	0

Figure 7-1. An array of five subscripted variables.

The A array shown in Figure 7-1 shows five different locations in memory that are set to zero. BASIC-PLUS sets numeric arrays or lists to zero when they are identified in the program. Unless you have an array of ten or fewer numbers, it is necessary to identify all of the arrays you plan to use in your program with a DIMENSION statement. This statement is

abbreviated DIM and generally appears at the beginning of a progr.
format is

```
line number   DIM   variable array name (maximum size of the array)
```

and we can dimension several arrays with one DIM statement as

10 DIM A(10), B(20)

which tells the computer to set aside ten spaces in memory for an array called A a.
spaces in memory for array, B.

Now let's look at a problem that illustrates the value of using subscripted variable.
handle an array. Let's assume we want to check our inventory list of the 15 most popula
bicycle parts to make sure that we have at least five of each part on hand. In real life we
would have many more parts, but the principle is the same. First, let's store the number of
parts in our bicycle inventory in the computer:

Example 7.1

```
10       REM USE OF SUBSCRIPTS TO STORE RELATED DATA VALUES
20       DIM A(15)
30       FOR I = 1 TO 15
40              READ A(I)
50       NEXT I
60       REM PRINTOUT OF 15 ELEMENTS IN THE ARRAY
70       FOR J = 1 TO 15
80              PRINT A(J);
90       NEXT J
200      DATA 12,7,10,1,3,5,6,2,0,9,13,4,8,7,6
900      END
```

Statement 20 in Example 7.1 tells the computer to reserve 15 locations in memory for an
array called, A. Actually, 16 locations are set aside in memory since the first location is
A(0), and the last location is A(15); however, we plan to use A(1) through A(15) to store the
number of parts that we have on hand for each of our popular 15 bicycle components.
Statement 40 is the key statement in this part of our program. This statement

40   READ A(I)

under control of the FOR I loop reads the numbers from the DATA statement and stores
these numbers in the fifteen locations of A as follows:

Value of I	Location	Storage
1	A(1)	12
2	A(2)	7
3	A(3)	10
.	.	.
.	.	.
15	A(15)	6

Since the value of I begins at 1, READ A(I) places the first number in the DATA statement, which is 12, in location A(1). The next pass through the FOR I loop sets I = 2, so 7 is
stored in location A(2). The process continues until all 15 values are stored in A(1) to A(15).
If we had wanted to store 1,000 inventory records, this short FOR I loop would have accomplished this process merely by setting the loop to FOR I = 1 to 1000. In that event, we

additional DATA statements. It is necessary to enclose parentheses around a constant or variable after any variable that is subscripted, such as array A. It is confusing and unwise to use a simple variable A and a subscripted variable array A in the same program.

If we had not used array A to store inventory information in example 7.1 and wanted to have these 15 items in memory at one time, our READ statement would have been long and would have appeared as follows without the FOR I loop:

30   READ A1,A2,A3,A4,A5,A6,A7,A8,A9,A0,B1,B2,B3,B4,B5

Further, as we continue to process data read into the program, the use of simple variables names would become very difficult.

7.2 SEARCHING ARRAYS

Now that we have stored information about the 15 bicycle parts inventory in A(1). . .A(15), let's continue our program to determine if we have at least five of each important bicycle part on hand.

Example 7.2

```
10        REM USING SUBSCRIPTS TO CONTROL AN INVENTORY OF BICYCLE PARTS
20        DIM A(15)
30        FOR I = 1 TO 15
40              READ A(I)
50        NEXT I
60        FOR J = 1 TO 15
70              IF A(J)<5 THEN PRINT 'PART#'J 'HAS'A(J)'ON HAND'
80        NEXT J
200       DATA 12,7,10,1,3,5,6,2,0,9,13,4,8,7,6
900       END

Ready

RUNNH
PART# 4 HAS 1 ON HAND
PART# 5 HAS 3 ON HAND
PART# 8 HAS 2 ON HAND
PART# 9 HAS 0 ON HAND
PART# 12 HAS 4 ON HAND
```

The program in Example 7.2 first reads in information about the number of parts on hand; then, beginning with statement 60, a search is made to see if we have fewer than five items on hand for any of these 15 bicycle parts. The key statement is:

70   IF A(J) < 5 THEN PRINT 'PART #' J 'HAS' A(J) 'ON HAND'

Since the FOR J loop started J = 1, the first part tested was A(1), bicycle part #1 which had 12 items on hand. Since the conditional statement 70 was false for this test (there were five or more parts on hand for part #1), the FOR J loop was incremented to 2 and part #2 was tested. When J = 4, A(J), the fourth data element, was compared with 5. Since A(4), part #4, had only one item on hand, a printout was made giving us the information that we wanted. With some changes in Example 7.2, a purchase order could be printed so that we could bring our bicycle inventory to the desired level by mailing the computer printout to our suppliers.

7.3 USING THE EXTEND MODE

Using the A(I) subscripted variable to describe a bike inventory is concise, but A(I) is not descriptive of the numbers we are storing in that array. BASIC-PLUS allows us to use longer variable names so that the variable name itself acts as a cue to tell us what is stored at a location. All one has to do is begin the program with:

5   EXTEND

which tells the computer that we want to EXTEND or lengthen variables. By using the EXTEND mode, we can use variable names that are up to 30 characters or digits long. These names can be simple or subscripted variables. We can use a period to make these names more readable, but we cannot use any spaces or other symbols within these longer variable names. For example:

40   READ BIKE.INVENTORY(I)

is a valid subscripted variable name that can be used instead of A(I) in statement 40 of example 7.2. Of course, we would need a new DIM statement to inform the computer of the new array name we are using as well as consistently using BIKE.INVENTORY throughout our program. Longer variable names in computer programs aid in readability and in documentation of programs, although longer names use more computer memory and take more space in program statements. The EXTEND mode also is more sensitive to spaces, and you will get more error messages until you become accustomed to the more rigid format requirements of the EXTEND mode. You should not use words in EXTEND mode that are spelled the same as BASIC-PLUS verbs or commands. (For a list of these "reserved" words refer to Appendix F.)

String variables can use the EXTEND mode, such as

90   READ STUDENT.NAME$(I)

where STUDENT.NAME$(I) is used as subscripted variable. You can switch from EXTEND to NO EXTEND mode within a program with the statement

500   NO EXTEND

but it is not considered a good programming practice. Some systems require that a continued statement line be terminated with an ampersand character (&) followed by the RETURN key when using the EXTEND mode.

7.4 SORTING ARRAYS

One common especially valuable application of the computer is to sort lists of numbers or arrange lists of names in alphabetical order. BASIC-PLUS handles either numerical or string sorting equally well. One method of sorting numbers is called the "bubble" sort. Figure 7-2 is a flowchart of the logic involved in the "bubble" sort. The logic of the "bubble" sort is quite simple; you move small numbers up the array and large numbers drop down. Figure 7-2 shows that an outer FOR loop controls the number of times an array is to be rearranged. Since we are sorting an array of 15 numbers, the FOR PASS loop forces the inner FOR PLACE loop to repeat the sorting process 14 times. The inner FOR PLACE loop compares two numbers each time this loop is repeated, so the first time 14 loops are made (15-PASS). The second time the inner FOR PLACE loop is entered from the FOR PASS loop, 13 loops are made (15-PASS). Thus, one less loop is made in successive passes through the inner loop, FOR PLACE, since the largest number in the array always drops to the bottom of the array with each pass.

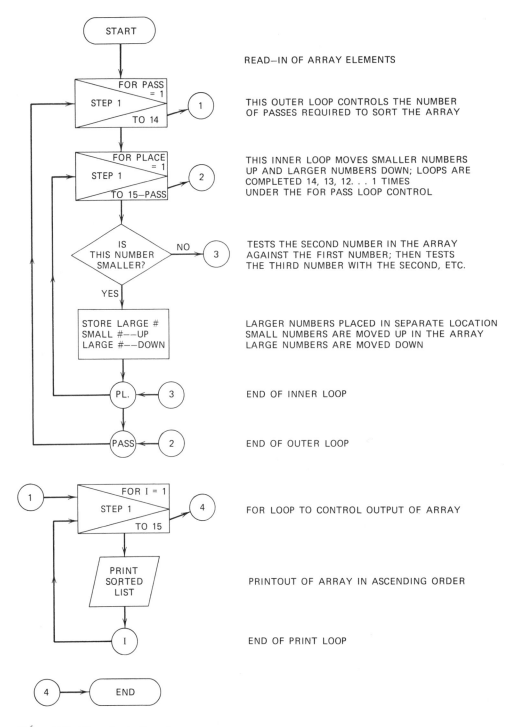

Figure 7-2. Flowchart of sorting an array.

Example 7.3 illustrates the use of the "bubble" sort using subscripts with the EXTEND mode. The name of the array is called, DATA.SORT, and the DIM statement identifies the size of this array at statement 30 immediately *after* statement 20 EXTEND. The sorting occurs within the inner FOR PLACE loop where numbers in the array are tested to see if the second number is smaller than the first number. If the second number is smaller, the larger number is placed in a location called, STORE; the smaller number is moved up one position in the array while the larger number is moved from STORE to one lower position in the

Example 7.3

```
10      REM USE OF SUBSCRIPTS USING EXTEND MODE TO SORT NUMBERS
20      EXTEND
30      DIM DATA.SORT(15)
40      FOR I = 1 TO 15
50          READ DATA.SORT(I)
60      NEXT I
70      REM SORT ROUTINE USING NESTED LOOPS
80      FOR PASS = 1 TO 14
90          FOR PLACE = 1 TO 15 - PASS
100             IF DATA.SORT(PLACE+1) < DATA.SORT(PLACE)
                THEN STORE = DATA.SORT(PLACE)\
                DATA.SORT(PLACE) = DATA.SORT(PLACE+1)\
                DATA.SORT(PLACE+1) = STORE
110             NEXT PLACE
120     NEXT PASS
130     REM PRINTOUT OF THE SORTED LIST
140     FOR POSITION = 1 TO 15
150         PRINT DATA.SORT(POSITION);
160     NEXT POSITION
200     DATA 4,5,9,6,3,15,2,1,13,10,7,8,12,11,14
900     END

Ready

RUNNH
 1  2  3  4  5  6  7  8  9  10  11  12  13  14  15
```

array. Notice how the use of descriptive names with the EXTEND mode helps both the programmer and others using the program to understand what is happening in the program.

Figure 7-3 shows how small numbers move up (bubble) with each pass while large numbers move down. Since the inner loop, FOR PLACE, always forces the largest number in the array to the lowest possible bottom position with each pass, one less loop is required for successive passes. So, 14 loops are made with the first FOR PLACE (14 comparisons test 15 numbers),then 13, until the 15 numbers are sorted in ascending order. Note that only seven

	DATA	PASS NUMBER													
		#1	#2	#3	#4	#5	#6	#7	#8	#9	#10	#11	#12	#13	#14
DATA, SORT(1)	4	4	4	4	3	3	2	1	1	1	1	1	1	1	1
DATA, SORT(2)	5	5	5	3	4	2	1	2	2	2	2	2	2	2	
DATA, SORT(3)	9	6	3	5	2	1	3	3	3	3	3	3	3		
DATA, SORT(4)	6	3	6	2	1	4	4	4	4	4	4				
DATA, SORT(5)	3	9	2	1	5	5	5	5	5	5					
DATA, SORT(6)	15	2	1	6	6	6	6	6	6						
DATA, SORT(7)	2	1	9	9	7	7	7	7	7						
DATA, SORT(8)	1	13	10	7	8	8	8	8							
DATA, SORT(9)	13	10	7	8	9	9	9								
DATA, SORT(10)	10	7	8	10	10	10									
DATA, SORT(11)	7	8	12	11	11										
DATA, SORT(12)	8	12	11	12											
DATA, SORT(13)	12	11	13												
DATA, SORT(14)	11	14													
DATA, SORT(15)	14														

Figure 7-3. Bubble sort of a list of numbers as ordered by Example 7.3.

passes are required although 14 passes are actually made by the computer to sort this array of 15 numbers. Seven passes complete the sort for this array because the lowest number in the array, one, is the eighth element of the array, and it takes seven passes to move it to the top position in the array.

7.5 TABLE ORGANIZATION

Tables are commonly used for showing income tax rates, transportation schedules, loan amortization tables, and in many other practical ways. There are hundreds of math and statistical tables that save time because we can select the information we want from a table in a matter of seconds. The computer is especially valuable in handling tables since it can retrieve data in microseconds.

A table is a two-dimensional array or matrix, since it can be viewed as having rows and columns. A table is a convenient way to store related numeric or string fields using one variable name. Since a table has two dimensions, rows and columns, a variable name identifying a specific location within that table must have two subscripts—one which identifies the row, the other which identifies the column. Let's use the variable name

TABLE(ROW,COLUMN)

where the first subscript, ROW, is the row location, and the second subscript, COLUMN, identifies the column of the TABLE. Unless you have a table with 10 or fewer rows and columns, it is necessary to identify the TABLE with a DIMENSION statement. It is good programming practice to identify all tables with a DIM statement, such as

10   DIM TABLE(2,3)

which tells the computer to reserve space in memory for TABLE with two rows and three columns. BASIC-PLUS sets numeric tables to zero and string tables to blanks when they are identified in the program.

We can store a single value in TABLE by

20   TABLE(1,2) = 9

where the number, 9, is stored in the first row and second column of TABLE.

Figure 7-4 shows the six locations of TABLE and how each location is identified. Notice that the number 9 stored in TABLE(1,2) replaced the zero while the other five locations in TABLE are set to zero. Figure 7-4 also shows that the first number in the subscript identifies the row of TABLE; the second number identifies the column of TABLE.

	COLUMN 1	COLUMN 2	COLUMN 3
ROW 1	TABLE(1, 1) 0	TABLE(1, 2) 9	TABLE(1, 3) 0
ROW 2	TABLE(2, 1) 0	TABLE(2, 2) 0	TABLE(2, 3) 0

Figure 7-4. A table with six locations (cells).

7.6 STORING DATA IN TABLES

Data can be stored in tables by using the READ/DATA statements or via the INPUT statement. Example 7.4 shows one way to read numbers into a table and a method for print out of these numbers in table form.

Example 7.4

```
10      REM TABLE READIN AND PRINTOUT USING DOUBLE SUBSCRIPTS
20      EXTEND
30      DIM TABLE(2,3)
40      READ TABLE(1,1),TABLE(1,2),TABLE(1,3),TABLE(2,1),TABLE(2,2),
            TABLE(2,3)
50      PRINT TAB(28);'TABLE'\ PRINT
60      PRINT TAB(13);'COLUMN 1      COLUMN 2      COLUMN 3'
70      PRINT 'ROW 1', TABLE(1,1),TABLE(1,2),TABLE(1,3)
80      PRINT 'ROW 2', TABLE(2,1),TABLE(2,2),TABLE(2,3)
200     DATA 1,2,3,4,5,6
900     END

Ready

RUNNH
                        TABLE

            COLUMN 1      COLUMN 2      COLUMN 3
ROW 1          1            2            3
ROW 2          4            5            6
```

Statement 30 in Example 7.4 defines the size of the TABLE by dimensioning it into two rows and three columns. Statement 40 reads the six numbers into the six locations in TABLE as follows:

TABLE(1,1) which is row 1, column 1

TABLE(1,2) which is row 1, column 2

TABLE(1,3) which is row 1, column 3

TABLE(2,1) which is row 2, column 1

TABLE(2,2) which is row 2, column 2

TABLE(2,3) which is row 2, column 3

Statements 70 and 80 print the TABLE in the way that we stored the number in the READ statement. Obviously, this method of reading and printing would not be practical for a large table since it is necessary to identify each cell in the table in both the READ and PRINT statements.

Let's look at a more general approach to reading data into a table and printing it. Example 7.5 uses FOR loops to read and print data in table format.

Example 7.5

```
10      REM TABLE READIN AND PRINTOUT USING FOR. . .NEXT LOOPS
20      EXTEND
30      DIM TABLE(2,3)
40      REM FOR LOOP TO READIN DATA
50      FOR ROW = 1 TO 2
60          FOR COLUMN = 1 TO 3
70              READ TABLE(ROW,COLUMN)
80          NEXT COLUMN
90      NEXT ROW
100     REM FOR LOOP TO PRINTOUT DATA
110     PRINT TAB(28);'TABLE'\ PRINT
120     PRINT TAB(13);'COLUMN 1      COLUMN 2      COLUMN 3'
130     FOR ROW = 1 TO 2
140         PRINT 'ROW';ROW;
150         FOR COLUMN = 1 TO 3
160             PRINT , TABLE(ROW,COLUMN);
170         NEXT COLUMN
180         PRINT
190     NEXT ROW
300     DATA 10,20,30,40,50,60
900     END

RUNNH
                        TABLE

            COLUMN 1      COLUMN 2      COLUMN 3
ROW 1          10            20            30
ROW 2          40            50            60
```

At first glance, it would appear that Example 7.5 is unnecessarily complex for handling this simple table. However, most tables that are useful in the real world will have many rows and columns, and Example 7.5 with only a few changes can handle the read-in and printout of large tables. Note that there is only one double subscripted variable name used to read in all values into the table—TABLE(ROW,COLUMN). The FOR loops identify the subscripts, ROW AND COLUMN, and these values can be set to vary with the size of any table. The PRINT statement also requires one variable name, TABLE(ROW,COLUMN), to handle output.

Now that we have been introduced to table input/output, let's examine approaches to retrieving selected data from tables.

7.7 RETRIEVING DATA FROM TABLES

With computer terminals in common use, the need for searching hard copy files (e.g. paper files or index cards) for frequently used information is becoming outmoded. Here is a simple example of computer retrieval of information from a shipping rate table.

Shipping rates are usually based on the distance the item is to be shipped and the weight of the item. Following is one small shipping rate table that is stored in the computer's memory:

| Distance | Weight Categories | | | |
	1 (<1#)	2 (1–3#)	3 (4–6#)	4 (7–10#)
1 (0–200 mi.)	.75	1.25	2.00	2.50
2 (201–500 mi.)	1.00	1.75	2.50	3.25
3 (501–up mi.)	1.25	2.50	3.22	4.00

Figure 7-5. Shipping rates for items up to 10 pounds.

The rows in Figure 7-5 represent three distance categories that affect rates—that is, the farther the distance shipped, the higher the rate. The columns represent weight categories. Once the table is read and stored in memory, it is necessary to tell the computer coded information about the item for which a rate is requested. This requires that we identify the row and column of the shipping rate table so that a table lookup occurs. The term, table lookup, is commonly used to describe retrieval of data from information stored in tabular form in memory.

Example 7.6 reads in the shipping rate table and requests coded data about the weight and distance for individual items to be shipped via INPUT statements. The read-in of the shipping rate is accomplished by nested FOR loops. Rates are read in by columns rather than by rows by using the FOR COLUMN loop to control the FOR ROW loop, since the data elements are placed for columnar arrangement. Had the FOR ROW loop been the controlling loop, the rate table would have been read in by rows and the table would have been inaccurate.

Table lookup is remarkably simple. Statement 130 prints out the distance and weight codes that have been inputted as well as the rate amount. By placing

TABLE(DISTANCE,WEIGHT)

in statement 130, the computer was instructed to lookup and print the value stored in the appropriate row (distance) and column (weight). The shipping rate table placed with Example 7.6 shows three shipping rates requested and the locations of these rates in the table. The first rate requested described an item with a weight code of 2 and a distance code of 3. Since distance represented rows and weight represented columns, the computer retrieved the

Example 7.6

```
10        REM PROGRAM TO RETRIEVE SHIPPING RATES FROM A TABLE
20        EXTEND
25        LINE.OUT$ ='DISTANCE CODE = ## WEIGHT CODE = ## RATE = $#.##'
30        DIM TABLE(3,4)
40        REM TABLE READIN OF SHIPPING RATES
50        FOR COLUMN = 1 TO 4
60              FOR ROW = 1 TO 3
70                    READ TABLE(ROW,COLUMN)
80              NEXT ROW
90        NEXT COLUMN
100       REM RETRIEVAL OF SHIPPING RATES USING THE INPUT STATEMENT
110       INPUT 'WEIGHT CODE =';WEIGHT
120       INPUT'DISTANCE CODE =';DISTANCE
130       PRINT USING LINE.OUT$, DISTANCE, WEIGHT, TABLE(DISTANCE,WEIGHT)
200       DATA .75,1,1.25,1.25,1.75,2.50,2,2.50,3.22,2.50,3.25,4
900       END

Ready

RUNNH
WEIGHT CODE =? 2
DISTANCE CODE =? 3
DISTANCE CODE =  3 WEIGHT CODE =  2 RATE = $2.50

Ready

RUNNH
WEIGHT CODE =? 1
DISTANCE CODE =? 1
DISTANCE CODE =  1 WEIGHT CODE =  1 RATE = $0.75

Ready

RUNNH
WEIGHT CODE =? 4
DISTANCE CODE =? 2
DISTANCE CODE =  2 WEIGHT CODE =  4 RATE = $3.25

Ready
```

	Shipping rate table			
Distance Code	Weight Code			
	1	2	3	4
1	.75 ²	1.25	2.00	2.50 ₃
2	1.00	1.75 ₁	2.50	3.25
3	1.25	2.50	3.22	4.00

value stored in row 3 column 2—$2.50. The second rate requested described an item with weight and distance codes of 1; thus, the computer retrieved the value stored in row 1, column 1—$0.75. The final rate requested was input with a weight code of 4 and a distance code of 2 which resulted in a table lookup of $3.25.

Tables can be used in many other ways. Chapter 11 explains matrix manipulation on a more sophisticated level.

Word List

Array. A list of related numeric or string fields.

Bubble Sort. A method of sorting numeric or string fields in either ascending or descending order.

Matrix. A two-dimensional array.

Subscripted Variable. Variables that store related numeric or string fields that can be referenced with one variable name having single or double subscripts.

Table Lookup. A form of data retrieval made from data stored in an array or table.

PROBLEMS

1. The following questions relate to the EXTEND mode:

   (a) What is the purpose of the EXTEND mode?
   (b) When is it best to use this mode?
   (c) What statement is necessary to have a program function using the EXTEND mode?
   (d) Correct invalid EXTEND mode variables in the following list:

   TOTAL-SALES

   CUSTOMERNAME $

   POINT.OF.SALES.TOTAL

   J.J.JONES$

   COUNTER (I,J)

   COLUMN(I + 1, 15)

   ROW9(20,X)

   A(B)

   NAME$(I,$)

2. Write one statement to set aside 20 locations in three arrays identified as A, B, C.

3. Write a series of statements that will read and store the following values in an array called LIST.ONE from a DATA statement:

   10   DATA 10,11,15,13,14,16,17,18,20,22,24,30,49,55,60

4. Write a series of statements that will read and store the following strings in an array called FIRST.NAME$:

   90   DATA JOHN, MARY, SUE, TOM, DICK, LEN, TAMI, HAL, MATT, TIM

5. Write a program to produce:

(a) A frequency distribution of test grades. There are 25 separate test results ranging in value from 15 to a high of 30. Use the following data to prepare a report that appears as follows:

BIS 56 QUIZ #4 RESULTS

TEST SCORE	FREQUENCY
30	0
29	2
28	3
.	.
.	.
15	1

   DATA   21,28,19,16,18,29,27,25,23,22,25,28,15,16,23,18,19,20,17
   DATA   29,27,28,24,25,19

(b) Add a third column to the output labelled PERCENTAGE which reports the percent frequency as a percentage.
(c) Add code which suppresses output for any test score whose frequency is zero.
(d) Output all test scores in descending order of their frequency.

6. Read a table into memory that will appear as follows:

10	50	30	40
20	30	40	50

Use the following DATA statement and store the values in a table called CROSS.TAB:

   DATA   10,50,30,40,20,30,40,50

7. Write a series of statements that will double each of the values in the table, CROSS.TAB, that you read in problem 6.

8. Write a series of statements that will print out the values of table, CROSS.TAB as described in problem 6 so that output appears as follows:

10	20
50	30
30	40
40	50

9. (a) Write a program which fills two tables in memory called TABLE1 and TABLE2 with numbers in each cell as shown below:

```
        15  20  30  30  99
TABLE1  16  25  50  40  11
        19  13  20  10  17

        12  13  14  16  18
TABLE2  21  31  41  61  81
        32  41  51  71  22
```

   (b) Once you have read and stored the above numbers in TABLE1 and TABLE2, add corresponding cells in these two tables and print their sums in the same format from TABLE3. Print all three tables so that a visual check on addition accuracy can be verified.

10. (a) Write a program which creates a table of part numbers and corresponding prices according to the following list:

Part#	Price
1100	22.55
1119	14.95
1210	9.99
1301	59.00
1416	29.50
1500	32.44
1510	17.60

   (b) Once you have stored part numbers with corresponding prices, write statements that will allow a user to retrieve a price for a specific part through the use of an INPUT statement. For example, the program should print:

STOCK NUMBER?

when the user lists 1119, the program should print:

$14.95

when the user requests a stock number that is not in the table, the program should print:

NO SUCH STOCK NUMBER EXISTS

11. A small forest of 80 trees, 8 rows and 10 columns, is represented by a two-dimensional array FOREST(8,10). The number in each location of the table has the following meaning:

```
     0:  empty place, no tree has been planted
    -1:  a dead tree
 1-100:  age of a planted tree (trees get planted as one-year-old seedlings)
```

Write a BASIC program which analyzes such a table and answers these questions:

   (a) How many trees have to be planted (that is, the sum of the empty places and places with dead trees)?
   (b) How many dead trees have to be removed?
   (c) How many trees can be harvested if the harvest age is between 30 and 100 years?

Here is the DATA for you to use in your program.

$$35,35,32,80,80,80,0,80,50,-1$$
$$20,20,-1,20,20,10,20,0,0,20$$
$$15,15,-1,15,15,15,0,0,30,15$$
$$35,40,-1,-1,15,0,0,15,20,35$$
$$0,0,5,0,75,40,30,10,30,30$$
$$30,75,40,75,0,0,75,0,10,5$$
$$75,10,40,30,75,5,-1,-1,5,5$$
$$-1,40,5,30,0,-1,20,20,40,-1$$
$$0,20,10,20,20,-1,20,20,10,0$$
$$15,15,20,0,20,-1,15,15,40,35$$

12. Write a program that will tabulate and print a weekly report showing sales made by three salesmen for four product lines. Use an input statement to allow daily recording of the sales made for each product line per each salesman. Keep running totals for each salesman and total sales for each product line. The output should appear as follows:

WEEKLY SALES OF FOUR PRODUCT LINES

SALESMAN	PRODUCT A	PRODUCT B	PRODUCT C	PRODUCT D	TOTALS
1	—	—	—	—	$ —
2	—	—	—	—	$ —
3	—	—	—	—	$ —
TOTALS	$ —	$ —	$ —	$ —	$ —

INPUT DATA:

MONDAY	1,10,15,9,22	(the first value is the salesman's #)	
	2,5,16,12,19	(the next four values represent units	
	3,19,5,16,29	sold for products A,B,C, & D)	
TUESDAY	1,15,11,10,17		
	2,8,15,14,22		
	3,21,6,18,19		
WEDNESDAY	1,19,20,21,18		
	2,16,19,20,28		
	3,20,7,19,23		
THURSDAY	1,11,29,17,9		
	2,15,16,21,19		
	3,19,8,26,30		
FRIDAY	1,12,15,17,31		
	2,14,16,18,19		
	3,16,15,13,5		

Chapter 8
Structured Programming in BASIC-PLUS

Objectives

You will learn:

The essentials of structured programming.

Fundamental program structures.

Avoiding the GO TO statements in sequence structure.

USE of IFTHENELSE statements for double decisions.

Use of ONGOTO statements for case decisions.

Building loop termination conditions in the FOR/NEXT statement.

Use of REM statements and indentation to structure a BASIC program.

The concept of Top-down design.

By this time you have acquired a solid background in the BASIC language. You should be able to write programs to solve a variety of problems, although your programs may be inefficient. Before more powerful BASIC statements are studied, let's examine the structure of a BASIC PROGRAM.

8.1 THE ESSENTIALS OF STRUCTURED PROGRAMMING

Until now your primary concern has been to get your programs to work. Your programs might be "clever," since you may need 10 statements while others need 20 statements to solve the same problem. In the past, computer memory was limited in size and processing speed was low, and people tried to write concise programs to conserve memory and speed processing. In the last decade the cost of developing programs has exceeded hardware costs. People have become more concerned with better methods of organizing programs so that programs are easier to write, read, and modify. This has resulted in an approach to programming which includes a structure to program design.

Example 8.1 illustrates two programming approaches to solve the same problem.

Example 8.1

Dr. Balfour has three students in his minicomputer course. He made ten assignments during the term. At the end of the term he collected all of the homework and found one assignment missing. He wanted to know which assignment was missing. Dr. Balfour asked Miss Karen Lin, his assistant, and John Anderson, one of this top students, to write programs to locate the missing assignment. Both Karen and John stored the records in a 29-element array. Each element records one assignment number which looks as follows:

A (1)	1
A (2)	2
A (3)	4
A (28)	9
A (29)	10

The following is John's program:

```
10      REM THIS IS A TRICKY PROGRAM
20      DIM A(29)
25      T = 0
30      FOR X = 1 TO 29
40          T = T + A(X)
45          IF T >= 10 THEN T = T - 10
50      NEXT X
60      PRINT T
70      PRINT 'THE MISSING HOME WORK IS NO.';10-T
```

Do you understand what John did in the above program? Perhaps not. Since John is mathematically inclined, he knows if he adds the assignment numbers in the array and keeps a modulus count of all the assignment numbers, the missing homework can be found by subtracting this count from 10.

Most of us are not as talented as John so let's look at Karen's program. Karen's program reflects the natural logic of performing this task. If she were to solve the problem, invariably she would examine the homework records one by one and tally the number of assignments completed as follows:

After she has examined all of the records, she would check each assignment to see which one has less than three tallys.

```
100     REM ********************************************************
105     REM *                                                      *
110     REM * THIS PROGRAM USES THE CONVENTIONAL WAY TO FIND THE   *
120     REM * MISSING HOMEWORK. REC IS AN ARRAY WHICH HOLDS THE    *
130     REM * RECORD OF HOMEWORK. COUNTER IS AN ARRAY WHICH HOLDS  *
135     REM * THE NUMBER OF COMPLETED ASSIGNMENTS                  *
138     REM *                                                      *
140     REM ********************************************************
150     EXTEND
160     DIM REC(29)
180     DIM COUNTER(10)
190     REM -------CLEAR THE COUNTER -------
220         FOR ASSIGNMENT = 1 TO 10
230             COUNTER(ASSIGNMENT) = 0
240         NEXT ASSIGNMENT
250     REM ------- COUNT EACH HOMEWORK -------
280         FOR X = 1 TO 29
290             ASSIGNMENT = REC(X)
300             COUNTER(ASSIGNMENT) = COUNTER(ASSIGNMENT) + 1
310         NEXT X
320     REM ----- CHECK THE COUNTERS -------
350         FOR ASSIGNMENT = 1 TO 10
360             IF COUNTER(ASSIGNMENT) < 3 THEN MISSING = ASSIGNMENT
370         NEXT ASSIGNMENT
380     REM ----- OUTPUT THE RESULT -----
410     PRINT 'THS MISSING HOMEWORK IS NO.';MISSING
420     END
```

Karen's program seems to be unnecessarily long; however, it is straightforward. It is easy to write, easy to understand, and easy to maintain. Maintenance of a program means modifying an existing program to suit a special need. For example, if there is more than one missing assignment, John's program wouldn't work while Karen's program, with a few changes, would.

Now, let's look at the type of structures used to organize programs. Three types of structures used in programming are:

1. Sequence structure.

2. Selection structure.

3. Iteration structure.

In the following three sections we will explain these three types of structures and illustrate how to use each type of structure.

8.2 SEQUENCE STRUCTURE

Sequence structure means the sequential flow of program logic. In flowchart form, the sequence structure appears as follows:

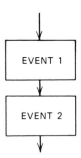

Notice that each event occurs sequentially. The event may be a single statement or a group of statements (module).[1]

In order to implement this step by step approach, every program should be carefully planned to avoid unnecessary branching. The GO TO statement should be eliminated, if possible. Example 8.2 illustrates unnecessary branching.

Example 8.2

Suppose a programming job consists of three tasks:

1. Print the header line.

2. Calculate and print the value of an expression.

3. Print a summary line.

Your program will look like this:

```
10      PRINT 'IS THIS A GOOD PROGRAM?'
20      PRINT '24 CUBED PLUS 10 IS'; 24**3+10
30      PRINT 'THAT'S ALL, CHARLIE BROWN'
99      END
```

As long as you use reasonable logic, you won't write a program like this:

```
10      GO TO 40
20      PRINT 'THAT'S ALL, CHARLIE BROWN'
30      GO TO 99
40      PRINT 'IS THIS A GOOD PROGRAM?'
50      PRINT '24 CUBED PLUS 10 IS'; 24**3+10
60      GO TO 20
99      END
```

The flow in the above example is obvious. As the program becomes complex, it is likely that you will have to branch back and forth, unless you plan ahead. In order to avoid the "spaghetti bowl" approach, design the logic flow of your program before you start coding.

---

[1] Modularity will be discussed in Chapter 9.

8.3 SELECTION STRUCTURE

Selection structure refers to conditional program flow. Based on specific conditions, the computer determines which path to take. Generally, selection structure can be classified into *double decision structure* and *multiple decision structure*.

8.3.1 Double Decision Structure and the IF. . . .THEN. . . .ELSE Statement

Many decisions in the world involve two-way alternatives—yes or no, true or false. One of two events will occur depending on whether or not a particular condition is met. This situation can be depicted by the following flowchart:

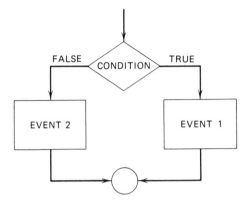

We have learned how to use the IF. . . .THEN statement to implement two-way alternatives. For example, we can use the following segment of coding to determine whether a student has upper-division standing (total units taken greater than 60) or lower division standing.

```
10      INPUT 'YOUR NAME';N$
20      INPUT 'TOTAL NUMBER OF UNITS';U
30      IF U>60 THEN 60
40      PRINT N$, 'YOU ARE CLASSIFIED AS LOWER-LEVEL STANDING'
50      GO TO 99
60      PRINT N$, 'YOU ARE WITH UPPER-LEVEL STANDING'
99      END
```

The selection structure is implemented at lines 30 through 60. The condition is tested at line 30. If the condition is true, a section of statements which include a false event, should be bypassed, and an unconditional jump to bypass the true event should be added at the bottom of false event, namely

50   GO TO 99

Care is required to jump around the alternatives. BASIC-PLUS provides a convenient feature to implement double-decision structure. With the IF. . . .THEN. . . .ELSE statement the above program can be revised as:

```
10      INPUT 'YOUR NAME';N$
20      INPUT 'TOTAL NUMBER OF UNITS';U
30      IF U>60
            THEN PRINT N$, 'YOU ARE WITH UPPER-LEVEL STANDING'
            ELSE PRINT N$, 'YOU ARE CLASSIFIED AS LOWER-LEVEL STANDING'
99      END
```

In the revised version, we just need one statement to implement the two-way alternative.

The GO TO statement at line 50 is eliminated here. The IF. . . .THEN. . . .ELSE statement takes the following format:

line number   IF condition   THEN statement   ELSE statement(s)

In the IFTHENELSE statement, the condition is evaluated first. If the condition is true, the statement following THEN is executed, otherwise, statements following the keyword ELSE are executed. *Caution:* While ELSE can be followed by a multiple statement, only one single statement may follow the keyword, THEN. As with the IFTHEN statement, if the statement following THEN or ELSE is a GO TO statement, the keyword GO TO can be omitted. For example:

10   IF X = 5 THEN 100 ELSE 200

is equivalent to

10   IF X = 5 THEN GO TO 100 ELSE GO TO 200

For the sake of readability, indent the IFTHENELSE statement as follows:

    10   IF Y = 1 (line feed)

(tab key)   THEN PRINT 'YES' (line feed)

(tab key)   ELSE PRINT 'NO' \ B = B + 1 (return)

If your terminal doesn't have a tab key, press the control key and letter I simultaneously; this will have the effect of tabulating.[2]

Many times, more than one task needs to be performed if the condition is true. Consider the following double-decision structure:

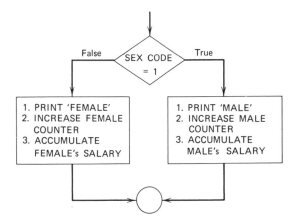

Since only one statement is allowed in the THEN clause,[3] the above double-decision can be coded in the following way:

---

[2] Avoid using the space bar for spacing. Because a BASIC line is limited to 255 characters, hitting the space bar 8 times counts for 8 blank characters which is equivalent to a single tab character.

[3] BASIC-PLUS-2 allows multiple statements following THEN. However, if the number of statements following THEN and ELSE are numerous, it may not be possible to fit the entire IFTHENELSE statement on one line. The double-decision structure should still be coded as the above indicates.

```
10              IF S = 1 THEN 30 ELSE 70
20      REM THEN
30              PRINT 'MALE'
40              M = M + 1
50              A1 = A1 + A
60              GO TO 110
70      REM ELSE
80              PRINT 'FEMALE'
90              F = F + 1
100             A2 = A2 + A
110     REM ENDIF 10
```

8.3.2 Multiple Decisions and the ON. . . .GO TO Statement

If IFTHENELSE statement is convenient when there are two alternatives to test. When there are more than two possibilities, it is called a case structure.

In the flowchart, it is represented as follows:

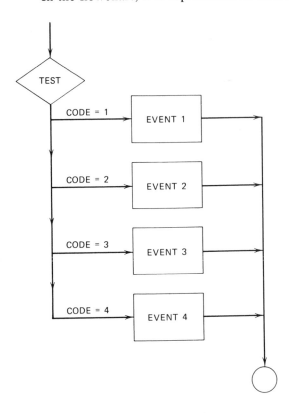

BASIC-PLUS has a multiple branching statement to implement the case structure, namely the ON. . . .GO TO. . . .statement. The format of this statement is

| line number   ON expression   GO TO list of line numbers |

The expression following the keyword ON will be evaluated. Depending on the result of evaluation, one of the locations listed following GO TO will be transferred. For example:

$$20 \quad ON \ X \ GO \ TO \ 100, \ 200, \ 300$$

causes a branch to:

   1. Line number 100, if X = 1.

   2. Line number 200, if X = 2.

   3. Line number 300, if X = 3.

IF X equals any other value of less than 1 or >= 4, an error message occurs:

?ON statement out of range at line 20

Fractional values are treated as integers rounded down if they fall within the range of the number of statements following GO TO.

Let's illustrate an application of the ON. . . .GO TO statement.

Example 8.3

Suppose the payrate of the sales staff in the Pine Company is calculated based on the following schedule:

Sale	Commission of % of Sale	Bonus
Less than 5,000	5	200
5,000—less than 10,000	6.5	500
10,000—less than 15,000	7	700
15,000—less than 20,000	10	1,000

   If the sales of 10 salesmen are given, and none of them sold $20,000 or more, the following program will calculate their pay for the month:

```
100     REM THIS PROGRAM WILL CALCULATE THE PAY OF SALES STAFF
110     H$ = 'NAME            SALE        COMMISSION     BONUS      PAY'
115     F$ = '\            \  ##,###      #,###          #,###      #,###'
117     PRINT H$ \ PRINT
120     FOR X = 1 TO 5
130         READ N$,S
140         ON S/5000+1 GO TO 150,200,250,300
150     REM CASE1: LESS THAN 5,000
160         C = S*0.05
170         P = C + 200
180         PRINT USING F$,N$, S, C, 200, P
190         GO TO 340
200     REM CASE2: 5,000 - LESS THAN 10,000
210         C = S*0.065
220         P = C + 500
230         PRINT USING F$, N$, S, C, 500, P
240         GO TO 340
250     REM CASE3: 10,000 - LESS THAN 15,000
260         C = S*0.07
270         P = C + 700
280         PRINT USING F$, N$, S, C, 700, P
290         GO TO 340
300     REM CASE4: 15,000 - LESS THAN 20,000
310         C = S*0.1
320         P = C + 1000
330         PRINT USING F$, N$, S, C, 1000, P
340     REM END CASE 140
350     NEXT X
360     DATA 'ADAMS', 7000, 'BLOOMFIELD', 4000
370     DATA 'EDMONSON', 19000, 'FELS', 10000
380     DATA 'JOHNSON', 17000
390     END
RUNNH
NAME            SALE        COMMISSION     BONUS      PAY

ADAMS           7,000       455            500        955
BLOOMFIELD      4,000       200            200        400
EDMONSON        19,000      1,900          1,000      2,900
FELS            10,000      700            700        1,400
JOHNSON         17,000      1,700          1,000      2,700
```

The loop enclosed in lines 120 through 350 is used to process data of the six salesmen. For each salesman, the data is read in at line 130. After the sales volume is stored at location S,

140   ON S/5000+1 GO TO 150, 200, 250, 300

will determine which event should occur. Since the difference in each

S/5000+1

will determine which case it is. You can verify the relationship by checking the following:

S	S/5000+1	Case	Line number to Branch
7000	2.4	2	200
4000	1.8	1	150
19000	4.8	4	300
10000	3.0	3	250
17000	4.4	4	300

Statements to handle all four cases are listed one after another. Each case starts with a REM statement and ends with a GO TO 340. Line 340 marks the end of this case structure.

The ON. . . .GO TO statement is convenient to use, if the case code is embedded in the data or if there is a relationship between data and the case number, as above. Otherwise, we need to use the nested IFTHENELSE to handle the multiple-decision case. For example, if the pay bracket of the PINE Company looks like this:

Sale	Commission as % of Sale	Bonus
Less than 3,000	5	200
3,000—less than 8,000	6.5	500
8,000—less than 15,000	7	700
15,000—less than 20,000	10	1,000

Line 140 should be replaced by

```
140        IF S < 3000
              THEN 150
              ELSE IF S < 8000
                      THEN 200
                      ELSE IF S < 15000
                              THEN 250
                              ELSE 300
```

The case structure implemented in terms of the nested IFTHENELSE is depicted by the following flowchart:

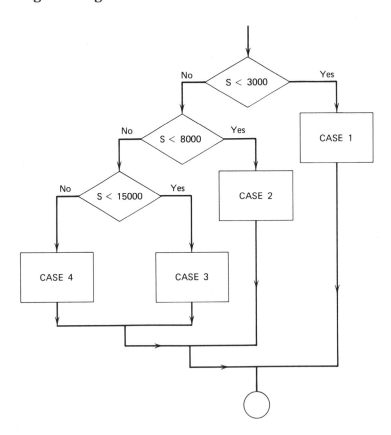

8.4 ITERATION STRUCTURE

The third fundamental structure in a program is the iteration structure, sometimes called a loop structure; that is, the same event should take place repetitively as long as a given condition holds true. The iteration structure is presented as follows:

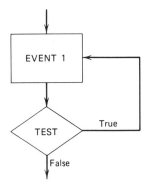

We have learned two approaches to building loops in the previous chapters:

1. Use the combination of GO TO and IF THEN statement.

2. Use the FOR/NEXT statement.

Let's use the first approach to rewrite the program on page 83 to sort 15 numeric values in order:

Example 8.4

```
100      REM A BUBBLE SORT WITHOUT USING FOR/NEXT STATEMENT
110      EXTEND
120      DIM DATA.SORT(15)
130      I = 1
140      IF I > 15 THEN 180
150      READ DATA.SORT(I)
160      I = I + 1
170      GO TO 140
180      PASS = 1
190      IF PASS > 15 THEN 300
200      PLACE = 1
210      IF PLACE > 15 - PASS THEN 280
220      IF DATA.SORT(PLACE+1) >= DATA.SORT(PLACE) THEN 250
230      STORE = DATA.SORT(PLACE)
240      DATA.SORT(PLACE) = DATA.SORT(PLACE+1)
250      DATA.SORT(PLACE+1) = STORE
260      PLACE = PLACE + 1
270      GO TO 210
280      PASS = PASS + 1
290      GO TO 190
300      I = 1
310      IF I > 15 THEN 360
320      PRINT DATA.SORT(I);
330      I = I + 1
340      GO TO 310
350      DATA 4,5,9,6,3,15,2,1,13,10,7,8,12,11,14
360      END
```

Now compare this program with the previous program in Chapter 7. The above program is a poor one because GO TO statements have been used at several places in the program to jump back for the purpose of achieving a loop effect. It is hard to follow, especially when a nested loop is involved. In the program in Chapter 7, with the use of FOR/NEXT statements which clearly mark the beginning and the end of a loop, a clear structure is provided. In addition, the lack of appropriate comments and indentation of the above program makes it more difficult to read.

In many situations we don't know how many times the loop should be executed in advance. We have to build a condition(s) within the *FOR* loop. Once a condition is met, repetition is terminated, which may require an abnormal exit from the loop. Let's consider the following simple example:

Example 8.5

We want to read a maximum of five data items and print the values, until a negative number is detected. The program may look as follows:

PROGRAM A

```
10       REM THIS PROGRAM HAS ONE ADDITIONAL EXIT INSIDE THE LOOP
20       FOR X = 1 TO 5
30           READ A
40               IF A < 0 THEN 99
50           PRINT A
60       NEXT X
70       DATA 1,54,34,-2,9
99       END
```

Program A is not a good program, since there is more than one exit in the loop (Line 40 and Line 60). If the loop is involved and several exits are embedded, clarity of the program is decreased. A well-organized program should just have one entry and one exit.

PROGRAM B

```
10      REM THIS PROGRAM USES FOR UNTIL STATEMENT
20      READ A
30      FOR X = 1 UNTIL A < 0
40          PRINT A
50          READ A
60      NEXT X
70      DATA 1,54,34,-2,9
99      END
```

PROGRAM C

```
10      REM THIS PROGRAM USES FOR WHILE STATEMENT
20      READ A
30      FOR X = 1 WHILE A >= 0
40          PRINT A
50          READ A
60      NEXT X
70      DATA 1,54,34,-2,9
99      END
```

In Program B the loop body, line 40 and line 50, was executed until A caught the negative value −2. When we exit from the loop, the counter X was 4; one number more than the actual number of times the loop body is executed. In Program B, we placed

50   READ A

at the bottom of loop body and one additional

20   READ A

is placed preceeding the loop. The reason for this will become apparent when we explain the function of the FORUNTIL statement. Program C uses the FORWHILE statement. The loop body is executed, while A has not caught the negative value.

Both the FORUNTIL and FORWHILE statements are useful variations of the FOR loop. The general format of FORUNTIL and FORWHILE loop is:

Line number   FOR variable = expression 1   STEP expression 2   UNTIL condition
                       loop body
Line number   NEXT variable

Line number   FOR variable = expression 1   STEP expression 2   WHILE condition
                       loop body
Line number   NEXT variable

Like the FORTO loop, the variable specified in the FOR statement and the NEXT statement must match. The STEP clause can be omitted, if the step value is 1.

The function of FORUNTIL and FORWHILE loop can be illustrated by the following flowchart:

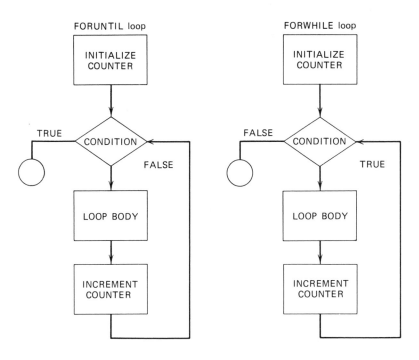

Before we give another example of the FORUNTIL loop, you are encouraged to compare the flowchart of the FORTO loop in order to avoid pitfalls.

Example 8.6

The MBI Company specializes in the production of minicomputers. The revenue function and cost function for model 9 are:

$$R(X) = 20 \cdot X \cdot \sqrt[3]{2^X}$$

$$C(X) = 2 \cdot X^3 - \frac{X^2}{2} + 100$$

Determine the break-even point for the MBI Company. The break-even point occurs when the revenue starts exceeding cost — $R(X) >= C(X)$. Mathematically, the equation is not easy to solve. What we can do is use a trial and error approach. Hence, the following program is necessary:

```
10      REM THIS PROGRAM WILL DETERMINE THE BREAK EVEN POINT
15      FOR X = 1 UNTIL R>C OR X>100
20          R = 20*X*(2**(1/3*X))
30          C = 2*X**3 - X**2/2 + 100
50      NEXT X
60      IF X <= 100
            THEN PRINT 'BREAK EVEN POINT IS';X-1
            ELSE PRINT 'NO BREAK EVEN POINT YET'
70      END


RUNNH
BREAK EVEN POINT IS 11

Ready
```

The production cost of Model 9 can be covered if the number of units to be produced is 11 or more. The program is straightforward, but special care is required in formulating the FORUNTIL statement.

$$15 \quad \text{FOR X} = 1 \text{ UNTIL R} > \text{C OR X} > 100$$

Instead of $R \geq C$, we set $R > C$ as one of the conditions for terminating the loop. Remember that the condition is evaluated before the loop body is executed. Initially, the location R and C are both 0. Therefore, if the condition to terminate looping is $R >= C$, the loop will not be executed at all. The second condition to terminate looping is

$$X > 100$$

In order to avoid infinite looping (R never exceeds C in this case), we have to set an upper limit for the counter X. As you can see the two exits of the loop are indicated clearly at the beginning of the loop, the clarity of the program is achieved by using the FORUNTIL statement.

8.4.1 A Short-cut Method for Looping

There are times when the body of a loop is very simple, so we do not need a formal loop to implement the repetitive task. The FORTO, FORUNTIL, and FORWHILE statement have their short-cut forms.

In a FORTO loop, the FOR statement can be written with the loop body on one line, and the NEXT statement can be omitted. Examine the following example:

Example 8.7

```
10      PRINT 'THE FOLLOWING LINE WILL BE DOUBLE SPACED'
20      PRINT FOR X = 1 TO 2
30      PRINT 'THIS LINE WILL BE UNDERLINED'
40      PRINT '-'; FOR X = 1 TO 28
99      END


RUNNH
THE FOLLOWING LINE WILL BE DOUBLE SPACED

THIS LINE WILL BE UNDERLINED
---- --------------------------------
Ready
```

Line 20 is used for double spacing, which is equivalent to:

$$\begin{array}{l} \text{FOR X} = 1 \text{ TO 2} \\ \quad \text{PRINT} \\ \text{NEXT X} \end{array}$$

Line 40 is another simple loop to generate 28 dashes, which is equivalent to:

$$\begin{array}{l} \text{FOR X} = 1 \text{ TO 28} \\ \quad \text{PRINT '—';} \\ \text{NEXT X} \end{array}$$

The general format of the short FORTO loop is:

Line number   statement FOR variable = expression 1 TO expression 2 STEP expression 3

As in the regular FOR loop, if the STEP clause is not specified, it is defaulted as STEP 1.

There are occasions when you do not need a counter to keep track of how many times the loop is executed. The single line task is repeated as long as certain conditions exist. In such a case, the short FORUNTIL and FORWHILE loop can be used. Consider the following example. Both programs below display the first negative data.

Example 8.8

Program A

```
10      READ A UNTIL A < 0
20      PRINT A
30      DATA 1,9,-4,8
99      END
```

Program B

```
10      READ A WHILE A >= 0
20      PRINT A
30      DATA 1,9,-4,8
99      END
```

The functions of Program A and B are identical. Line 10 in both programs will repeat reading a value in A and terminate the reading when a negative A is detected. The short FORUNTIL and FORWHILE form are,

```
Line number   statement UNTIL condition
```

```
Line number   statement WHILE condition
```

Notice that neither the key word FOR nor NEXT appears in the short form. As you can see, when the task inside the loop is simple, using short-cut methods adds to the clarity of your program.

8.5 REM STATEMENT AND INDENTATION TO STRUCTURE THE PROGRAM

We have learned how to organize the three fundamental structures with BASIC-PLUS statements in the previous sections. The REMARK statement is also useful for structuring programs. Unlike some other programming language, such as PL1 and PASCAL, BASIC is not designed for structured programming. With the help of the REM statement, some *artificial* statements can be formulated. For example, after a long nested IF statement, a REM ENDIF can be attached to mark the logical end of the IF statement:

```
10   IF A = 1
            THEN B = B+1
            ELSE IF C = 1
                      THEN 100
                      ELSE PRINT 'OK'
20   REM ENDIF 10
```

Another example of artificial statements has been shown in the previous section. The example shown on page 97 uses the following three artificial statements to highlight the double decision structure:

```
20   REM   THEN
70   REM   ELSE
110  REM   ENDIF 10
```

The original purpose of the REM statement is to document a program. A well-structured program is also well documented. You want to explain the program to yourself and to others. Hence, a box of REM statements should be used at the beginning of your program, which normally includes:

1. Name of the program.

2. Author of the program.

3. Date the program is written.

4. Purpose of the program.

5. INPUT information.

6. OUTPUT requirements.

7. Algorithm to process data.

8. Explanation of major variables.

Indentation is an effective method for improving the readability of your program and highlighting the structure of your program. Good indentation is especially helpful in detecting the errors in nested loops and nested IF statements. Since BASIC-PLUS is very generous in spacing your instructions, you are allowed to set up your own indentation standards. The example illustrated in the following section suggest ways in which to use REM statements and indentation to structure your program.

8.6 TOP-DOWN DESIGN

Programming tasks are by their nature complex. The method for implementing three fundamental structures has been discussed. Now, we need a systematic approach for the design of the program. A top-down approach allows us to concentrate on the main scheme of the program at an early stage in the design. The details for subtasks at a lower level can be filled in later.

Now, let us use an example to review the various aspects of a well-structured program:

Example 8.9

Dr. Mann determines the grades in his Introduction to Data Processing course on the following basis:

1. Best two out of three test scores will be averaged for each student.

2. Letter grades:

   A is given for average of 90 or better

   B is given for average of 80 to 90

   C is given for average of 70 to 80

   F is given for average less than 70

Dr. Mann would like to write a BASIC program to generate a grade report. Now, let's analyze the problem.

Level 1 Every program has a fundamental framework, consisting of three parts:

Set up

Repetitive Processing

Wrap up

Level 2 The major tasks of the three parts in the problem include:

Set up

1. Print heading lines.

2. Clear accumulation counter.

3. Build data block.

4. Priming read.

Repetitive processing

1. Read a record.

2. Determine the lowest score to be thrown away.

3. Calculate the average.

4. Determine letter grade.

5. Print results.

6. Accumulate class averages.

Wrap up

1. Calculate class average.

2. Print class average.

3. Mark end of the program.

Level 3 Repetitive processing of student records should be implemented in a FOR/NEXT loop; a condition to terminate the loop will be built. All other subtasks are quite straightforward, except determination of the lowest score and letter grade. Two flowcharts can be used to describe the algorithm of these two subtasks:

Determine the smallest among T1, T2, and T3

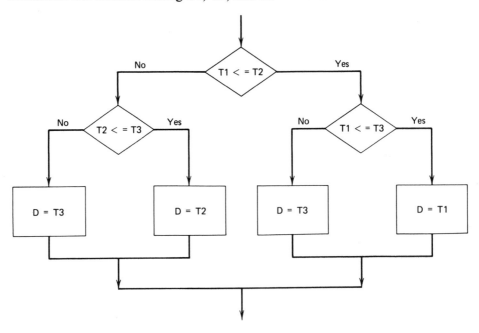

Determine the letter grade from average A

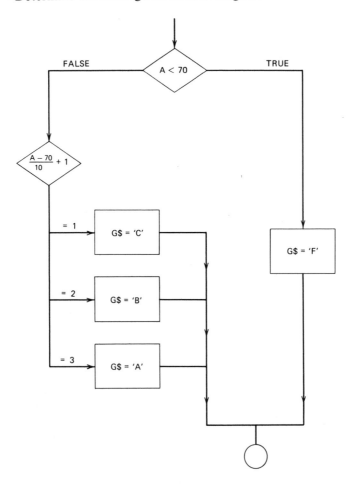

Based on the above analysis, the program will look as follows:

```
100    REM *******************************************************
110    REM *                                                     *
120    REM * PROGRAM:      GRADE REPORT                          *
130    REM * AUTHOR:       SHU-JEN CHEN                          *
140    REM * DATE:         AUGUST 20, 1979                       *
150    REM * PURPOSE:      THIS PROGRAM WILL SELECT THE BEST TWO *
160    REM *               TEST SCORES OUT OF THREE, DETERMINE   *
170    REM *               LETTER GRADE AND COMPUTE CLASS AVERAGE*
180    REM * INPUT:        RECORD OF EACH STUDENT INCLUDING      *
190    REM *               NAME AND 3 TEST SCORES; N$,T1,T2,T3   *
200    REM * OUTPUT:       A TABLE OF STUDNET'S NAME, AVERAGE    *
210    REM *               LETTER GRADE AND A SUMMARY LINE       *
220    REM * VARIABLES:    A=AVERAGE                             *
230    REM *               C= CLASS TOTAL OF AVERAGES            *
240    REM *               A1=CLASS AVERAGE                      *
245    REM *               D = THE LOWEST SCORE                  *
250    REM *                                                     *
260    REM *******************************************************
270    REM ------ SET UP ------
280       PRINT 'NAME', 'AVERAGE', 'GRADE'
290       PRINT
300       G = 0
310       READ N$, T1, T2, T3
320    REM ------ REPETITIVE PROCESSING ------
330       FOR X = 1 UNTIL N$ = 'DUMMY'
340          IF T1 <= T2
                 THEN IF T1 <= T3
                         THEN D = T1
                         ELSE D = T3
                 ELSE IF T2 <= T3
                         THEN D = T2
                         ELSE D = T3
350          REM * END IF
360          T = T1 + T2 + T3 - D
370          A = T/2
380          IF A < 70 THEN 390 ELSE 430
390          REM THEN
400                     G$ = 'F'
410                     GO TO 540
430          REM ELSE
440                     ON (A-70)/10+1 GO TO 450,480,510
450                     REM CASE1: 70 - LESS THAN 80
460                        G$ = 'C'
470                        GO TO 550
480                     REM CASE2: 80 - LESS THAN 90
490                        G$ = 'B'
500                        GO TO 550
510                     REM CASE3: 90 OR OVER
520                        G$ = 'A'
530                        GO TO 550
540                     REM END CASE
550          REM END IF
560          G = G + A
570          PRINT N$,A,G$
580          READ N$, T1, T2, T3
590       NEXT X
600    REM ------ WRAP UP ------
610       A1 = G/(X-1)
620       PRINT
630       PRINT 'CLASS AVERAGE', A1
640       DATA 'BROWN J.', 56, 76, 77, 'MCDONALD A.', 83, 82, 85
650       DATA 'DEAN M.', 88, 78, 98, 'SAWYER A.', 56, 77, 66
660       DATA 'COOPER G.', 23, 10, 11, 'DUMMY', 0, 0, 0
670       END
```

```
RUNNH
NAME            AVERAGE         GRADE

BROWN J.        76.5            C
MCDONALD A.     84              B
DEAN M.         93              A
SAWYER A.       71.5            C
COOPER G.       17              F

CLASS AVERAGE 68.4
```

Notice that a box of REM statements is used to describe the program. The set-up section includes lines 270–310 and the DATA block at the bottom of the program. Since we used a FORUNTIL loop for repetitive processing, a priming read preceeding the loop is needed so that once the trailer is detected, the processing segment will not proceed further.

Following the priming read, the loop starts with the second subtask: determining the smallest score, D. The nested IFTHENELSE statement (line 340) to select the lowest score is indented, and an artificial END IF statement is attached. Lines 360 and 370 calculate the average. The IFTHENELSE statement at line 380 classifies the grades into two categories—failing grades are processed beginning at line 390 and failing grades are processed beginning at line 430.

The subtask of printing the individual's grade and accumulating class averages are subsequently coded. The first task of the repetitive loop, reading a record, is placed at the end of the loop (Line 580).

The wrap-up section is simple. Keep in mind that the number of records being processed is X-1 not X and do not forget the END statement.

Word List

Case Structure. Multiple-decision structure, such as used in the ON. . .GOTO statement.

Double-decision Structure. Two possible alternatives are evaluated.

Iteration Structure. Repetition of a program loop that depends on a given condition.

Multiple-Decision Structure. More than two possible alternatives are evaluated.

Selection Structure. Two or more conditions are evaluated before a branch is made.

Sequence Structure. The flow of instructions is organized in logical, sequential steps.

Top-down Design. Development of the main scheme of a program at an early stage in program design.

PROBLEMS

1. Explain why it is important to write a well-structured program.
2. Indicate under what circumstances the IFTHENELSE statement is preferred to the ONGOTO statement in terms of implementing the case structure.
3. Sketch the output of the following program segments:

   (a) 10   FOR X = 1 TO 10
       20   PRINT X
       30   NEXT X
   (b) 10   FOR X = 1 UNTIL X = 10
       20   PRINT X
       30   NEXT X
   (c) 10   FOR X = 1 WHILE X <> 10
       20   PRINT X
       30   NEXT X

4. Write one statement to implement the following branching:

   1. GO TO 100, IF $-20 <= A < -15$

   2. GO TO 200, IF $-15 <= A < -10$

   3. GO TO 300, IF $-10 <= A < -5$

   4. GO TO 400, IF $-5 \ <= A < \ 0$

5. Use REM statements and indentation to improve the structure of the following program segments:

(a) IF X = 3 THEN PRINT 'OK' ELSE PRINT 'WRONG'
 \ Y = Y+1 \ GO TO 10

(b) IF S$ = 'FEMALE' THEN IF A <= 20 THEN IF H$ = 'TENNIS'
 THEN IF H >= 67 THEN IF W <= 120 THEN PRINT "I WANT HER"

(c) 10   FOR X = 1 UNTIL X = 10
 20   FOR Y = 1 UNTIL Y = 10
 30   PRINT X*Y;
 40   NEXT Y
 50   PRINT
 60   NEXT X

(d) 10   FOR X = 1 TO 100
 20   READ A$, S
 30   IF A$ = 'DOLL' THEN 40 ELSE ON S GO TO 32,34,36
 32   PRINT 'MARRIED' \ GO TO 40
 34   PRINT 'SINGLE' \ GO TO 40
 36   PRINT 'DIVORCED' \ GO TO 40
 40   NEXT X

6. Use the short-cut method for looping to do the following tasks:
(a) Read values in a 5 by 4 table.
(b) Find the first multiple of 13, which is greater than 200.

7. The following program will read a maximum of 15 values presented in the DATA statement and calculate the average of positive values. The accumulating process will stop if the running total exceeds 100. The following program works but is poorly structured. Restructure the program to accomplish the above goal.

```
10      X = 0
20      X = X+1
30      IF X > 15 THEN 100
40      READ C
50      IF C < 0 THEN 40
52      Y = Y + 1
55      T = T + C
60      IF T < 100 THEN 20
70      GO TO 130
80      DATA 3,-69,4,65,4,6,7,8,9,10,22,12,13,44,-5
100     IF X <= 15 THEN 120
110     PRINT 'AVERAGE IS'; T/(Y-1)
120     GO TO 199
130     PRINT 'RUNNING TOTAL EXCEEDS 100, I QUIT'
199     END
```

8. Use the FORUNTIL loop to solve the equation

$$X^2 + 2X - 15 = 0$$

Start searching at X = 0 and keep checking at steps of 0.5.

9. Revise Example 8.3 to allow sales volume exceeding $20,000. The commission is 20% of the sale for sales >= $20,000, and no bonus is paid in this case.

10. Write a program to compute the powers of 2. Your output should appear as

POWER OF 2 TO 1 IS   2
POWER OF 2 TO 2 IS   4

. . . .

. . . .

Notice what happens at the
end of your 2's power table.

11. A mail-order house is designing a one-size T-shirt. A survey sample reveals the size of a group of women:

$$7,8,9,11,13,5,6,7,7,6,5,9,10,13,7,8$$

Write a program to determine which size should be used as a standard to design the one-size shirt. (Hint: You should not design the T-shirt based on the average size, which fits no one. Select a size which will fit the largest number.)

12. Mr. Hughes, director of a computer center, is considering promoting one person on his staff to be the new assistant. The ideal candidate is either a person called "Von Neumann" or someone who majored in "computer science" and has more than five years experience. The information about his staffs appears as follows:

Name	Major	Experience in Years
Harper	English	10
Davidson	Math	3
Lener	Greek	20
Galey	Computer Science	3
Beck	Computer Science	7
Von Neuman	Latin	0

Write a well-structured program to search the *first* ideal person found in the data block.

13. The students at PASCAL University are classified into

Year level	Total units taken
Freshman	0–35
Sophomore	36–70
Junior	71–105
Senior	106–140

Make up a set of at least 10 data records including the student's name and number of units taken. Write a well-structured program to:

1. Determine and print the year level of each student.

2. Determine and print the average number of units for each year level.

14. Record the number of cans of beer consumed by your friends in one week. Write a well-structured program to

1. Generate the distribution table as follows:

Number of Cans Drunk	Number of Persons
None	XX
1–3	XX
4–7	XX
8–15	XX
over 15	XX
Total	XXX

    2. Find the one who drank the most beer and print his name.

15. Write a well-structured program to process checking accounts. The information you have includes:

    1. Customer's name.

    2. Old balance.

    3. Number of transactions.

    4. Deposits and withdrawals (withdrawals are recorded negative values).

The output should include:

    1. Name of the customer.

    2. Old balance.

    3. Deposits to this account.

    4. Total withdrawals from this account.

    5. New balance.

At the end of the table, the following statistics should be printed

    1. Total number of transactions.

    2. Total deposits.

    3. Total withdrawals.

    4. Total balance.

16. A good friend can frequently read your mind. Write a well-structured program to check your friends. In your program, you place five single-digit numbers in the DATA statement, and let your friend guess them one by one. For each number, allow three changes for guessing. If he/she fails in all three guesses, it is considered wrong. At the end of the program you can rate your friendship as

Degree of friendship	Number of correct guesses
Buddy	5
Close friend	4
Special friend	3
Good friend	2
Soso friend	1
No friendship	0

17. Write a well-structured program to compute the gross pay earned by workers at Redwood, Inc. You are to compute each employee's pay based on the following categories: 1 = $2.95; 2 = $3.75; 3 = $4.95; 4 = $6.75. Gross pay is computed by multiplying the hourly pay of one of the above codes by the number of hours worked. You are to keep a running total of the entire payroll and print that total at the end. You are also to print the number and pay of each employee as shown below:

Gross Pay of Redwood, Inc.

Employee Number	Amount
1	$XXX.XX
2	XXX.XX
•	XXX.XX
•	XXX.XX
8	XXX.XX
TOTAL PAYROLL	$XXXX.XX

Information for each employee is coded as follows:
3,40 would indicate that this employee had a pay code of 3 or $4.95 per hour; the 40 represents the total number of hours worked during the week

DATA   1,30,   3,40,   2,37,   4,25,   2,40,   3,39,   4,40,   1,40,   9,99

You are to number employees in sequential order starting with employee #1 coded as 1,30 (pay code #1; 30 hours). Compute and print the first data line of output and accumulate his pay total for final use in printing the total payroll. The last two numbers (9,99) act as a flag that the payroll has been completed.

Chapter 9
Functions and Subroutines

Objectives   You will learn:

The need for functions and subroutines.

To use built-in functions.

Computer simulation.

To define your own functions.

To modulize your program by using subroutines.

More about top-down design.

Programs frequently include sections requiring the repetition of a formula or a series of statements. For example, you may want to convert temperatures from Fahrenheit to Celsius and print four average temperatures. The program may look as follows:

Example 9.1

```
10      PRINT 'WINTER', 'SPRING', 'SUMMER', 'AUTUMN'
20      PRINT (50-32)*5/9, (70-32)*5/9, (85-32)*5/9, (72-32)*5/9
30      END
```

As you can see, it was necessary to repeat the formula

$$\frac{(\text{degree in Fahrenheit} - 32) \times 5}{9}$$

four times at line 20. This can be a very tedious job as the part of coding to be repeated becomes more complex. In order to save memory space and programming effort, you should learn to use functions and subroutines.[1]

9.1 BUILT-IN FUNCTIONS

BASIC has two types of functions: built-in functions and user-defined functions.

Let's discuss the built-in functions first. Quite often, in making a calculation, you have to consult a mathematical table to find the square root of 101 or natural logarithm of 34. Obviously, it would take several instructions to compute a square root or a logarithm value.

BASIC has a predefined set of the commonly used mathematical functions. If you wish to use a function, you need to call up that function and provide a value as an argument.

$$\text{LET A} = \text{SQR (101)}$$

will store the square root of 101 in location A

$$\text{LET B} = \text{LOG(34)}$$

will store the natural logarithm value of 34 in location B. Notice that BASIC's built-in functions have three-letter names. The argument must be enclosed in parentheses. The argument

---

[1]BASIC-PLUS-2 has a SUBPROGRAM feature, which will be discussed in Chapter 12.

does not need to be a constant; it can be any kind of expression. We can also amend the LET statement so that the function can be referenced directly in an expression to the right-hand side of the equal sign.

Now, let's list the table of BASIC-PLUS's built-in functions before we give some examples.

Function	Description
ABS(X)	Absolute value of X
SGN(X)	The sign of X, if X > 0 then SGN(X) = 1 if X = 0 then SGN(X) = 0 if X < 0 then SGN(X) = −1
INT(X)	Largest integer less than or equal to X
RND(X)	A random number between 0 and 1
SQR(X)	Positive square root of X
EXP(X)	Value of e raised to the power of X
LOG(X)	Natural logarithm of X
SIN(X)	Sine value of X (in radians)
COS(X)	Cosine value of X (in radians)
TAN(X)	Tangent value of X (in radians)
ATN(X)	Arctangent value (in radians) of X
LOG10(X)	Common logarithm of X

Figure 9-1. Available Built-in Functions in BASIC-PLUS.

9.2 DISCUSSION OF MATHEMATICAL FUNCTIONS

9.2.1 ABS Function

The ABS function returns the magnitude of X. For example, regardless of whether X is +5 or −5, its absolute value is 5. Consider the following example:

Example 9.2

```
10      REM THIS PROGRAM WILL PRINT THE ABSOLUTE VALUES
            OF THE INTEGERS FROM -5 TO 5
20      FOR X = -5 TO 5
30          A = ABS(X)
40          PRINT A;
50      NEXT X
60      END


RUNNH
 5  4  3  2  1  0  1  2  3  4  5
Ready
```

9.2.2 SGN Function

You might want to know whether a number is positive or negative. The SGN function enables you to do this by identifying all the positive numbers as 1, negative numbers as −1, and zero as 0.

Example 9.3

```
10      REM THIS PROGRAM WILL DISPLAY THE SIGN VALUES OF 5 DATA
20      FOR I = 1 TO 5
30          READ X
40          PRINT SGN(X),
50      NEXT I
60      DATA -100,3.14,-3.18,0,100
70      END
```

```
RUNNH
-1              1               -1              0               1

Ready
```

Notice that, in line 40 we

$$\text{PRINT SGN(X),}$$

Hence, every time line 40 is encountered, the current value of X will be evaluated, and the sign value of that number will be printed.

9.2.3 SQR Function

SQR function will return the positive square root of the argument. The argument for the SQR function must not be negative; otherwise, an error message will be printed. For example:

$$10 \quad X = SQR\,(-100)$$

will cause the following message to be printed:

$$\% \text{ IMAGINARY SQUARE ROOT AT LINE } 10\text{[2]}$$

Let's have an example of using the SQR function;

Example 9.4

If three sides of a triangle are known, the area of that triangle can be calculated by the following formula:

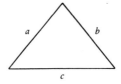

$$\text{Area} = \sqrt{s\,(s-a)\,(s-b)\,(s-c)} \quad \text{where } s = \frac{a+b+c}{2}$$

The following program will calculate the area of a triangle, which has three sides, 8, 7, and 12, respectively.

---

[2]An error message preceded by the question mark '?' is a fatal error. Execution cannot continue unless the user removes the cause of the error. Error messages preceded by a percent sign '%' are warnings. Execution of the program can continue but may not generate the expected results.

```
10      EXTEND
20      READ A,B,C
30      S = (A+B+C)/2
40      AREA = SQR(S*(S-A)*(S-B)*(S-C))
50      PRINT 'AREA ='; AREA
60      DATA 8,7,12
99      END
```

```
RUNNH
AREA = 26.9061
```

9.2.4 EXP Function

The EXP (Exponential) function accepts a numerical argument and calculates the value of 2.71828 (which is e, natural number) to the power of that argument. The following example shows the application of the EXP function,

Example 9.5

People arrive at a self-service car wash shop at the rate of nine cars each hour. The probability that the next car will arrive within 10 minutes can be calculated by using the following formula (Exponential distribution):

$$\text{Probability} = 1 - e^{-9(10/60)}$$

The following program will instruct the computer to do the calculation for you:

```
10      EXTEND
20      PROBABILITY = 1 - EXP(-9*(10/60))
30      PRINT PROBABILITY
40      END
```

```
RUNNH
.77687
```

As you can see from the output of the above program, there is a 78% chance that the next car will arrive within 10 minutes.

9.2.5   LOG and LOG10 Function

The LOG function returns the natural logarithm of the argument. The argument must be positive; otherwise an error message will be displayed.

% Illegal argument in LOG

The LOG10 function returns the common logarithm (base 10).
The LOG function is the inverse of EXP function.
The following program shows the relationship between LOG and EXP function.

Example 9.6

```
10        PRINT LOG(2.71828)
20        PRINT EXP(LOG(3.5))
30        PRINT LOG(EXP(3.5))
40        END
```

```
RUNNH
 .999999
 3.5
 3.5
```

Line 10 printed the value of log 2.71828, which is close to 1. Line 20 outputs the value of a mathematical expression

$$e^{\log(3.5)}$$

Since logarithm and exponentiation offset each other, the value is 3.5. Notice that at line 20 the argument of EXP function is another function, e.g., LOG. EXP(LOG(3.5)) which is evaluated in the following steps:

Step 1:   LOG(3.5) = 1.25276

Step 2:   EXP(1.25276) = 3.5

LOG and EXP function are useful in scientific applications. Many economic models and management science problems are also involved with the calculation of log and/or exp value.

9.2.6 Trigonometric Functions

SIN, COS, TAN are used to calculate the sine, cosine, and tangent values, respectively, of an angle. It is important to remember that the argument must be expressed in radians. The relationship between degree and radians is

1 degree = 0.0174533 radians

Here is an example of trigonometric function.

Example 9.7

As a professor in the School of Business and an outstanding skier, Professor Iloffsky is interested in the cost of building a ski lift gondola. The information he has is:

1. The length of the hill is 1200 feet.

2. The distance between the hill foot and the end of gondola is 800 feet.

3. The hill angle is 140°.

4. The cost of building the gondola is $180 per foot.

The above information can be depicted as follows:

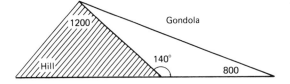

Before the cost can be computed, we have to find out the length of gondola, C, which can be determined by using the following formula:

$$C = \sqrt{1200^2 + 800^2 - 2 \times 1200 \times 800 \times COS(140°)}$$

The following program will do the calculation:

```
10      EXTEND
20      C = SQR(1200**2 + 800**2 - 2*1200*800*COS(140*0.0174533))
30      COST = 180 * C
40      PRINT 'COST OF BUILDING THE PROPOSED GONDOLA IS'; COST
50      END


RUNNH
COST OF BUILDING THE PROPOSED GONDOLA IS 339185
```

Notice that the formula to calculate C is expressed at line 20. The argument of the SQR is an expression containing constants and another function, COS. Also notice that the argument of the COS function must be expressed in radian measures. Hence, 140° is multiplied by 0.0174553.

The ATN[3] (Arctangent) function is used to find the size of an angle, provided the tangent value of this angle is known. The ATN function produces the size of the angle in radian measure. If you want to convert it into degree measures, the following equation can be used.

$$1 \text{ radian} = 57.2957795 \text{ degree}$$

Consider the following example:

Example 9.8

```
10      INPUT 'PLEASE ENTER AN ARCTANGENT VALUE'; X
20      PRINT 'ANGLE WHOSE TANGENT IS'; X; 'IS'; ATN(X); 'RADIAN'
30      PRINT 'ANGLE WHOSE TANGENT IS'; X; 'IS'; ATN(X)*57.2957795; 'DEGREE'
40      END


RUNNH
PLEASE ENTER AN ARCTANGENT VALUE? 1
ANGLE WHOSE TANGENT IS 1 IS .785398 RADIAN
ANGLE WHOSE TANGENT IS 1 IS 45 DEGREE
```

9.3 APPLICATION OF INT AND RND FUNCTION

We purposefully left out the discussion of INT and RND functions in the previous section. INT and RND function are two of the most useful mathematical functions in business applications.

9.3.1 INT function

The INT returns the largest integer value, which is equal or less than the argument. For example

---

[3] ATN is the only inverse function, the value of arcsine and arccosine can be determined by employing trigonometrical relationships.

$$INT(1.33) = 1$$
$$INT(3.99) = 3$$
$$INT(\ 0) = 0$$
$$INT(-1.23) = -2$$

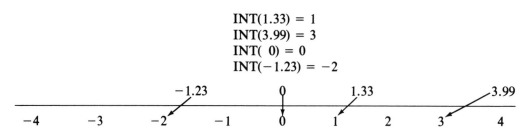

We use the INT function not only for truncating the fractional part of the number. It can also be used to round a number to a specific number of decimal places. For instance, the following instruction will round a positive number, X, to the nearest hundredth and store it in location X1

$$10 \quad X1 = INT\ (X*100+0.5)/100$$

If X = 1.234 then X1 = 1.23; a round down case
If X = 1.236 then X1 = 1.24; a round up case.

Let's see more precisely how the rounding mechanism works. The computer evaluated the right-hand side of the equation in the following steps:

1. Multiply X by 100

$$\begin{array}{r} 1.234 \\ \times\ \ 100 \\ \hline 123.4 \end{array} \qquad \begin{array}{r} 1.236 \\ \times\ \ 100 \\ \hline 123.6 \end{array}$$

2. Add 0.5 to the previous result

$$\begin{array}{r} 1.234 \\ +\ \ .5 \\ \hline 123.9 \end{array} \qquad \begin{array}{r} 123.6 \\ +\ \ .5 \\ \hline 124.1 \end{array}$$

A carry

3. Take integer part of the number resulting from Step 2

$$123 \qquad\qquad 124$$

4. Divide the integer by 100

$$1.23 \qquad\qquad 1.24$$

In general, if you want to round a positive number, X, to N decimal places, the following formula can be used:

$$INT(X*10**N + 0.5)/(10**N)$$

Consider the following example:

Example 9.9

```
10      X = 1.54926
20      PRINT ' N', 'ROUNDED NUMBER'
30      FOR N = 0 TO 4
40        PRINT N, INT(X*10**N +0.5)/(10**N)
50      NEXT N
60      END


RUNNH
N               ROUNDED NUMBER
0               2
1               1.5
2               1.55
3               1.549
4               1.5493
```

Notice, when N=0, the expression on line 40

$$INT(X*10**0 + 0.5)/(10**0)$$

rounded 1.54926 up to 2. If you just used a plain INT(X), the fractional part will be simply truncated and 1 is the result.

One other direct application of the INT function is to check whether a number is odd or even.

```
10      INPUT X
20      IF X-INT(X/2)*2 = 0
            THEN PRINT 'EVEN'
            ELSE PRINT 'ODD'
30      GO TO 10
```

```
RUNNH
? 5
ODD
? 16
EVEN
? -5
ODD
? ^C
```

Do you understand why line 20 works?

9.3.2 RND Function

The RND function is important in computer simulation. It returns a random number between 0 and 1 (0 inclusive, but 1 exclusive). It is displayed as a six-digit fractional number. The following example will generate five random numbers.

Example 9.10

```
10      FOR I = 1 TO 5
20          PRINT RND,
30      NEXT I
40      END
```

```
RUNNH
 .204935      .229581      .533074      .132211      .995602
```

You can imagine the procedure of generating random numbers assuming there were 1 million tickets, numbered from 0.000000 to 0.999999 in a box and you drew five of them. Each ticket has an equal chance of being selected. This is the essence of random numbers.

Notice that RND did not require an argument. Although BASIC-PLUS's random number function has two forms, RND and RND(X), in fact, they act exactly the same.

One caution: If you run Example 9.10 again, you will get the same set of random numbers. It is helpful for debugging a program. In many situations, however, you might want to have a different set of random numbers for each run. In that case, one statement should be added before you use the RND function, which takes the following format:

```
Line number      RANDOM
```

Now you can see by adding

5 RANDOM

in Example 9.10, you will get a different set of random numbers when you run the program for the second time.

```
5       RANDOM
10      FOR I = 1 TO 5
20          PRINT RND,
30      NEXT I
40      END
```

```
RUNNH
 .707689        .245901        .106203        .424108        .588821

Ready

RUNNH
 .51896         .113551        .010666        .420384E-1     .156236
```

Frequently, you won't want to use the RND function in its raw form. For example, if you want to draw an integer between 10 and 20 (inclusive), you have to combine the INT function and RND function. In general, if you want to generate an integer between L(lower limit) and U(upper limit), the following formula must be used.

$$INT((U-L+1)*RND)+L$$

Let's use an example to illustrate the use of the above formula.

Example 9.11

Dr. Miller teaches three sections of BASIC programming. He numbers his students in the three sections as

Section 1	1–30
Section 2	31–55
Section 3	56–75

Dr. Miller does not want to call the roll every day. He just wants to check roll by randomly selecting one person in each class. Hence, he wrote the following BASIC program to determine who should be called the next day:

```
10      RANDOM
20      PRINT 'SECTION 1', INT((30-1+1)*RND)+1
30      PRINT 'SECTION 2', INT((55-31+1)*RND)+31
40      PRINT 'SECTION 3', INT((75-56+1)*RND)+56
50      END
```

```
RUNNH
SECTION 1       28
SECTION 2       41
SECTION 3       63
```

Line 10 is absolutely necessary in this program because Dr. Miller certainly does not want to check the same person every day. The expression to generate a random number between 1 and 30 to select a student in section 1 is set in the PRINT statement at line 20. We substitute the lower limit, 1 and the upper limit, 30 in the formula. A number, 28, is generated. Similarly, Line 30 selected number 41 and line 40 selected number 63 for the first time the program is executed.

CAI is gaining popularity rapidly. The computer can be used to provide students with d
specific subject areas. In this section, we will show a program which helps first-grade pu
in practicing basic subtraction on numbers up to 10. Each time the program is run, the pt
will be given a set of 10 questions one by one. At the end, the score will be displayed. Be
fore we list the coding let's have a flowchart to illustrate the logic of this program:

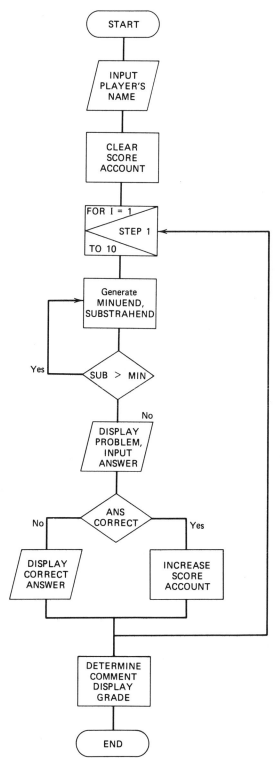

Example 9.12

```
10        REM THIS PROGRAM IS USED TO PRACTICE BASIC SUBTRACTION
20        RANDOM
30        EXTEND
40        INPUT 'WHAT IS YOUR NAME';N$
50        SCORE = 0
60        FOR I = 1 TO 10
65            MINUEND = INT((10+1)*RND)
70            SUBTRAHEND = INT((10+1)*RND)
80            IF SUBTRAHEND > MINUEND THEN 65
90            PRINT 'QUESTION';I
100           PRINT MINUEND; '-'; SUBTRAHEND; '=';
110           INPUT DIFFERENCE
120           IF MINUEND - SUBTRAHEND = DIFFERENCE
                  THEN ANSWER$ = 'CORRECT'
                  ELSE ANSWER$ = 'WRONG'
130           PRINT ANSWER$
140           IF ANSWER$ = 'CORRECT'
                  THEN SCORE = SCORE + 1
                  ELSE PRINT 'THE CORRECT ANSWER IS';MINUEND-SUBTRAHEND
150       NEXT I
160       IF SCORE >= 8
                  THEN COMMENT$ = 'YOU HAVE DONE A GOOD JOB'
                  ELSE COMMENT$ = 'YOU NEED MORE PRACTICE'
170       PRINT SCORE; 'CORRECT OUT OF 10'
180       PRINT N$, COMMENT$
190       END
```

Study the flowchart and program carefully so that you can follow the logic of the CAI program. In order to generate a different set of questions every time the program is executed, we have to place

$$20 \quad \text{RANDOM}$$

before the RND function is used. The loop enclosed in line 60 and 150 will produce 10 questions. The formula used to generate minuend and subtrahend on line 65 and 70 looks a little different from the formula discussed in the previous section. Since the random numbers we wanted to generate are between 0 and 10, the formula can be simplified. Line 80 is used to make sure that no negative numbers will appear so that the first grader can handle it.

9.4 USER-DEFINED FUNCTIONS

We have covered the standard mathematical functions in the earlier sections of this chapter. If a formula is frequently used in your program, you can invent your own function and use it over and over again in your program. For example, if it is necessary to evaluate the following formula:

$$X^4 - X^2 + 1 + 2/X$$

for various X values, say, 1 and 4, you can define a function as follows:

$$10 \quad \text{DEF FNA(X)} = X**4 - X**2 + 1 + 2/X$$

Later, when you want to use this function, you can call it by name FNA and specify the X value, for instance:

$$20 \quad B = FNA(1)$$
$$30 \quad C = FNA(4)$$

will cause the value of

$$1^4 - 1^2 + 1 + 2/1$$

to be stored in location B, which is 3, and the value of

$$4^4 - 4^2 + 1 + 2/4$$

to be stored in location C, which is 241.5.

9.4.1 General Format of Defining a Function

BASIC-PLUS provides the capability of defining single-line functions and multiple-line functions. We will postpone the discussion of multiple line functions to Chapter 12. Defining a single-line function takes the following format:

> Line number   DEF   Function name (Argument List) = Expression

Line # : The define function statement can be placed anywhere in the program, *even after the function is used*. The reason is that the define function statement is a nonexecutable statement just like the DATA statement. *It does not* compute anything; it just informs the computer that a certain expression will go by a specific name. From the viewpoint of structured programming, it is recommended that you place the function definition statement at the beginning of the program.

DEF: DEF is the key word for the function definition statement.

Function Name: The function name can be any legal variable name[4] preceded by two letters, FN. For example.

> FNA
> FNA1
> FNALABERT (if the extend mode is used)

Argument List: The argument list must be enclosed in parentheses. It can be up to five numeric variables, separated by commas. The argument here is just a placeholder—a *dummy argument*. When the function is used, the *actual argument* will substitute for it. While the dummy argument must be a variable, the actual variable can be a constant, variable, or a combination. Consider the following example:

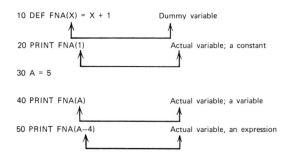

```
10 DEF FNA(X) = X + 1          Dummy variable

20 PRINT FNA(1)                Actual variable; a constant

30 A = 5

40 PRINT FNA(A)               Actual variable; a variable

50 PRINT FNA(A—4)             Actual variable, an expression
```

The expression at the righthand side of the equal sign involves dummy variables. It tells the computer what calculations to make.

---

[4] The variable used as function name can't be a subscripted variable.

9.4.2 Application of Defined Function

Now, let's have some examples to show the user-defined function feature of BASIC-PLUS. First, let's rewrite Example 9.1. We can simply define a function to convert the temperature from Fahrenheit to Celsuis measure, without repeating the formula four times.

Example 9.13

```
5       DEF FNT(H) = (H-32)*5/9
10      PRINT 'WINTER', 'SPRING', 'SUMMER', 'AUTUMN'
20      PRINT FNT(50), FNT(70), FNT(85), FNT(72)
30      END
```

```
RUNNH
WINTER          SPRING          SUMMER          AUTUMN
  10             21.1111        29.4444          22.2222
```

Example 9.14

Dr. Carter is a professor of economics and the owner of the Pub at the University Center. He is considering selling his business. One of his employees, Miss Brown, is offering him $20,000 in cash. Professor King in the math department promises to pay him $3,000 per year for the next 10 years. Which offer is the more attractive?

Dr. Carter knows quite well that $3,000 next year certainly will be worth less than that same amount now; $3,000 in five years will be worth even less. He believes that the inflation rate will stay at the same level for the next 10 years, but he doesn't know what that rate will be. His estimates are 6%, 10%, or 13%.

Based on his estimates of various inflation levels, he wants to write a program to calculate the *present value* of Professor's King's offer. The formula to calculate the present value is:

$$\text{Present Value} = 3000 \times \frac{1 - (1+I)^{-10}}{I} \text{ (I is inflation rate)}$$

Dr. Carter's program will look as follows:

```
10      REM THIS PROGRAM IS USED TO CALCULATE THE PRESENT VALUE
20      DEF FNA(I) = 3000*(1-(I+1)**(-10))/I
30      F$ = '     ##%                        $##,###'
40      PRINT 'INFLATION RATE', "PRESENT VALUE OF PROF. KING'S OFFER"
45      PRINT
50      PRINT USING F$, 6,  FNA(0.06)
60      PRINT USING F$,10,  FNA(0.10)
70      PRINT USING F$,13,  FNA(0.13)
80      END
```

```
RUNNH
INFLATION RATE                  PRESENT VALUE OF PROF. KING'S OFFER

    6%                               $22,080
   10%                               $18,434
   13%                               $16,279
```

Based on the output of the program, Dr. Carter should accept Professor King's offer, provided he is optimistic about the inflation. Because, for an inflation rate of 6%, Professor King's offer is worth $22,080 today, which exceeds what Miss Brown wants to pay. Otherwise, he will not take Professor King's offer.

Let's have a quick look at the program. Since the formula to calculate present value will be used more than one time in the program, it is worthwhile to define a function representing that relationship (see line 20). When we want to use it, we simply plug the real argument in; for example,

FNA(0.06)

FNA(0.10)

FNA(0.13)

9.4.3 Multiple Argument Function

So far we have illustrated the single argument function. BASIC-PLUS allows us to define a function for a maximum of five variables. The following example should explain the use of the multiple argument function.

Example 9.15

In dealing with inventory policy, you will be facing a dilemma: either place the order more often to reduce storage costs or order a large amount at one time to reduce reorder costs. There is a formula which calculates the optimal size of an order.[5]

$$\sqrt{\frac{2\ B\ Q}{K}}$$

where B is cost per order
   Q total number of items needed in a period of time
   K is cost of storing a unit for a period of time

German Deli Co. carries the following inventory items:

Item	Total Demand	Cost per Order	Unit Storing Cost
Wine	1000	$25	$1.00
Beer	3000	$20	$0.50
Leberwurst	500	$10	$0.80
Sauerkraut	4000	$30	$0.50
Chocolate	100	$40	$0.50

The program to calculate the optimal size per order for each item should look as follows:

---

[5] Consult a management science book about the assumptions of this mathematical model.

```
10      REM THIS PROGRAM WILL CALCULATE THE OPTIMAL REORDER SIZE
20      EXTEND
30      DEF FNS(B,Q,K) = SQR(2*B*Q/K)
40      TITLE$ = 'G E R M A N    D E L I    C O'
50      HEAD1$ = 'ITEM         TOTAL  COST PER   UNIT STORING   SIZE OF'
60      HEAD2$ = '             DEMAND  ORDER         COST        ORDER'
70      L$ =       '\           \ ####     $##       $#.##         ###'
80      PRINT TAB(15);TITLE$ \ PRINT \  PRINT
90      PRINT HEAD1$ \ PRINT HEAD2$ \ PRINT
100     FOR X = 1 TO 5
110         READ ITEM$,B,Q,K
120         SIZE = FNS(B,Q,K)
130         PRINT USING L$, ITEM$,Q,B,K,SIZE
140     NEXT X
150     DATA 'WINE',25,1000,1
160     DATA 'BEER',20,3000,0.5
170     DATA 'LEBERWURST',10,500,0.8
180     DATA 'SAUERKRAUT',30,4000,0.5
190     DATA 'CHOCOLATE',40,1500,0.3
199     END


RUNNH
            G E R M A N    D E L I    C O


ITEM        TOTAL  COST PER   UNIT STORING   SIZE OF
            DEMAND  ORDER         COST        ORDER

WINE        1000    $25        $1.00          224
BEER        3000    $20        $0.50          490
LEBERWURST   500    $10        $0.80          112
SAUERKRAUT  4000    $30        $0.50          693
CHOCOLATE   1500    $40        $0.30          632
```

We define the formula to calculate optimal reorder size as FNS at line 30. Function FNS contains three arguments: B, Q and K. At the righthand side of the function definition, we used a square root function (SQR) as part of the expression. In addition to the built-in functions, any user-defined function can also be used in the expression.

For example, the following two statements have the same effect as line 30.

```
25  DEF FNA(B,Q,K) = 2*B*Q/K
35  DEF FNS(B,Q,K) = SQR(FNA(B,Q,K))
```

We set up the title, header lines, and the format of report lines at lines 40–70. After the headers have been printed, the loop, lines 100–140 read a set of data, calculate size by using the function FNS, and then output the result. At line 120, when we call function FNS, we used Q,B,K as real arguments, which are identical to the dummy arguments in the function definition. When you call a function, you must match actual variables with dummy variables. For instance:

```
195  PRINT FNS(W,X,Y,Z)
```

will cause the following error message to be printed:

?ARGUMENTS DON'T MATCH AT LINE 195

because function FNS is expecting three actual arguments, not four. You should also use care in the sequence of the arguments. If you put the actual argument in the wrong place, the computer will not give you any error message, but the result will be wrong. For example, the computer will interpret the arguments in the following function call:

FNS(25,1,1000)

as

$$B \text{ (cost per order)} = 25$$
$$Q \text{ (total demand)} = 1$$
$$K \text{ (unit storing cost)} = 1000$$

If this should represent the information about wine, it is a logic error.

9.5 SUBROUTINES

A function is used when a formula needs to be repeated many times in a program. Similarly, when a group of statements needs to be used several times in a program, we need a *subroutine*. A subroutine is a block of statements (any number of statements) put aside from the mainroutine and used for the purpose of simplifying the coding and adding to the clarity of the program. The computer transfers the control back and forth between the mainroutine and subroutine. This situation can better be depicted as follows:

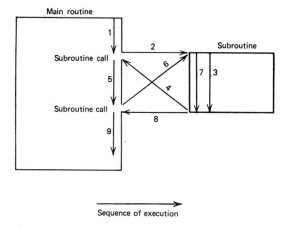

Example 9.16

Consider the situation when you want to triple space after each printed line. Since the procedure for printing three blank lines needs to be used over and over again, why not put it in a subroutine.

```
100     REM THIS IS A SIMPLE PROGRAM TO ILLUSTRATE SUBROUTINE
110     PRINT 'THIS IS LINE 1'
120     GOSUB 200
130     PRINT 'THIS IS LINE 2'
140     GOSUB 200
150     PRINT 'THIS IS THE LAST LINE'
199     STOP
200     REM SUBROUTINE TO TRIPLE-SPACE
210     FOR X = 1 TO 3
220           PRINT
230     NEXT X
240     RETURN
999     END
```

```
RUNNH
THIS IS LINE 1

                ──────▶ triple space


THIS IS LINE 2

                ──────▶ triple space


THIS IS THE LAST LINE
Stop at line 199
```

In the above example, we instructed the computer to transfer the control to the subroutine after the first line has been printed by

120   GOSUB   200

Then, line 200 is encountered, which is just a remark statement. The loop, lines 210–230, will be executed to produce the first three blank lines.

240   RETURN

Control will be transferred to the instruction immediately following the one which called the subroutine, for example, line 130. After the second line has been printed, line 140 GOSUB 200 again will send the computer to 200, do the loop, and then return to line 150 to print the last line. Then, the program stops at line 199.

9.5.1 Key Statements for Subroutines

We notice that

GOSUB
RETURN

are the two key words for construction of a subroutine. The general format of these two statements looks as follows:

Line number	GOSUB	line number
Line number	RETURN	

The GOSUB statement can do two things:

1. Transfer the control to the line number specified, which is usually the first line number in the subroutine.[6]

2. Keep track of return address by internally recording the line number immediately following the GOSUB statement.

At the end of a subroutine, we must have a RETURN statement that will send the computer back to the line immediately following the most recent GOSUB statement. At least one RETURN should be put at the end of a subroutine. More than one RETURN statement can be placed in the subroutine. Once a RETURN statement is encountered, the computer will *return*.

Theoretically, subroutines can be placed anywhere in your program, but, from the standpoint of structured programming, they should be placed at the end of your program. Hence,

199   STOP

is necessary to separate the main routine and subroutine. Otherwise, the subroutine will be executed for a third time and an error message

?RETURN WITHOUT GOSUB

will be caused.[7]

---

[6] This may not be the first line.

[7] When we use a STOP statement to terminate the execution, the END statement is still mandatory.

Now you can realize the advantage of the GOSUB/RETURN statements. If a programming language does not have this feature, your program will look as follows:

```
100      REM THIS IS THE PROGRAM WITHOUT SUBROUTINE
110      PRINT 'THIS IS LINE 1'
120      Y = 1 \ GO TO 200
130      PRINT 'THIS IS LINE 2'
140      Y = 2 \ GO TO 200
150      PRINT 'THIS IS THE LAST LINE'
199      STOP
200      REM THIS IS THE SECTION TO TRIPLE-SPACE
210      FOR X = 1 TO 3
220          PRINT
230      NEXT X
240      IF Y = 1 THEN 130
250      IF Y = 2 THEN 150
999      END
```

Without the capability of retaining the return address, we have to set a code before transferring the control to the subroutine:

$$120 \qquad Y=1 \setminus GO\ TO\ 200$$
$$140 \qquad Y=2 \setminus GO\ TO\ 200$$

and at the end of the subroutine, we have to use IF/THEN statements to determine where to return. If the subroutine is used many times, this becomes a tedious task.

9.5.2 More Examples of Subroutines

Subroutines can be executed repeatedly but need not produce the same value each time. Let's consider the following two examples:

Example 9.17

```
100      REM THIS IS A SUBROUTINE TO ILLUSTRATE THE VARIOUS ENTRY POINTS
110      GOSUB 200
120      GOSUB 230
130      GOSUB 220
199      STOP
200      REM THIS IS A SUBROUTINE TO PRINT LINES
210          PRINT 'LINE 1'
220          PRINT 'LINE 2'
230          PRINT 'LINE 3'
240      RETURN
999      END
```

```
RUNNH
LINE 1 ──────────→ result of 110   GOSUB 200
LINE 2
LINE 3
LINE 3 ──────────→ result of 120   GOSUB 230
LINE 2 ──────────→ result of 130   GOSUB 220
LINE 3
Stop at line 199

Ready
```

As you can see, we can enter the middle of the subroutine. We can also exit from the middle of a subroutine, provided a RETURN statement is reached, as the following example will illustrate:

Example 9.18

It is usually necessary to compute the value of $_nC_r$ binomial coefficient in a probability or statistics problem. $_nC_r$ is the number of all possible combinations for n distinct objects taken r at a time. The formula to calculate $_nC_r$ is

$$_nC_r = \frac{n!}{r!\,(n-r)!}$$

Where $n! = n.(n-1).(n-2).\ldots\ldots\ldots 2.1$ (n factorial), and $0! = 1$. Hence, in order to calculate $_nC_r$, the factorial values must be computed. For example,

$$_5C_3 = \frac{5}{3! \times 2!}$$
$$= \frac{5.4.3.2.1}{(3.2.1) \times (2.1)} = 10$$

The following program will allow us to INPUT any n and r and calculate the value of $_nC_r$:

```
100     REM THIS PROGRAM WILL CALCULATE THE BINOMIAL COEFFICIENT
105     EXTEND
110     PRINT'PLEASE ENTER N AND R VALUES'
120     PRINT "N AND R MUST BE INTEGER, R CAN'T BE GREATER THAN N"
130     INPUT 'N VALUE';N
140     INPUT 'R VALUE';R
150     IF N<>INT(N) OR R<>INT(R) OR R>N OR R<0 OR N<0 THEN 110
160     Y = N \ GOSUB 200 \ NFACTORIAL = YFACTORIAL
170     Y = R \ GOSUB 200 \ RFACTORIAL = YFACTORIAL
180     Y = N-R \ GOSUB 200 \ NMINUSRFACTORIAL = YFACTORIAL
190     RESULT = NFACTORIAL / (RFACTORIAL * NMINUSRFACTORIAL)
195     PRINT'RESULT =';RESULT
199     STOP
200     REM THIS IS THE SUBROUTINE TO CALCULATE YFACTORIAL
210     YFACTORIAL = 1
220     IF Y = 0 THEN 260
230     FOR NUMBER = Y TO 1 STEP -1
240         YFACTORIAL = YFACTORIAL*NUMBER
250     NEXT NUMBER
260     RETURN
999     END
```

```
RUNNH
PLEASE ENTER N AND R VALUES
N AND R MUST BE INTEGER, R CAN'T BE GREATER THAN N
N VALUE? 5
R VALUE? 3
RESULT = 10
Stop at line 199
```

The subroutine, lines 200 to 260, is used to compute the y factorial. Since a factorial is the product of a sequence of integers, we have to initialize the accumulation counter, YFACTORIAL with value 1, instead of 0 at line 210. By the definition of factorial, for Y = 0, its factorial is 1; hence, a test is made at line 220 to determine whether or not the following steps should be performed. If Y=0, we need to jump to 260 to exit from the subroutine immediately.[8] The loop, lines 230 to 250, will build up the product. Verify the logic yourself. The subroutine can be depicted as follows:

---

[8]It may be more convenient to replace 220 by

IF Y=0 THEN RETURN

However, in structured programming, we prefer having one exit from the subroutine.

Now, let's explain the main routine. We printed the instruction at lines 110 and 120. Lines 130 and 140 ask for input. We use line 150 to validate the input data. We understand, if N is an integer, then

$$N = INT(N)$$

If any of the five simple conditions, which are coupled by OR, is met, the program will ask you to enter the values again. Statements 160, 170, and 180 calculate the n factorial, r factorial, and (n−r) factorial, respectively. Before the subroutine is called, Y value must be set. After the factorial is computed, it must be stored in an appropriate location. Therefore, each of these three lines consist of three components. We notice that the variable Y and YFACTORIAL in the subroutine are used in a similar way as dummy arguments in a function. For different Ys, each subroutine call produces a different YFACTORIAL. Line 190 then calculates the final result, which is displayed at line 195. The STOP statement should not be left out.

9.5.3 Nested Subroutines

So far we have shown a BASIC program with a single subroutine. There can be as many subroutines as memory space allows. Subroutines may be paralleled or nested as the illustration below shows. This is analogous to the FOR/NEXT loop. A subroutine usually starts with REM statement, and a RETURN statement must be used to mark the end of a subroutine.

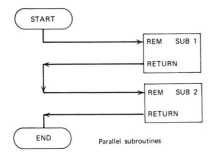

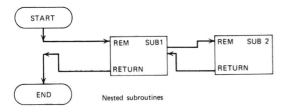

Figure 9-2. Nested subroutines.

Of course, for a large program the parallel structure and nested structure can be combined. What we have to remember is that when a subroutine is called, it always returns to the statement immediately following the one that calls it. We will see some applications in the following section.

9.5.4 Multiple Destination Subroutine Branching

In the previous chapter, we used the ON GOTO statement to implement the case structure of a BASIC program. Similar to the ON GOTO statement, there is a ON GOSUB statement, which allows us to transfer the control to one of the subroutines or any part of a subroutine. Consider the following example:

```
10      REM THIS PROGRAM ILLUSTRATES THE MULTIPLE DESTINATION
                SUBROUTINE  BRANCHING
20      INPUT 'WHICH SUBROUTINE DO YOU WANT TO EXECUTE';X
30      ON X GOSUB 100,200
99      STOP
100     REM------SUBROUTINE 1------
110         PRINT 'BASIC IS EASY'
199     RETURN
200     REM------SUBROUTINE 2------
210         PRINT 'COMPUTING IS FUN'
220     RETURN
999     END

Ready

RUNNH
WHICH SUBROUTINE DO YOU WANT TO EXECUTE?   1
BASIC IS EASY
Stop at line 99

Ready

RUNNH
WHICH SUBROUTINE DO YOU WANT TO EXECUTE?   2
COMPUTING IS FUN
Stop at line 99
```

The general format of the multiple destination subroutine branching statement is

```
Line number    ON   expression    GOSUB   line numbers
```

The expression following the key word ON will be evaluated. Depending on the value of the expression, control is then transferred to the subroutine which begins at one of the line numbers listed. When line 30 is executed, the value of X should be either 1 or 2, otherwise an error message

?ON statement out of range at line 30

will be printed. The ON GOSUB statement is very convenient in structuring a program.

9.6 FURTHER CONSIDERATIONS OF STRUCTURING A PROGRAM: MODULARITY AND TOP-DOWN DESIGN

We have shown how to structure your program in Chapter 8. A well-organized program depends largely on whether or not a complex program can be broken into several simple tasks. A module is a group of instructions used to perform a certain task. The subroutine capability makes modularity possible. Modules can be written and corrected independently. In order to implement modularity, we use the top-down approach to break the tasks. A program can be broken into several tasks. The tasks, in turn, will be broken into subtasks. The stepwise refinement simplifies coding and improves the clarity of the program, which is necessary for communication among programmers involved in the same project. Hence, the subroutine is not only used to avoid repetitive coding but also to structure the program. We will use an example to show the modularity and the top-down design concept in this section.

Example 9.19

Suppose data of the ages of 50 mini-town residents are given. We want to write a program to analyze the age structure of mini-town. Our job includes:

1. Constructing a distribution table.

2. Calculating the mean.

3. Calculating the standard deviation.

4. Determining the median.

5. Determining the range.

This is a typical statistical problem. The program can be organized as follows:

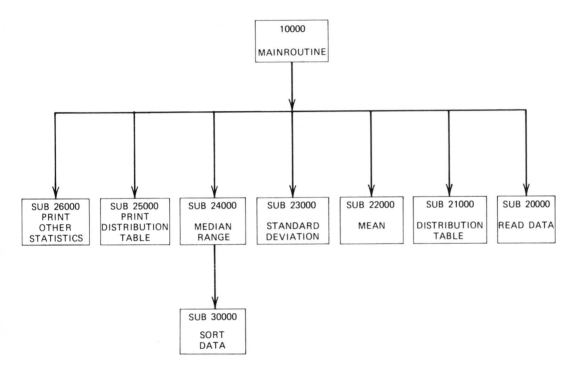

Three major steps in data processing are:

INPUT

PROCESS

OUTPUT

Hence, we need separate modules to do the I/O. Printing the distribution table is a little complicated. Therefore, we have two subroutines to do the output, SUB 25000 and SUB 26000. The process of data can be broken down into following tasks:

1. Making up a distribution table to show number of residents in each age class; for example, 0 − less than 10, 10 − less than 20, and so on.

2. Computing the mean, which is the average age.

3. Computing the standard deviation, which is defined as

$$\sqrt{\frac{\text{total squared differences from mean}}{50}}$$

4. Determining median and range. Median is the middle value. Since we have 50 values, median will be the average of 25th and 26th value. Range is the difference between the highest value and the lowest value. In order to obtain the lowest, middle, and highest value, data should be sorted. Hence, a subroutine for sorting data will be used in the course of performing this task. The sort routine (SUB 30000) is nested in the module to determine median and range.

Now, let's take a look at the program and its output.

```
10000     REM *****************************************************************
10010     REM *                                                               *
10020     REM * AUTHOR:    SHU-JEN CHEN                                        *
10030     REM * DATE:      MARCH 20, 1980                                      *
10040     REM * PURPOSE:   USING 50 DATA OF MINI TOWN RESIDENT'S AGES          *
10050     REM *            TO PRODUCE                                          *
10060     REM *              1. DISTRIBUTION TABLE                             *
10070     REM *              2. MEAN                                           *
10080     REM *              3. STANDARD DEVIATION                             *
10090     REM *              4. MEDIAN                                         *
10100     REM *              5. RANGE                                          *
10110     REM *                                                               *
10120     REM *****************************************************************
10130     REM FOLLOWING IS THE MAIN ROUTINE
10140     EXTEND
10150     DIM RAWDATA(50),FREQUENCY(8)
10160     GOSUB 20000              !READ DATA INTO RAWDATA TABLE
10170     GOSUB 21000              !MAKE UP FREQUENCY TABLE
10180     GOSUB 22000              !CALCULATE THE MEAN
10190     GOSUB 23000              !CALCULATE STANDARD DEVIATION
10200     GOSUB 24000              !DETERMINE MEDIAN AND RANGE
10210     GOSUB 25000              !PRINT FREQUENCY TABLE
10220     GOSUB 26000              !PRINT OTHER STATISTICS
10230     STOP
20000     REM SUBROUTINE TO READ DATA INTO RAWDATA TABLE
20010        FOR X = 1 TO 50
20020           READ RAWDATA(X)
20030        NEXT X
20040     RETURN
21000     REM SUBROUTINE TO MAKE UP DISTRIBUTION TABLE, FREQUENCY
21010        FOR CLASS = 1 TO 8
21020           FREQUENCY(CLASS) = 0
21030        NEXT CLASS
21040        FOR X = 1 TO 50
21050           CLASS = INT(RAWDATA(X)/10) + 1
21060           FREQUENCY(CLASS) = FREQUENCY(CLASS) + 1
21070        NEXT X
21080     RETURN
22000     REM SUBROUTINE TO CALCULATE THE MEAN
22010        TOTAL = 0
22020        FOR X = 1 TO 50
22030           TOTAL = TOTAL + RAWDATA(X)
22040        NEXT X
22050        MEAN = TOTAL/50
22060     RETURN
23000     REM SUBROUTINE TO CALCULATE STANDARD DEVIATION
23010        DIFFERENCESUM = 0
23020        FOR X = 1 TO 50
23030           DIFFERENCE = (RAWDATA(X) - MEAN)**2
23040           DIFFERENCESUM = DIFFERENCESUM + DIFFERENCE
23050        NEXT X
23060        DEVIATION = SQR(DIFFERENCESUM/50)
23070     RETURN
24000     REM SUBROUTINE TO DETERMINE MEDIAN AND RANGE
24010     GOSUB 30000              !SORT DATA IN RAWDATA TABLE
24020        MED1 = 50/2           !FIRST MEDIAN POSITION
24030        MED2 = 50/2+1         !SECOND MEDIAN POSITION
24040        MEDIAN = (RAWDATA(MED1) + RAWDATA(MED2)) /2
```

```
24050            LOW = RAWDATA(1)
24060            HIGH = RAWDATA(50)
24070            RANGE = HIGH - LOW
24080            RETURN
25000     REM SUBROUTINE TO PRINT DISTRIBUTION TABLE
25010            TITLE$ = 'AGE OF RESIDENTS IN MINI TOWN'
25020            DASH$ = '-------------------------------------------------------------'
25030            HEAD1$= '                    CLASS      ABSOLUTE      RELATIVE      '
25040            HEAD2$= ' CLASS      BOUNDARY      CLASS        CLASS        '
25050            HEAD3$=  '                              FREQUENCY   FREQUENCY    '
25060            L$    = '   #    LESS THAN ##        ##          #.##    '
25070            PRINT TAB(10);TITLE$
25080            PRINT \ PRINT
25090            PRINT DASH$
25100            PRINT HEAD1$
25110            PRINT HEAD2$
25120            PRINT HEAD3$
25130            PRINT DASH$
25140            PRINT
25150            FOR CLASS = 1 TO 8
25160                 BOUNDARY = CLASS * 10
25170                 RELATIVE = FREQUENCY(CLASS)/50
25180                 PRINT USING L$, CLASS, BOUNDARY,
                          FREQUENCY(CLASS), RELATIVE
25190            NEXT CLASS
25200            PRINT \ PRINT DASH$
25210     RETURN
26000     REM SUBROUTINE TO PRINT STATISTICS
26010            F$    = ' \                  \ =   ##.##'
26020            PRINT USING F$,'MEAN',MEAN
26030            PRINT USING F$,'STANDARD DEVIATION',DEVIATION
26040            PRINT USING F$,'MEDIAN',MEDIAN
26050            PRINT USING F$,'RANGE',RANGE
26060     RETURN
30000     REM SUBROUTINE TO SORT DATA IN RAWDATA TABLE IN ORDER
30010            FOR PASS = 1 TO 49
30020                 FOR PLACE = 1 TO 50-PASS
30030                      IF RAWDATA(PLACE+1) < RAWDATA(PLACE)
                               THEN TEMP = RAWDATA(PLACE)\
                                    RAWDATA(PLACE) = RAWDATA(PLACE+1)\
                                    RAWDATA(PLACE+1) = TEMP
30040                 NEXT PLACE
30100            NEXT PASS
30110     RETURN
32000     DATA 15,2,34,78,45,23,21,34,54,32,65,76,5,44,15,26
32010     DATA 13,66,3,2,47,44,45,34,23,12,13,26,23,37,25,18
32020     DATA 12,19,30,20,21,24,14,13,70,7,3,72,45,22,35,5,22,35
32767     END
```

```
RUNNH
          AGE OF RESIDENTS IN MINI TOWN
```

CLASS	CLASS BOUNDARY	ABSOLUTE CLASS FREQUENCY	RELATIVE CLASS FREQUENCY
1	LESS THAN 10	7	0.14
2	LESS THAN 20	10	0.20
3	LESS THAN 30	12	0.24
4	LESS THAN 40	8	0.16
5	LESS THAN 50	6	0.12
6	LESS THAN 60	1	0.02
7	LESS THAN 70	2	0.04
8	LESS THAN 80	4	0.08

```
MEAN                  =   29.38
STANDARD DEVIATION    =   20.14
MEDIAN                =   23.50
RANGE                 =   76.00
Stop at line 10230
```

Since this is a large program, we decided to use a five-digit line number. Lines 10000 to 10230 constitute the main program. We first used a series of REM statements to document the program. After the extend mode is declared, the array to store data, RAWDATA, and the array to store the frequency, FREQUENCY, is defined at line 10150. Since we group the ages in an interval of 10, and we assume that there is no one older than 79 in mini-town, FREQUENCY contains eight elements. Then, the subroutines are called one by one to perform the tasks. Finally, the program stops at line 10230

The first subroutine, lines 20000 to 20040, to read data into RAWDATA is self-explanatory. Subroutine 21000 to 21080 needs a bit of explanation. Since the setup of a distribution table involves a counting process, we have to initialize all the counters in the FREQUENCY array with zero. This is done in the loop lines 21010–21030. Then we check data in the raw-data table one by one, determine which class it belongs to (line 21050), and then increase the corresponding class (line 21060). (Verify the logic here yourself!). After we return from this subroutine, FREQUENCY table will look as follows:

FREQUENCY (1)	7
FREQUENCY (2)	10
FREQUENCY (3)	12
FREQUENCY (4)	8
FREQUENCY (5)	6
FREQUENCY (6)	1
FREQUENCY (7)	2
FREQUENCY (8)	4

The subroutine to calculate the mean starts with line 22000 and ends with 22060. In order to get the standard deviation, we have to take the difference of each individual data from the mean and square it, which is stored in DIFFERENCE, (line 23030). The differences are accumulated at line 23040. When this procedure has been done 50 times, line 23060 will compute the standard deviation.

At the beginning of the subroutine to determine median and range, we call subroutine 30000–30110 to sort the data in RAWDATA table in ascending order. The sorting algorithm used in subroutine 30000 is the bubble sort, which has already been discussed in Chapter 7.

24010   GOSUB 30000

The RAWDATA table looks as follows

RAWDATA (1)	2
RAWDATA (2)	2
⋍	⋍
RAWDATA (25)	23
RAWDATA (26)	24
⋍	⋍
RAWDATA (50)	78

The rest of the instructions in this module to determine the median and the range are not hard to understand.

After all calculations have been completed, we go to subroutine 25000 to print the distribution table. After the title, header lines, and format of the lines inside the table are defined at lines 25010 through 25060,[9] the header lines are printed. Then, we print the lines for each class, which is done in the loop 25150 to 25190. Notice that, in addition to the absolute frequency, we also print the relative frequency, which reveals residents in a certain age class. Hence, a calculation for relative frequency is done at line 25170.

Printing of the bottom lines is straight forward. After setting a format, line 26010, the statistics are printed.

Data are placed at the end of the program. Notice, we use 32767 as a line number for the END statement, which is the largest a PDP 11 computer can accept.

Word List

Built-In Function. A built-in program that is available for computing the value of a function, such as finding a square root, random number, and so on.

Module. A group of instructions used to perform a specific task.

Multiple Argument Function. A function in BASIC-PLUS that allows the user to define a function for a maximum of five variables.

Subroutine. A block of statements placed separate from the main program.

User-Defined Function. Through the use of a special statement, the user can define his own unique functions within a program.

PROBLEMS

1. Explain why functions and subroutines are necessary

2. Determine values assigned to the variables below

   (a) 10   X=INT(3.14159)

   (b) 20   Y=ABS(SGN(−3))

   (c) 30   Z1=SGN(ABS(−3))

   (d) 40   A4=SQR(101)

   (e) 50   C5=SQR(ABS(4−8))

   (f) 60   V2=EXP(−3)

   (g) 70   W=LOG(ABS(−5.5))

   (h) 80   B=LOG10(10)

3. Determine values assigned to the variables below

   (a) 10   D = COS(1.27)

   (b) 20   E1 = TAN(.52)

   (c) 30   F = SIN(45 * .0174533)

   (d) 40   G = ATN(50)

   (e) 50   H3 = TAN(ATN(1))

---

[9] You will learn a better way to define DASH$ in Chapter 10.

4. Obviously, interest compounded daily generates more money than the same interest compounded annually. A smart person will ask people to compound his deposit every hour, every minute, even every second, continuously. If you are able to do so, for 12% nominal interest rate, your effective interest rate will be 12.7497%. In general, if the nominal interest rate is R, then the effective interest rate will be

$$e^R - 1 \qquad \text{(where e is natural number)}$$

Write a program to display the effective rates for the nominal rate 6%, 7%, 8%, and 10%

5. Write a program to determine whether a number (entered by INPUT statement) is a multiple of 10.

6. Write a program to generate 10 random integer numbers between 20 and 60, inclusive.

7. Write a program to generate 1,000 random numbers; average the 1,000 random numbers; check to see if the average is close to 0.5.

8. Write a program to simulate flipping two coins 100 times. The program should record the occurence of 0,1, and 2 heads. The output should look as follows:

Number of heads	Occurence
0	XX
1	XX
2	XX
TOTAL	100

9. If a RANDOM statement is included in the program listed in problem 8, will the result vary from run to run?

10. The terminal at the computer lab has a 10% chance of being "down" every day. Suppose there are 20 terminals, write a program to simulate number of "down" terminals for 10 days. Your output may look as follows:

Day	Number of Down Terminal
1	2
2	3
3	0
. . . .	
10	1

11. Write a BASIC program to find the height of a redwood tree in the illustration below. A 300-foot rope is stretched from the top of the tree as shown. Hint: The SIN function is needed for this program.

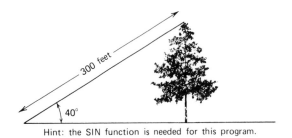

Hint: the SIN function is needed for this program.

12. Supply statement defining functions for equations below:

(a) $Y = X^2 - 2X + 4$

(b) $Z = LOG(X+10)$

(c) $W = \dfrac{X^4 - 5}{X^3 + 2X + 1}$

(d) $X1 = INT(X*10**N + 0.5)/10**N$

(e) $R = INT((U-L+1)*RND)+L$

(f) $G = \dfrac{W}{2.D^2}$

(g) $C = \sqrt{A^2 + B^2}$

13. For $f(x) = x^4 - 2x^2 + 2x + 1$, compute and display the function values in steps of $1/2$ on the interval of $(1,4)$.

14. For any quadratic equation, $ax^2 + bx + c = 0$, the two roots are

$$X1 = \frac{-b - \sqrt{a^2 - 4bc}}{2ac}$$

$$X2 = \frac{-b + \sqrt{a^2 - 4bc}}{2ac}$$

Write a program to input any quadratic equation (just the coefficients a, b, and c), and determine the two roots.

15. Miss Lucy decides to save $100 every month. She deposits her money at CITIZEN bank, which offers her a 6% interest rate, compounded monthly. Write a program to determine her balance at the end of third, fifth, and tenth years. (Hint: The balance at the end of Nth year is

$$100 \times \frac{1-(1+0.06/12)^{12N}}{1-(1+0.06/12)}$$

16. Determine the output of the following program:

```
10    GOSUB 100
20    GOSUB 200
30    GOSUB 100
99    STOP
100   PRINT "TO BE   ";
199   RETURN
200   PRINT "OR NOT   ";
299   RETURN
999   END
```

17. Sketch the output of the following program:

```
10      GOSUB 100
20      A = 1 \ B = 10 \ C = 1 \ GOSUB 200
30      A = 10 \ B = 1 \ C = −1 \ GOSUB 200
40      GOSUB 100
99      STOP
100     REM SUBROUTINE 1
110     PRINT TAB(30);'*'
120     RETURN
200     REM SUBROUTINE 2
210        FOR X = A TO B STEP C
220            PRINT TAB(30−X);'*';TAB(30+X);'*'
230        NEXT X
240     RETURN
999     END
```

18. Write a program to find the MAXMIN of a 4 by 3 table. MAXMIN is defined as the largest value of the smallest values in each row. For example:

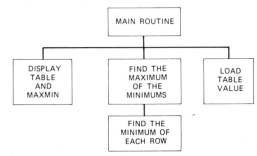

Your program may be organized as follows:

19. Write a *well-structured* payroll program for the Great Eastern Co. Make up the payroll information about 10 employees on your own. You should include:

   Name.

   Hours worked.

   Payrate.

   Number of dependents.

You are required to generate an attractive payroll report, which indicates

   Name.

   Gross pay.

   Net pay.

The gross pay is number of hours worked multiplied by pay rate. Time-and-a-half is to be paid for hours over 40. Exemption for each dependent is $20, provided gross pay is greater than the total of exemption. For the difference between gross pay and total exemption, a tax of 20% is assessed.

Your program should also include validation of the data, which means:

1. Hours worked should not be greater than 100.

2. Payrate must be in the range of $2.50 and $12.00, inclusive.

3. Number of dependents would never exceed 10.

If any violation of the above three limitation occurs, an error message should be printed.

Chapter **10**
Character Strings

Objectives   You will learn:

About string arrays.

The CHANGE statement and ASCII function.

To use functions for extracting substrings.

To link strings.

To search for characters.

To convert numeric strings to numbers.

Other string functions.

Character strings were defined and discussed briefly in Chapter 2, and some examples of handling strings for formatting output were given in Chapter 6. Recall that a string is one or more alphanumeric characters treated as a unit. BASIC-PLUS provides special statements and functions that allow varied manipulation of characters that are useful in many situations.

The maximum length of a character string will vary with different systems. In BASIC-PLUS, the string size is limited only by space in memory.

Strings must include a dollar sign ($) as part of the string name as

> 10   S$ = 'TIM STRAHAN'

and the EXTEND mode can be used to provide a more descriptive string name as

> 10   EXTEND
> 20   NAME1$ = 'TIM STRAHAN'

Strings can be assigned characters as shown above with the abbreviated LET statement or with an INPUT statement as

> 30   INPUT NAME1$

(Note: Since NAME is a BASIC reserved word, it
         should not be used as a string variable name)

where NAME1$ is a string variable name. The INPUT statement allows you to type in a string that will fit on one line.

The READ and DATA statements can also be used to handle strings as follows:

Example 10.1

```
5          REM READIN AND PRINTOUT OF STRINGS
8          EXTEND
10         READ NAME.TITLE$, ADDRESS$, CITY.STATE.ZIP$
20         PRINT NAME.TITLE$\ PRINT ADDRESS$\ PRINT CITY.STATE.ZIP$
30         DATA 'MS. ROSE SIEMENS', 'STAR ROUTE', 'BLUE LAKE, CA.   95525'
90         END

Ready

RUNNH
MS. ROSE SIEMENS
STAR ROUTE
BLUE LAKE, CA.   95525
```

Notice that strings can be alphabetic characters, special symbols, or numerics in any combination. Quote marks must be used before and after strings when strings contain commas, spaces, or begin with a number.

10.1 STRING ARRAYS

Strings can be stored in arrays and tables in the same way that numbers are stored. Since characters are stored in strings, the string array name must include a $ and a DIM statement is required, such as

10   DIM A$(20)

which sets aside 21 locations in memory (locations 0 to 20) for a string array called A$. Let's use the bubble sort to arrange names in alphabetical order by using a string array. (Refer to Chapter 7 for a review of the bubble sort process if necessary.)

Example 10.2 reads five names into a string array called NAME.SORT$, sorts these names in alphabetical order, and prints the sorted list of names. Note that the DATA statements use quotes around each name in order to get an accurate reading of each name. For example, if we had placed

SMITH, THOMAS A.

without quotes in the DATA statement, the READ statement would have placed

SMITH

in the first location of NAME.SORT$ and

THOMASA.

as the second name because the comma would have signaled the end of the first data field.
Note the sorting sequence of the names in output:

SMITH, THOMAS
SMITH, THOMAS A.
SMITH, THOMAS A. JR.
SMITH, THOMAS ANDREW
SMYTHE, THOMAS A.

The sorting of names is based on an assignment of numbers to characters based on the ASCII code (American Standard Code for Information Interchange). Note that SMITH, THOMAS precedes SMITH, THOMAS A. because a blank character is assigned an ASCII code of 32 which is smaller than any alphabetic character.

Example 10.2

```
10      REM *********************************************************
20      REM
30      REM PURPOSE:   TO SORT NAMES IN ALPHABETICAL ORDER
40      REM               USING THE BUBBLE SORT
45      REM
50      REM *********************************************************
60      EXTEND
70      DIM NAME.SORT$(5)
80      REM READIN OF NAMES INTO THE ARRAY NAME.SORT
90      FOR LOCATION = 1 TO 5
100           READ NAME.SORT$(LOCATION)
110     NEXT LOCATION
120     REM THE NAME.SORT ROUTINE
130     REM
140     FOR PASS = 1 TO 4
150           FOR PLACE = 1 TO 5 - PASS
160                 IF NAME.SORT$(PLACE+1) < NAME.SORT$(PLACE)
                    THEN STORE$ = NAME.SORT$(PLACE)\
                    NAME.SORT$(PLACE) = NAME.SORT$(PLACE+1)\
                    NAME.SORT$(PLACE+1) = STORE$
170           NEXT PLACE
180     NEXT PASS
190     REM
200     REM PRINTOUT ROUTINE OF NAMES IN ALPHABETICAL ORDER
210     REM
220     FOR PRINTOUT = 1 TO 5
230           PRINT NAME.SORT$(PRINTOUT)
240     NEXT PRINTOUT
300     DATA 'SMITH, THOMAS A.', 'SMYTHE, THOMAS A.', 'SMITH, THOMAS A. JR.'
320     DATA 'SMITH, THOMAS ANDREW', 'SMITH, THOMAS'
900     END

Ready

RUNNH
SMITH, THOMAS
SMITH, THOMAS A.
SMITH, THOMAS A. JR.
SMITH, THOMAS ANDREW
SMYTHE, THOMAS A.
```

Figure 10-1 shows some of the ASCII number assigned to commonly used characters. Since the letter, 'A', is assigned an ASCII code of 65 and the letter 'B' a code number of 66, a relational test of

$$\text{'A'} < \text{'B'}$$

will result in A being considered a smaller value. Thus, sorting of characters works on the same principle and uses the relational operators described in Chapter 4.

10.2 THE CHANGE STATEMENT AND ASCII FUNCTION

The CHANGE statement changes alphanumeric characters in strings to ASCII code numbers and stores these numbers in a numeric array. For example,

```
10   DIM N(20)
20   N$ = 'A'
30   CHANGE N$ TO N
```

results in the ASCII code for 'A' which is 65 to be placed in a numeric array called N. The array, N, is not subscripted in the CHANGE statement since all the characters stored in the string name, N$, are converted to ASCII numbers and stored in array, N, using the number of locations required depending on the length of the string that is changed. In addition, the CHANGE statement stores in the first location of the N array, N(0), the number of characters changed into numbers. If there were 12 characters in a string that were being changed, N(0) would have a numeric 12.

Character	ASCII	Character	ASCII	Character	ASCII
blank	32	A	65	N	78
0	48	B	66	O	79
1	49	C	67	P	80
2	50	D	68	Q	81
3	51	E	69	R	82
4	52	F	70	S	83
5	53	G	71	T	84
6	54	H	72	U	85
7	55	I	73	V	86
8	56	J	74	W	87
9	57	K	75	X	88
comma	44	L	76	Y	89
period	46	M	77	Z	90

Figure 10-1. ASCII code for selected characters.

The CHANGE statement can also be used to convert the ASCII code number to the alphanumeric characters represented by

30   CHANGE N TO N$

which would change the ASCII code of the character stored in N to the associated characters.

Example 10.3 shows a conversion of 10 alphabetic characters to their equivalent ASCII code numbers and the printout of these numbers.

Example 10.3

```
1        REM CHANGING CHARACTERS TO ASCII CODE NUMBERS
5        EXTEND
10       DIM ALPHA.NUMBERS(10)
20       READ ALPHA$
30       CHANGE ALPHA$ TO ALPHA.NUMBERS        !(CHANGES CHARACTERS TO
                                                  NUMBERS)
40       FOR COUNTER = 0 TO ALPHA.NUMBERS(0)
50           PRINT ALPHA.NUMBERS(COUNTER);
60       NEXT COUNTER
90       DATA 'ABCDEFGHIJ'
900      END

Ready

RUNNH
 10   65   66   67   68   69   70   71   72   73   74
```

Statement 30 changes all characters stored in ALPHA$ to equivalent ASCII code numbers and stores these 10 numbers in an array called ALPHA.NUMBERS. The printout shows that the first element, ALPHA.NUMBERS(0), stores the number of characters converted (10 in this example, characters A - J).

Example 10.4 illustrates the use of the CHANGE statement and tests to determine if a car license number ends in an even or odd number. This program assumes a license number with the following formats:

AAA 999   or   999 AAA   or   AAAAAAA

Example 10.4

```
1       REM **********************************************************
2       REM
3       REM PURPOSE: TO TEST FOR ODD-EVEN LICENSE PLATES USING THE
4       REM               CHANGE STATEMENT AND ASCII FUNCTION
5       REM
6       REM **********************************************************
10      EXTEND
20      DIM NUMBER(7)
30      COUNTER = 0
40      INPUT 'WHAT LICENSE NUMBER DO YOU WANT CHECKED'; LICENSE$
45      REM   LINE 50 CHANGES A STRING INTO AN ARRAY CALLED NUMBER
50      CHANGE LICENSE$ TO NUMBER
55      REM   TESTING THE THIRD AND SEVENTH CHARACTER FOR NUMBERS
60      FOR I = 3 TO NUMBER(0) STEP 4
70              IF NUMBER(I) >= ASCII('0') AND
                        NUMBER(I) <= ASCII('9') THEN GO SUB 200
80      NEXT I
90      PRINT 'LICENSE NUMBER IS ';LICENSE$
100     IF COUNTER = 0 THEN PRINT 'THIS IS A PERSONALIZED PLATE'
110     STOP
200     REM SUBROUTINE TO TEST FOR EVEN OR ODD NUMBERED PLATE
205     COUNTER = COUNTER + 1
210     IF NUMBER(I) - 2 * INT(NUMBER(I)/2) = 0
                THEN PRINT 'THIS PLATE ENDS WITH AN EVEN NUMBER'
                        ELSE PRINT 'THIS PLATE ENDS WITH AN ODD NUMBER'
220     RETURN
900     END

Ready

RUNNH
WHAT LICENSE NUMBER DO YOU WANT CHECKED? ZOE 167
THIS PLATE ENDS WITH AN ODD NUMBER
LICENSE NUMBER IS ZOE 167
Stop at line 110

Ready

RUNNH
WHAT LICENSE NUMBER DO YOU WANT CHECKED? 234 BAD
THIS PLATE ENDS WITH AN EVEN NUMBER
LICENSE NUMBER IS 234 BAD
Stop at line 110

Ready

RUNNH
WHAT LICENSE NUMBER DO YOU WANT CHECKED? RAREGEM
LICENSE NUMBER IS RAREGEM
THIS IS A PERSONALIZED PLATE
Stop at line 110
```

where AAA represents any alphabetic characters and 999 represents any numeric characters. The license plate with all alphabetic characters is a personalized plate and may have from two to seven characters.

Statement 60 in program 10.4 is a FOR I loop to test the third and seventh characters in a license plate. After changing the license plate characters to numbers in statement 50, statement 70

70   IF NUMBER(I) >= ASCII('0') AND
NUMBER(I) <= ASCII('9') THEN GO SUB 200

tests NUMBER(I) against the ASCII codes for numeric characters ranging from zero to nine. When either the third or seventh character in the license plate is a number, a branch is made to a subroutine to test whether or not the number is even or odd. ASCII, as used in statement 70, is a string function which converts the first character of a string placed in parentheses immediately following the function name, ASCII. If we had used

80   PRINT ASCII(LICENSE$)

the output would be the ASCII code number for 'Z', which is 90, the first character stored in LICENSE$, since our first input string was the license number, ZOE 167.

10.3 FUNCTIONS FOR EXTRACTING SUBSTRINGS

BASIC-PLUS string functions are similar to the math functions described in Chapter 9; however, string functions are designed to aid in the manipulation of nonnumeric characters as well as numeric characters.

There are times when it is necessary to extract parts of strings, such as the first or last name of a person, from a string which may include other related information.

The LEFT function is
LEFT(A$,N)

where A$ is the main string and N is an integer indicating the number of characters to be extracted.

Example 10.5

```
5       REM USING THE LEFT STRING FUNCTION
8       EXTEND
10      PERSON$ = 'JAMES CHEN'
20      PRINT LEFT(PERSON$,5)
900     END

Ready

RUNNH
JAMES
```

extracts the leftmost five characters from the string, PERSON$, and prints the substring, JAMES.

The MID(middle) function is related to the LEFT function but results in the extraction of a substring from a specified middle section of a main string. The MID function is

MID(A$,N1,N2)

where A$ is the main string, N1 is the first character position in the substring, and N2 is the number of characters of the substring that are to be processed. For example:

Example 10.6

```
5       REM USING THE MID STRING FUNCTION
8       EXTEND
10      ALPHA$ = 'ABCDEFGHIJ'
20      PRINT MID(ALPHA$,4,4)

Ready

RUNNH
DEFG
```

Line 20 identifies a substring of the main string, ALPHA$, which begins with the fourth character and extracts four characters, DEFG.

The RIGHT function is used to extract a substring from the right portion of a main string. The RIGHT function is

RIGHT(A$,N)

where A$ is the main string and N is the first character position of the substring; all remaining characters in the main string beginning with location N are included in the substring as shown in the following example:

Example 10.7

```
4       REM USING THE RIGHT STRING FUNCTION
8       EXTEND
10      ALPHA$ = 'ABCDEFGHIJ'
40      PRINT RIGHT(ALPHA$,8)
900     END

Ready

RUNNH
HIJ
```

Line 40 identifies and prints a substring of ALPHA$ beginning at the eighth character and continues until all remaining characters in the string are printed.

When errors are made in specifying the range of the three substring functions of LEFT, MID, and RIGHT, output will reflect errors by either printing the entire string or no characters (a null string). When fractional values are used to describe a substring location, BASIC-PLUS truncates numbers to integers.

10.4 LINKING STRINGS

You can take substrings from main strings, insert spaces or other symbols, and then link them together. This process is called *concatenation*. For example:

10   PRINT '509' + '20' + '7371'

produces

509207371

as a linked string that is printed. The plus sign (+) acts as a link (concatenation) symbol.

Example 10.8

```
1       REM USE OF THE LEFT, MID, AND RIGHT STRING FUNCTIONS TO
            INSERT HYPHENS IN A SOCIAL SECURITY NUMBER
10      READ R$
15      REM STORE THE 9 LEFTMOST CHARACTERS IN S$
20      S$ = LEFT(R$,9)
25      REM STORE 3 LEFTMOST CHARACTERS OF SUBSTRING S$ IN L$
30      L$ = LEFT(S$,3)
35      REM STORE 4TH AND 5TH CHARACTERS OF S$ IN M$
40      M$ = MID(S$,4,2)
45      REM STORE LAST FOUR CHARACTERS OF S$ IN R$
50      R$ = RIGHT(S$,6)
60      PRINT L$ + '-' + M$ + '-' + R$
90      DATA '509207371LEE HENDERSON'
900     END

Ready

RUNNH
509-20-7371
```

Example 10.8 illustrates an application of linking strings. Statement 90, the DATA statement, includes one string with a social security number and a name. Since social security numbers are hard to read without spaces between subgroups of numbers, it is common practice to imbed hyphens within the number. Statement 20 extracts the social security number from the string R$ and stores it in location S$. Statement 30 stores the three leftmost digits of S$ in L$; statement 40 stores the fourth and fifth numbers in M$; and statement 50 stores the last four digits of the number in R$. Thus, we have taken the nine-digit social security number and stored sections of the number in three locations:

$$L\$ = \text{'509'}$$
$$M\$ = \text{'20'}$$
$$R\$ = \text{'7371'}$$

Now it is simply a matter of inserting hyphens between these three substrings and linking them together to produce a more readable number. Statement 60 handles this process by using

$$+ \text{ '—' } +$$

between each of the substrings. We tell the computer to link together the three substrings with hyphens.

10.5 SEARCHING STRINGS

There is a special string function called INSTR (in string), which searches for the location of a specific character or characters within a string. The function is written

$$INSTR(N,A\$,B\$)$$

where N is an integer that signals the computer where you wish to begin your search within the string; A$ is the main string and can be either a quoted string or a string variable; B$ is the substring and can be either a quoted string or a string variable. For example:

Example 10.9

```
5       REM USING THE INSTR FUNCTION TO SEARCH A STRING
10      A$ = 'JOHN SMITH'
20      PRINT INSTR(1,A$,' ')
90      END

RUNNH
  5
```

Statement 20 instructs the computer to search the main string, A$, beginning at the first character position. The search is directed toward finding a blank within the string, since we have placed quotes around a blank, ' '. The printout produces a 5 that tells us that the blank in string, A$, is located in the fifth character position. We could have searched for a specific alphabetical character, comma, or any other valid alphanumeric symbol. If the character we are searching for does not exist in the string, the printout is zero. If either of the strings specified in the INSTR function are null strings, the printout is one(1). Recall that a null string is one that contains no characters; that is, its length is zero. Note that

$$10 \quad PRINT \; INSTR(1,A\$,\text{'H'})$$

would print 3, since it will find only the first occurrence of the letter, 'H'.

Example 10.10

```
1       REM ********************************************************
2       REM
3       REM THIS PROGRAM USES THE INSTR, LEFT, RIGHT, AND SPACE
4       REM STRING FUNCTIONS TO PLACE A PERSON'S LAST NAME FIRST
5       REM WITH A COMMA AND SPACE INSERTED
6       REM
7       REM*********************************************************
10      REM
20      INPUT 'NAME';N$
25      REM SEARCH OF N$ TO LOCATE THE POSITION OF AN IMBEDDED SPACE
30      F = INSTR(1,N$,' ')
35      REM PLACE CHARACTERS IN N$ TO THE LEFT OF THE SPACE IN F$
40      F$ = LEFT(N$,F-1)
45      REM PLACE CHARACTERS IN N$ TO THE RIGHT OF THE SPACE IN L$
50      L$ = RIGHT(N$,F+1)
60      PRINT L$ + ',';SPACE$(3);F$
900     END

Ready

RUNNH
NAME? 'JAMES CALLAHAN'
CALLAHAN,    JAMES
```

Example 10.10 uses the INSTR function to locate the space in the string called, N$, which is used for a name field. The name is input as

'JAMES CALLAHAN'

and statement 30 searches the string, N$, to locate the position of the first space in the string. Statement 40 extracts all characters in N$ to the left of the space (the first name, JAMES) and places this substring in location F$. Statement 50 extracts all characters in the main string to the right of the space (the last name, CALLAHAN) and places this substring in location L$. Finally, statement 60 prints the last name first with three spaces inserted, followed by the first name. The SPACE$ function is used in statement 60 and is a convenient method of inserting spaces for string output. The function is written as follows:

SPACE$(N)

where N is a positive integer that indicates how many spaces are to be inserted in the string.

10.6 CONVERTING NUMERIC STRINGS TO NUMBERS

There are times when it is convenient to store numbers as part of a string. Yet we may wish to use the numeric strings for computational purposes. BASIC-PLUS has a VAL function that converts numbers in strings to numeric values which can be used arithmetically. The function is written as

VAL(A$)

where A$ is a string or substring composed of numbers. If A$ has any nonnumeric characters, an error message results. For example:

Example 10.11

```
5        REM USING THE VAL FUNCTION TO CONVERT STRINGS TO NUMBERS
10       A$ = '500'
20       A1 = VAL(A$)
30       PRINT 'THE STRING '; A$; ' CONVERTS TO THE NUMBER';A1
900      END

Ready

RUNNH
THE STRING 500 CONVERTS TO THE NUMBER 500
```

Statement 20 converts A$ into a number that can be used with any arithmetic operator.

Example 10.12 uses the VAL function to compute individual student ratings of faculty teaching effectiveness and computes the class average rating. Statement 80 extracts individual string characters and converts them to numeric values before adding them to SUB.TOTAL. Statements 100 to 115 compute the average of each student's ratings of an instructor and prints the average. Finally, statement 140 computes and prints the average rating for the class.

Example 10.12

```
1        REM ************************************************************
2        REM
3        REM THIS PROGRAM COMPUTES STUDENTS' RATING OF A PROFESSOR
4        REM ON FIVE DIFFERENT ITEMS USING THE STRING VAL FUNCTION
5        REM TO CONVERT STRINGS TO NUMBERS
6        REM
7        REM************************************************************
10       EXTEND
20       SUB.TOTAL, TOTAL = 0
30       REM COMPUTING AND PRINTOUT OF INDIVIDUAL STUDENT'S RATING
40       FOR J = 1 TO 50
50            READ RATINGS$
60            IF RATINGS$ = '9' THEN 130
65            REM THE FOR I LOOP EXTRACTS INDIVIDUAL STRING
                        CHARACTERS AND PLACES THEM AS NUMERIC VALUES
                        IN SUB.TOTAL
70            FOR I = 1 TO 5
80            SUB.TOTAL = SUB.TOTAL + VAL(MID(RATINGS$,I,1))
90            NEXT I
100           AVERAGE = SUB.TOTAL/5\  TOTAL = TOTAL + AVERAGE
110           PRINT ' STUDENT #';J; 'RATING IS'; AVERAGE
115           SUB.TOTAL = 0
120      NEXT J
130      REM PRINTOUT OF AVERAGE OF ALL STUDENTS RATING A PROFESSOR
140      PRINT TAB(20);'CLASS RATING IS'; TOTAL/(J-1)
200      DATA 13233,24332,22133,22332,22133,9
900      END

Ready

RUNNH
 STUDENT # 1 RATING IS 2.4
 STUDENT # 2 RATING IS 2.8
 STUDENT # 3 RATING IS 2.2
 STUDENT # 4 RATING IS 2.4
 STUDENT # 5 RATING IS 2.2
                  CLASS RATING IS 2.4

Ready
```

10.7 OTHER STRING FUNCTIONS

The CHR$(character) function is the inverse of the ASCII function explained earlier in this chapter. One can place the ASCII numeric code for a character in parenthese following this function name and a printout will produce the related ASCII character. For example:

Example 10.13

```
5       REM USING THE CHR$ STRING FUNCTION TO PRINT CHARACTERS
10      PRINT CHR$(44)
20      PRINT CHR$(10)
30      PRINT CHR$(77)
99      END

Ready

RUNNH
,


M
```

Line 10 prints the ASCII character for code 44 which is a comma (,); line 20 leaves a blank, since the ASCII character for code 10 is a line feed key which acts as double space; and line 30 prints the letter, M, the ASCII character for 77. The CHR$ function is particularly useful for handling strings that contain non-printing characters such as the line feed key used in statement 20.

The LEN(length) function acts as a counter to determine the number of characters in a string. For example:

Example 10.14

```
1       REM USING THE LEN STRING FUNCTION TO COUNT THE NUMBER OF
                CHARACTERS IN A STRING
5       EXTEND
10      FULL.NAME$ = 'MAUREEN SPRANKLE'
20      PRINT LEN(FULL.NAME$)
900     END
RUNNH
 16
```

Notice that the LEN function counted 16 spaces in the string, FULL.NAME$, including spaces. The LEN function can be used with the IF THEN statement to effect a branch based on the length of a string. For example:

40   IF LEN(FULL.NAME$) = 16 THEN 90

causes a branch to statement 90 if FULL.NAME$ includes 16 characters.

The STRING$ function is similar to the SPACE$ function explained earlier except that it permits output of characters other than spaces. The format for STRING$ is

STRING$(A,B)

where A is an integer that indicates the length of the string, and B is the ASCII numeric code of the desired character. Let's print five periods (.) using this function:

Example 10.15

```
5        REM USING THE STRING$ STRING FUNCTION TO PRINT A SELECTED
                  NUMBER OF SYMBOLS
10       PRINT STRING$(5,46)
99       END

Ready

RUNNH
. . . . .
```

The ASCII numeric code of 46 represents a period (.); thus, statement 10 instructed the computer to PRINT five periods.

There are other string functions that are available in BASIC-PLUS. Some of the functions are used in connection with string arithmetic and allow the user to perform basic arithmetic operations with large numbers printed in output having more than six significant digits. You should check your local time-sharing system manual to determine the availability of string arithmetic functions.

You can make your own string functions in the same way that you did for numeric functions. (See Chapter 9 for a discussion of user defined functions.)

String functions can be used in more extensive ways for editing character strings, using the functions described in this chapter; however, a specially designed text editor, such as the one described in Chapter 13, simplifies the editing process.

Word List

ASCII code. The American standard code for information exchange. See Figure 10-1 for a partial listing.

Concatenation. The process of linking strings.

String Functions. Special BASIC functions which can be used to manipulate strings.

Substrings. A part of a string, such as a name that is extracted from a record stored as a string.

PROBLEMS

1. (a) Write a program to READ and PRINT the strings listed below in the DATA statement, using the string names of A$, B$, C$. The output should be placed on three lines in the usual envelope address format.

   DATA 'MS. JENSHU ADAMS', '1400 E. 24TH STR.', 'FULLERTON, CA. 92634'

   (b) Modify the above program to use descriptive string names, using the EXTEND mode.

2. Print in output the first character only of each word in the following string:

   AMERICAN AUTOMOBILE ASSOCIATION

3. (a) Write a program that will read your name and print the ASCII code numbers for each character in your name, as well as the total number of characters and spaces in your name.

   (b) Add statements to the program in 3a above that will print your name in reverse order, character by character including spaces.

4. Write a program that will produce 10 sentences, using three parts of speech in the sequence of subject - verb - object. Select words at random to produce different word combinations.

  DATA DOGS, CATS, RATS, PEOPLE (use these as subjects)

  DATA HATE, AVOID, LIKE, ENJOY (use these as verbs)

  DATA STRANGERS, BAIT, PEOPLE, OTHERS (use these as objects)

5. Write a program that will read the following string and print information about:

  (a) The number of words in the string.
  (b) The length of the string, including spaces.

  DATA 'PUT YOUR PEN WHERE YOUR MOUTH IS.'

6. Modify the program in problem 5 to:

  (1) Count the number of words with two, three, four, and five letters in the string.
  (2) Remove all blanks from the string and compact it

7. Write a program that will compute the grade point averages of students where student records are stored as strings. Use four points for an A; three points for a B; two points for a C; one point for a D; no points for an F. Note that the number of grades for each student will vary from three to five.

  DATA 'GREG FEENEY,ABB', 'JOAN WRIGHT,CBBDF', 'BARRY FLOWER,ABAC'

8. Write a program that will process employee records stored in strings and compute the gross pay, a social security tax deduction of .0665, and the adjusted gross pay (where adjusted gross pay = gross pay − social security tax deduction).

  The general format of your data will be the employee name, total hours worked in the period, and the hourly pay rate

  DATA 'TRESA BIEHN,30,6.50', 'KAY HOLLYMAN,40,6.25', 'FRANK DEAN,39,9.85', DATA 'KENT DOUGLASS,35,10.95'

  The output format should be as follows, including totals for numeric fields

  ABC CORPORATION SCHEDULE

  EMPLOYEE HOURS WORKED PAY RATE GROSS PAY SOCIAL SEC. NET PAY
  TOTALS

9. Write a program that can deal a card deck of 52 cards for a bridge hand, or 13 cards each to four people. Be sure to include a test to determine that no two similar cards are dealt in the hand.

  Suggestion: Store suit names, CLUBS, DIAMONDS, HEARTS, SPADES in one string array. Store card values, A, 2, 3, 4, 5, 6, 7, 8, 9, 10 J, Q, K in a second string array. Use the random number function to select a suit; then use it again to select a card value

  Hint: Keep track of cards selected at random by using a 52-element numeric array so that no two similar cards are dealt.
  The following formula can be valuable in determining which of the 52 cards has been selected at random:

Card selected = card value + 13(suit-1); for example, if the card value is 5 and the suit is 4 (spades), the 44th card in the deck has been selected (e.g., the 5 of spades).

Numbers   1–13 are CLUBS (A, 2, 3, ... K)
   14–26 are DIAMONDS
   27–39 are HEARTS
   40–52 are SPADES

Chapter **11**
Matrix Manipulation

Objectives

The relationship between tables and matrices.

Approaches to loading values in a matrix.

Ways of displaying the contents of a matrix.

Arithmetic operations of matrices.

Functions of a matrix.

Solving simultaneous equations with matrices.

In BASIC-PLUS, it is possible to work on a one-dimensional array as well as a two-dimensional table. Mathematically, we use the term vector for array and matrix for table. In algebra, we use a pair of brackets to enclose a vector or a matrix, which can be depicted as follows:

$$\begin{bmatrix} 10 \\ 20 \\ -7 \\ 3 \\ 4 \end{bmatrix} \longleftarrow \text{a column vector}$$

$$\begin{bmatrix} 12, & 34, & -3.14159, & 0 \end{bmatrix} \longleftarrow \text{a row vector}$$

$$\begin{bmatrix} 1 & 23 & 45 & -7 \\ 20 & 15 & -9 & 0 \\ 12 & -6 & 0 & 88 \end{bmatrix} \longleftarrow \text{a 3 by 4 matrix}$$

A matrix is a rectangular arrangement of objects. Actually, a vector is a special form of matrix in which there is only one column or one row. In this chapter, we will use the term, matrix, both for one-dimensional arrays and for two-dimensional tables. Matrix manipulation has been the subject of study in mathematics for sometime. In recent years, matrices have been applied to other fields, such as economics, business and biology.

Elementary applications using a matrix were introduced in Chapter 7. We used the nested loop and subscripted variables to access the individual elements in a table. This approach can be tedious for some matrix operations. For example, if you want to multiply a matrix by another matrix, you need to use a three-layered loop. BASIC is one of the few programming languages that includes several matrix operations as part of the language. In other words, we do not need to process the elements of a matrix individually but can treat the whole matrix as an entity. The general format for matrix manipulating is

> Line number   MAT   an action

11.1 DEFINING A MATRIX

Recall that the DIM statement is used to define a matrix. For example,

10   DIM A(5,4)

defines a matrix of 5 by 4; 5 rows and 4 columns. We reference the entire matrix as A and use subscripts to distinguish individual elements in the matrix. For instance, A(2,3) references the element on the second row and third column.

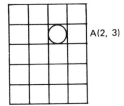

A(2, 3)

As mentioned before, one-dimensional arrays can be treated as a matrix. For example, we can define a five-element column vector as

10 DIM A(5,1)

and a 10-element row vector as

10 DIM B(1,10)

In many situations, the size of a matrix is not known at the time you write your program. You cannot use variables to indicate the size of a matrix when you first define it. For example, the following program segment will not work

```
10      DIM A(X,Y)
20      INPUT X,Y
```

even if the values of X and Y are assigned before matrix A is defined because the size of a matrix (the number of columns and rows) must be specified by numeric values in parentheses following the matrix name. One way to get around this problem is to define a large matrix at the beginning of your program and change the size of that matrix later. We will discuss this point in the next section.

11.2 LOADING VALUES IN A MATRIX

Like a simple variable, we can use READ and INPUT statement to assign values to cells in the matrix. In order to read a matrix in the form of

$$A = \begin{bmatrix} 12 & 34 & 5 & 6 \\ -4 & 0 & 15 & 34 \\ 99 & 19 & -7 & 0 \end{bmatrix}$$

The following nested loop should be used:

Example 11.1

```
10      DIM A(3,4)
20      FOR X = 1 TO 3
30         FOR Y = 1 TO 4
40            READ A(X,Y)
50         NEXT Y
60      NEXT X
70      DATA 12,34,5,6,-4,0,15,34,99,19,-7,0
99      END
```

Treating matrix A as an entity, we can use a single matrix statement to replace the nested loop. The program above can be shortened to

```
10      DIM A(3,4)
50      MAT READ A
70      DATA 12,34,5,6,-4,0,15,34,99,19,-7,0
99      END
```

The MAT READ statement fills the matrix *row by row*.

50   MAT READ A

instructs the computer to fill the first row of matrix A with first four items of data, the second row with next four items of data and the third row with the remaining four items. The general format of reading matrices is

```
Line number      MAT READ   List of matrix names
```

More than one matrix can be read in one MAT READ statement, but the names of matrices must be separated by commas. Consider the following program segment.

Example 11.2

```
10      DIM A(3,4), B(2,3)
20      MAT READ A,B
30      DATA 1,2,3,4,5,6,7,8,9,10,11,12,13,14,15,16,17,18
99      END
```

In line 20, matrix A will be filled first and then matrix B. Hence, after execution of line 20, the two matrices look as follows:

A

1	2	3	4
5	6	7	8
9	10	11	12

B

13	14	15
16	17	18

If there are not enough data to satisfy both matrix A and B, an error message

?OUT OF DATA AT LINE 20

will be displayed.

Matrices can be redimensioned when we load the values into a matrix. The example below illustrates the redimension feature of BASIC-PLUS.

Example 11.3

```
10      DIM A(10,10)
20      MAT READ A(2,3)
30      DATA 10,20,30,40,50,60
99      END
```

Originally, we reserved a 10 by 10 matrix in the memory. When we load values into matrix A, it is redimensioned as a 2 by 3 matrix.[1] We specify the new dimension in a MAT READ statement. After line 20 is executed, MATRIX A has the following form:

10	20	30
40	50	60

11.2.1 MAT INPUT

MAT INPUT permits the entry of values of a matrix from a terminal while the program is running. Like the ordinary INPUT statement, MAT INPUT will print a question mark on the terminal. After the question mark appears, you have to enter the values as indicated in the following example:

Example 11.4

```
10      DIM A(2,4)
20      MAT INPUT A
30      END


RUNNH
?  9,-4,3,5,5,3,2,0
```

After line 20 is executed, matrix A contains the folllowing values:

9	-4	3	5
5	3	2	0

The general format of MAT INPUT statement is:

Line number   MAT INPUT   List of matrices

You may not be able to remember how many values have been entered; fortunately, BASIC-PLUS has the capability to check it. Example 11.5 shows how you can check if the proper number of values have been entered.

---

[1] One restriction for matrix redimension is that the total number of elements in the new matrix can't exceed those in the old matrix.

Example 11.5

```
10      DIM A(5,4)
20      PRINT 'PLEASE ENTER ELEMENTS OF MATRIX A';
30      MAT INPUT A
40      IF NUM = 5 AND NUM2 = 4
                THEN PRINT 'YOU HAVE FILLED THE MATRIX'
                ELSE PRINT 'YOU DID NOT FILL THE MATRIX'\
                     PRINT 'NUMBER OF ROWS YOU HAVE ENTERED IS';NUM\
                     PRINT 'NUMBER OF ELEMENTS IN LAST ROW IS';NUM2
999     END
```

```
RUNNH
PLEASE ENTER ELEMENTS OF MATRIX A? 1,2,3,4,5,6,7,8,9,10,
? 11,12,13,14,15,16,17,18,19,20
YOU HAVE FILLED THE MATRIX
```

A 5 by 4 matrix is defined at the beginning of the program. Twenty values are expected to be entered at line 30. Every time a MAT INPUT statement is encountered, BASIC-PLUS will automatically provide two locations to keep track of the number of values being entered. Location *NUM* will record the number of rows being filled, and NUM2 records the number of elements in the last row. For example, if we run the above program for a second time and just enter 13 values for matrix A, locations NUM and NUM2 appear as follows:

```
RUNNH
PLEASE ENTER ELEMENTS OF MATRIX A? 1,2,3,4,5,6,7,8,9,10,11,12,13
YOU DID NOT FILL THE MATRIX
NUMBER OF ROWS YOU HAVE ENTERED IS 4
NUMBER OF ELEMENTS IN LAST ROW IS 1
```

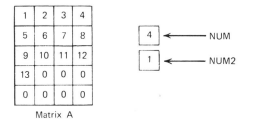

Matrix A

Situations may arise when the size of a matrix is determined only on execution of the program. The following example illustrates how the size of a matrix is changed during the run.

Example 11.6

Mini Data Service Corp. will reserve space in a matrix to store inventory information about selected styles of shoes for Walker's Shoes Inc.

```
10      EXTEND
20      DIM A(20,20)
30      INPUT 'NAME OF THE SHOES'; SHOES.NAME$
40      INPUT 'NUMBER OF SIZES'; TOTAL.SIZE
50      INPUT 'NUMBER OF WIDTHS'; TOTAL.WIDTH
60      MAT INPUT A(TOTAL.SIZE,TOTAL.WIDTH)
70      END
```

```
RUNNH
NAME OF THE SHOES? EUREKA
NUMBER OF SIZES? 6
NUMBER OF WIDTHS? 3
? 0,4,0,1,5,3,5,5,5,6,3,4,7,0,2,5,4,2
```

Since Mini Data Service Corp. is not sure about the inventory size, a large matrix is reserved at the beginning of the program. Lines 40 and 50 specify the number of rows and number of columns for the matrix. When MAT INPUT is encountered, the size of the matrix is changed to a DIM A(6, 3) Notice that like the MAT READ statement, the redimension can be achieved by attaching the size specification to the matrix name:

60   MAT INPUT A(TOTAL.SIZE,TOTAL.WIDTH)

We can use constants as well as variables to specify the *new* size, provided the values of the variables have been assigned, as we did at lines 40 and 50.

11.2.2 Initializing the Values in a Matrix

Zero matrix, summation matrix, and identity matrix are matrices of special form.
    A zero matrix contains all zeros. For example, a 2 × 3 zero matrix looks as follows:

0	0	0
0	0	0

A summation matrix contains all ones. The following is a 3 × 4 summation matrix:

1	1	1	1
1	1	1	1
1	1	1	1

An identity matrix is a square matrix (same number of rows and columns), which has all zero elements except along the main diagonal where the elements are set equal to one. A 3 × 3 identity matrix should look as follows:

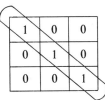

main diagonal
(from top left to bottom right)

In order to set up a special matrix, neither the MAT READ nor the nested loop should be used to assign values. BASIC-PLUS provides several instructions for generating a special matrix. Consider the following example:

```
10      DIM A(2,3),B(3,4),C(3,3)
20      MAT A = ZER
30      MAT B = CON
40      MAT C = IDN
50      END
```

After the program is executed, a zero matrix of size 2 by 3, named A; a summation matrix of size 3 by 4, named B; and a identity matrix of size 3 by 3 called C are established. The general format of generating a special matrix is

> Line number   MAT   name of the matrix = function name

Matrix function ZER will initialize a zero matrix; CON will initialize a summation matrix; and IDN a identity matrix. The size of the matrix can also be redefined in the matrix initialization statement by attaching the size specification to the function name. For example, if we change line 40 to

$$40 \quad MAT\ C = IDN(2,2)$$

then, a 2 by 2 identity matrix is set up, which looks as follows:

MAT ZER statement is used to zero-out a matrix. The application of MAT CON and MAT IDN instructions will be presented later in the chapter.

11.3 DISPLAYING A MATRIX

Data that have been stored in a matrix can be displayed by the MAT PRINT statement, which takes the following format:

> Line number   MAT PRINT   Matrix name

Consider the following example:

Example 11.7

```
10      DIM A(3,4)
20      MAT READ A
30      MAT PRINT A
40      DATA 1,2,3,4,5,6,7,8,9,10,11,12
50      END


RUNNH
 1
 2
 3
 4
 5
 6
 7
 8
 9
 10
 11
 12
```

Notice that each element in matrix A was printed on a separate line. While we can read in several matrices in one MAT READ statement, MAT PRINT only outputs one matrix for each statement. Part of the matrix can be printed by subscripting the matrix name. For example, after line 20, the matrix was set up as follows:

1	2	3	4
5	6	7	8
9	10	11	12

If we want to print the *upper left* portion of the matrix, the MAT PRINT statement should look as follows:

```
        30      MAT PRINT A(2,3)
RUNNH
   1
   2
   3
   5
   6
   7
Ready
```

Caution is required here. Unlike the MAT READ statement, the subscripts following the MAT PRINT statement do not redefine the matrix but indicate what cells in the upper left portion of the matrix should be printed.

We printed elements of matrix A on a separate line in the previous example. In the MAT PRINT statement, if the matrix name is followed by a semicolon (;), elements will be printed in a compact fashion. If the matrix name is followed by a comma (,), the elements are printed across the line with one element in each zone. Consider the following:

Example 11.8

```
10      DIM A(3,4)
20      MAT READ A
30      MAT PRINT A,
40      MAT PRINT A;
50      DATA 1,2,3,4,5,6,7,8,9,10,11,12
60      END
```

```
RUNNH
   1             2             3             4

   5             6             7             8  ◄────── generated by MAT PRINT A,

   9            10            11            12


   1  2  3  4

   5  6  7  8  ◄────── generated by MAT PRINT A;

   9  10  11  12
```

If spacing other than zone or compact fashion is required, the MAT PRINT statement cannot be used.

11.4 MATRIX ARITHMETIC OPERATIONS

Matrices can be conveniently set to equal another matrix, added, subtracted, and multiplied by the MAT statement, provided the dimension of the matrices are appropriately defined.

Redefining the dimension is not allowed in matrix arithmetic operations. Only one operation can be performed in one matrix operation statement.

11.4.1 Simple Matrix Assignment

One matrix can be set to be equal to another matrix. The BASIC statement to accomplish this takes the following format:

> Line number   MAT   matrix name = matrix name

For example, after the following program is executed:

Example 11.9

```
10        DIM A(3,4),B(3,4)
20        MAT READ A
30        MAT B = A
40        DATA 3,6,2,0,12,4,9,5,71,34,0,9

Ready
```

both matrix A and matrix B will contain the same elements

3	6	2	0
12	4	9	5
71	34	0	9

Matrix A

3	6	2	0
12	4	9	5
71	34	0	9

Matrix B

Notice, in the matrix assignment statement the matrix on the righthand side is the original matrix and matrix on the left hand side is the resulting matrix. The concept here is similar to the LET statement.

11.4.2 Matrix Addition and Subtraction

Addition of two matrices of similar size can be accomplished by adding the corresponding elements of two matrices and placing the sum in a third matrix. All three matrices should have the same dimension. Subtraction of two matrices is accomplished by the same method: corresponding elements are subtracted. The general format of matrix addition and subtraction is:

> Line number   MAT   matrix name = matrix name + matrix name
> Line number   MAT   matrix name = matrix name − matrix name

Consider the following example:

Example 11.10

```
10        DIM A(3,4),B(3,4),C(3,4),D(3,4)
20        MAT READ A,B
30        MAT C = A + B
40        MAT D = B - A
50        PRINT 'MATRIX A' \ MAT PRINT A,
60        PRINT 'MATRIX B' \ MAT PRINT B,
70        PRINT 'MATRIX C' \ MAT PRINT C,
80        PRINT 'MATRIX D' \ MAT PRINT D,
90        DATA 12,0,4,6,-9,4,3,-7,2,1,6,0
100       DATA 5,8,10,0,-3,5,6,20,-5,-2,0,7
999       END
```

```
RUNNH
MATRIX A
 12           0           4           6

 -9           4           3           -7

 2            1           6           0


MATRIX B
 5            8           10          0

 -3           5           6           20

 -5           -2          0           7


MATRIX C
 17           8           14          6

 -12          9           9           13

 -3           -1          6           7


MATRIX D
 -7           8           6           -6

 6            1           3           27

 -7           -3          -6          7


Ready
```

11.4.3 Scalar Multiplication

There are two types of multiplication in matrix arithmetic; namely, scalar multiplication and matrix multiplication. Scalar multiplication is performed by multiplying each element of a matrix by a scalar. For example, in the following scalar multiplication, the scalar value is 10.

$$10 \times \begin{bmatrix} 1 & 2 & 3 \\ 4 & 5 & 6 \\ 7 & 8 & 9 \end{bmatrix} = \begin{bmatrix} 10 & 20 & 30 \\ 40 & 50 & 60 \\ 70 & 80 & 90 \end{bmatrix}$$

The format for scalar multiplication in BASIC-PLUS is

> Line number   MAT   matrix name = (expression)* matrix name

The scalar in BASIC-PLUS can be a constant, a variable, or combination of both; in general, an expression, such as

```
10      MAT B = (10)*A
20      MAT B = (X)*A
30      MAT B = (X + 10/2)*A
```

The scalar expression must be enclosed in parentheses. The matrix on the righthand side is the original matrix; the one on the lefthand side is the resulting matrix. Both matrices must have the same dimension.

Example 11.11

The example below indicates the application of scalar multiplication. Suppose the average temperatures during four seasons in three major cities is stored in the following table:

	Winter	Spring	Summer	Fall
New York	45	55	80	55
Chicago	25	56	75	55
Los Angeles	58	67	80	70

We want to write a BASIC program to convert the temperatures from Farenheit to Celsius. We have learned several approaches to handle temperature conversion in previous chapters. Treating the temperature table as a whole, we can conveniently use matrix arithmetic to perform the conversion. We recall that the formula for conversion is

$$C = (F - 32)*(5/9)$$

```
10      REM THIS PROGRAM CONVERT THE FOUR SEASONS AVERAGE TEMPERATURES
20      REM OF 3 MAJOR CITIES FROM FARENHEIT MEASURE TO CELSIUS MEASURE
30      DIM A(3,4),B(3,4),C(3,4)
40      MAT READ A
50      MAT B = CON
60      MAT B = (32)*B
70      MAT C = A - B
80      LET X = 5/9
90      MAT C = (X)*C
100     MAT PRINT C,
110     DATA 45,55,80,55,25,56,75,55,58,67,80,70
999     END
```

```
RUNNH
   7.22222       12.7778       26.6667       12.7778

  -3.88889       13.3333       23.8889       12.7778

  14.4444        19.4444       26.6667       21.1111


Ready
```

We read in the temperatures into matrix A at line 40. Each element in A must be subtracted from 32. This is accomplished by setting a matrix with all 32s

50   MAT B = CON

1	1	1	1
1	1	1	1
1	1	1	1

32	32	32	32
32	32	32	32
32	32	32	32

60   MAT B = (32)*B

and subtracting it from the original matrix A. After the subtraction, matrix C contains:

13	23	48	23
−7	24	43	23
26	35	48	38

A scalar value, 5/9, is multiplied by each cell in matrix C, at line 100. Thus the conversion is completed.

11.5 MATRIX MULTIPLICATION

Matrix multiplication is more complex than other matrix arithmetic. The elements of the resulting matrix are derived by adding the products of the row elements from one matrix and the corresponding column elements of the second matrix. To illustrate the mechanics of matrix multiplication, let's show how a 2 by 3 matrix A is multiplied by a 3 by 2 matrix B.

$$\begin{bmatrix} a_{11} & a_{12} & a_{13} \\ a_{21} & a_{22} & a_{23} \end{bmatrix} \times \begin{bmatrix} b_{11} & b_{12} \\ b_{21} & b_{22} \\ b_{31} & b_{32} \end{bmatrix} = \begin{bmatrix} a_{11} \cdot b_{11} + a_{12} \cdot b_{21} + a_{13} \cdot b_{31} & a_{11} \cdot b_{12} + a_{12} \cdot b_{22} + a_{13} \cdot b_{32} \\ a_{21} \cdot b_{11} + a_{22} \cdot b_{21} + a_{23} \cdot b_{31} & a_{21} \cdot b_{12} + a_{22} \cdot b_{22} + a_{23} \cdot b_{32} \end{bmatrix}$$
$$A \quad \times \quad B \quad = \quad C$$

As you can see, the resulting matrix, C, is a 2 by 2 matrix. Dimensions of matrices in matrix multiplication require special caution. As a general rule, the number of columns in the first matrix, A, must be equal to the number of rows in the second matrix, B. The resulting matrix, C, will have the same number of rows as matrix A and the same number of columns as matrix B. Here is how a 3 by 3 matrix is multiplied by a 3 by 2 matrix:

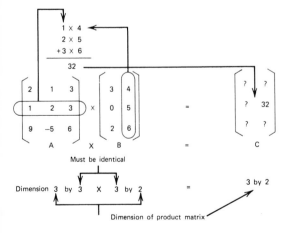

Obviously, several statements are required to perform matrix multiplication. Fortunately, a simple matrix statement can be used in the BASIC language, which takes the following format:

Line number	MAT matrix name = matrix name * matrix name

Now, let's use an example to illustrate matrix multiplication.

Suppose the number of cars, which Jerry's Ford Inc. sold last year are as follows

	Pinto	Mustang	Fairmont	Granada	LTD
1st quarter	10	24	3	4	5
2nd quarter	2	14	5	2	7
3rd quarter	10	10	4	2	1
4th quarter	1	13	4	5	6

The price list for each model is

Pinto	$4200
Mustang	$5675
Fairmont	$4010
Granada	$6025
LTD	$8000

Write a BASIC program to compute the

1. Total revenue in each quarter.

2. Total revenue last year.

3. Total number of cars sold each quarter.

The program should look as follows:

Example 11.12

```
10        EXTEND
20        DIM QUANTITY.TABLE(4,5)
30        DIM PRICE.TABLE(5,1)
40        DIM QUARTER.REVENUE.TABLE(4,1)
50        DIM YEAR.REVENUE.TABLE(1,1)
60        DIM QUARTER.QUANTITY.TABLE(4,1)
70        REM TOTAL REVENUE OF EACH QUARTER
80            MAT READ QUANTITY.TABLE
90            MAT READ PRICE.TABLE
100           MAT QUARTER.REVENUE.TABLE = QUANTITY.TABLE*PRICE.TABLE
110           PRINT 'QUARTER REVENUE TABLE'
120           MAT PRINT QUARTER.REVENUE.TABLE
130       REM TOTAL REVENUE LAST YEAR
140           MAT A = CON(1,4)
150           MAT YEAR.REVENUE.TABLE = A*QUARTER.REVENUE.TABLE
160           PRINT 'TOTAL REVENUE'
170           MAT PRINT YEAR.REVENUE.TABLE
180       REM TOTAL NUMBER OF CARS SOLD EACH QUARTER
190           MAT B = CON(5,1)
200           MAT QUARTER.QUANTITY.TABLE = QUANTITY.TABLE*B
210           MAT B = CON(5,1)
220           PRINT 'QUARTER QUANTITY TABLE'
230           MAT PRINT QUARTER.QUANTITY.TABLE
240       DATA 10,25,3,4,5,2,14,5,2,7,10,10,4,2,1,1,13,4,5,6
250       DATA 4200,5675,4010,6025,8000
260       END
```

Example 11.2 *(Continued)*

```
RUNNH
QUARTER REVENUE TABLE
 260005
 175950
 134840
 172140

TOTAL REVENUE
 742935

QUARTER QUANTITY TABLE
 47
 30
 27
 29


Ready
```

The number of cars sold are read into QUANTITY.TABLE (4 by 5). Prices are read into PRICE.TABLE (5 by 1). The total sale of each quarter is obtained by

100   MAT QUARTER.REVENUE.TABLE = QUANTITY.TABLE*PRICE TABLE

$$
\begin{bmatrix} 260005 \\ 175950 \\ 134840 \\ 172140 \end{bmatrix}
=
\begin{bmatrix} 10 & 24 & 3 & 4 & 5 \\ 2 & 14 & 5 & 2 & 7 \\ 10 & 10 & 4 & 2 & 1 \\ 1 & 13 & 4 & 5 & 6 \end{bmatrix}
\times
\begin{bmatrix} 4200 \\ 5675 \\ 4010 \\ 6025 \\ 8000 \end{bmatrix}
$$

The total revenue is the sum of the four quarter revenues. This can be computed by multiplying the QUARTER.REVENUE.TABLE by an appropriate summation matrix:

150   MAT YEAR.REVENUE.TABLE = A*QUARTER.REVENUE.TABLE

$$
742935
=
\begin{bmatrix} 1 & 1 & 1 & 1 \end{bmatrix}
\times
\begin{bmatrix} 260005 \\ 175950 \\ 134840 \\ 172140 \end{bmatrix}
$$

Notice that YEAR.REVENUE.TABLE has only one element. In order to make matrix multiplication possible, YEAR.REVENUE.TABLE needs to be defined as a 1 by 1 matrix instead of a single variable. As the name reveals, the summation matrix (where all elements are one) can be used to sum the elements in the other matrix. We set up a 1 by 4 summation matrix at line 140. When this is multiplied with QUARTER.REVENUE.TABLE, the sum of the later is obtained.

Similar techniques can be used to obtain the total number of cars sold in each quarter. Instead of using a nested loop to sum the rows of QUANTITY TABLE, matrix multiplication can be used.

200   MAT QUARTER.QUANTITY.TABLE = QUANTITY.TABLE*B

$$
\begin{bmatrix} 47 \\ 30 \\ 27 \\ 29 \end{bmatrix}
=
\begin{bmatrix} 10 & 24 & 3 & 4 & 5 \\ 2 & 14 & 5 & 2 & 7 \\ 10 & 10 & 4 & 2 & 1 \\ 1 & 13 & 4 & 5 & 6 \end{bmatrix}
\times
\begin{bmatrix} 1 \\ 1 \\ 1 \\ 1 \\ 1 \end{bmatrix}
$$

11.6 MATRIX INVERSE AND SIMULTANEOUS LINEAR EQUATION

In the previous sections we have discussed matrix addition, subtraction and multiplication. Matrix division has a somewhat different meaning in matrix alegebra. Thus, dividing a number is equivalent to multiplying the inverse of that number:

$$10/5 = 10 \times \frac{1}{5}$$

Similarly, dividing a matrix can be achieved by multiplying the inverse of that matrix. The inverse of matrix A, written as A^{-1} is a unique matrix such that when the inverse matrix is multiplied by the original matrix, A, the product is an identity matrix of the same size. Mathematically, this relationship can be expressed as

$$A \times A^{-1} = I$$

Notice that only the square matrix can be inverted, and the inverted matrix is also a square matrix of same size. For example, if

$$A \quad = \quad \begin{bmatrix} 3 & 1 & 5 \\ 3 & 2 & 1 \\ 0 & 1 & 2 \end{bmatrix}$$

then

$$A^{-1} \quad = \quad \begin{bmatrix} 1/6 & 1/6 & -1/2 \\ -1/3 & 1/3 & 2/3 \\ 1/6 & -1/6 & 1/6 \end{bmatrix}$$

because the relation

$$\begin{matrix} & A & \times & A^{-1} & = & I \end{matrix}$$

$$\begin{bmatrix} 3 & 1 & 5 \\ 3 & 2 & 1 \\ 0 & 1 & 2 \end{bmatrix} \times \begin{bmatrix} 1/6 & 1/6 & 1/2 \\ -1/3 & 1/3 & 2/3 \\ 1/6 & 1/6 & 1/6 \end{bmatrix} = \begin{bmatrix} 1 & 0 & 0 \\ 0 & 1 & 0 \\ 0 & 0 & 1 \end{bmatrix}$$

holds true

Finding the inverse matrix is a very tedious task, both by hand and by computer. Fortunately, creating an inverse matrix in a BASIC program can be achieved by the following statement:

```
Line number    MAT    matrix name = INV (matrix name)
```

The matrix name on the right side of the original matrix must be enclosed in parenthesis. BASIC-PLUS allows the inverted matrix to carry the same name as the original matrix. We can use the following instructions to invert the above matrix A:

Example 11.13

```
10      DIM A(3,3),B(3,3)
20      MAT READ A
30      MAT B = INV(A)
40      PRINT 'ORIGINAL MATRIX, A'
50      MAT PRINT A,
60      PRINT 'THE INVERTED MATRIX, B'
70      MAT PRINT B,
80      DATA 3,1,5,3,2,1,0,1,2
99      END
```

```
RUNNH
ORIGINAL MATRIX, A
 3              1              5

 3              2              1

 0              1              2


THE INVERTED MATRIX, B
 .166667        .166667       -.5

-.333333        .333333        .666667

 .166667       -.166667        .166667


Ready
```

Notice that not every square matrix can be inverted. If the matrix cannot be inverted, a message

?MATRIX CAN'T BE INVERTED AT LINE 30

will be displayed.[2]

Now, let us have an application of matrix inversion:

Example 11.14

As a vegetarian, Teresa eats only fruits, but she seldom remembers the price of each kind of fruit she purchases. Suppose the purchases made in the last three days are as follows:

	Apple	Number of pounds Banana	Strawberry		Total Amount
Day 1	3	4	2		$8.20
Day 2	2	5	1		$5.85
Day 3	1	1	5		$5.25

---

[2] Even if the matrix inverse operation is completed, it may not be suitable for inversion in a mathematical sense. We can add one instruction to check the accuracy of matrix inversion:

        35   IF DET = 0 THEN PRINT 'MATRIX INVERSION IS NOT APPROPRIATE'

DET is a build-in function, which will return the determinant of a matrix.

We would like to write a program to help Teresa by figuring the price of each type of fruit purchased.

If we use P_1 to indicate price of apples, P_2 to indicate price of bananas and P_3 to indicate price of strawberries, as a college student, you should be able to write the following system of linear equations to represent the situation:

$$3P_1 + 4P_2 + 2P_3 = 8.2$$
$$2P_1 + 5P_2 + P_3 = 5.85$$
$$P_1 + P_2 + 5P_3 = 5.25$$

With the knowledge you have about matrix arithmetic, you can rewrite the above equations in the form of a matrix

$$\begin{bmatrix} 3 & 4 & 2 \\ 2 & 5 & 1 \\ 1 & 1 & 5 \end{bmatrix} \times \begin{bmatrix} P_1 \\ P_2 \\ P_3 \end{bmatrix} = \begin{bmatrix} 8.2 \\ 5.85 \\ 5.25 \end{bmatrix}$$

$$A \qquad \times \qquad P \qquad = \qquad T$$

To solve this equation for P, we need to divide matrix T by A, in other words, we need to multiply the inverse of matrix A, A^{-1}, by T. Thus,

$$P = A^{-1} \times T$$

With this analysis in mind, it is not hard to write a BASIC program to find the solution for Teresa.

```
10      REM ****************************************************
20      REM *                                                  *
30      REM * PURPOSE:   THIS PROGRAM SOLVES A SYSTEM OF LINEAR *
40      REM *            EQUATIONS. THERE ARE 3 UNKNOWNS AND 3  *
50      REM *            EQUATIONS. THE PARTICULAR APPLICATION IS*
60      REM *            TO DETERMINE THE PRICE OF 3 TYPES OF   *
70      REM *            FRUIT FOR TRESA                        *
80      REM * AUTHOR:    SHU-JEN CHEN                           *
90      REM * DATE:      MARCH 25, 1980                         *
100     REM * VARIABLE:  A = A 3X3 MATRIX CONTAINING NUMBER OF  *
120     REM *                FRUIT PURCHASE IN LAST THREE DAYS  *
130     REM *            T = AMOUNTS SPENT IN LAST THREE DAYS   *
140     REM *            A1 = INVERSE OF A                      *
145     REM *            P1 = PRICE OF FRUIT                    *
150     REM *                                                  *
160     REM ****************************************************
170     DIM A(3,3),A1(3,3),T(3,1),P(3,1),P1(1,3)
180     MAT READ A,T
190     MAT A1 = INV(A)
200     MAT P = A1*T
210     PRINT TAB(12);'PRICE OF FRUIT'
220     PRINT 'APPLE','BANANA','STRAWBERRY'
230     MAT PRINT P,
240     DATA 3,4,2,2,5,1,1,1,5
250     DATA 8.2,5.85,5.25
260     END


RUNNH
            PRICE OF FRUIT
APPLE       BANANA        STRAWBERRY
 2           .25           .6

Ready
```

The above program is straightforward. Only sequential structure is involved—no looping, no decision. If the matrix operation feature did not exist, a large number of statements would be necessary to accomplish matrix inversion and multiplication.

One more matrix function needs to be mentioned. You might want to interchange rows and columns of a matrix. A MAT TRN statement will do the job for you. For example, if

$$A = \begin{bmatrix} 1 & 2 & 3 & 4 \\ 5 & 6 & 7 & 8 \\ 9 & 10 & 11 & 12 \end{bmatrix}$$

then   10   MAT B = TRN(A)   will cause

$$B = \begin{bmatrix} 1 & 5 & 9 \\ 2 & 6 & 10 \\ 3 & 7 & 11 \\ 4 & 8 & 12 \end{bmatrix}$$

where A is a 3 by 4 matrix and B is a 4 by 3 matrix. The general format for matrix transpose is:

> Line number   MAT   matrix name = TRN(matrix name)

Vector. A column or row of objects; these may be numbers or strings.

Identity Matrix. A table with the same number of rows and columns which has all zeros except along the main diagonal where elements are set to one.

Inverse Matrix. A unique matrix such that when the inverse matrix is multiplied by the original matrix, the product is an identity matrix.

Matrix. A rectangular arrangement of numbers or strings; a table.

Scalar. A value which can be a constant, variable, or a combination of both used in a matrix or vector.

Summation matrix. A table containing all ones.

Zero Matrix. A table containing all zeros.

PROBLEMS

1. Assume that matrix A is to be loaded with the following values:

1	4	7	10
2	5	8	11
3	6	9	12

   If MAT INPUT is used to enter the data, what is the correct sequence of values when you key them in?

2. Mike, John, and Andy go to a stationery store. Suppose Mike buys five pencils, one box of crayons, and three rulers; John buys three pencils, two boxes of crayons, and one ruler; Andy buys two pencils, three boxes of crayons, and one ruler. Write matrix statements to depict this situation.

3. Sketch the output of the following program

```
10   DIM A(4,4)
20   MAT READ A(5,3)
30   MAT PRINT A(3,3)
40   DATA 4,8,0,4,1,5,17,9,2,0.5,3,5,6,15,12
99   END
```

4. Write a program that will print the results of adding and then subtracting the following two matrices:

A

1	5	0
−3	0	3
−5	8	2

B

−3	7	9
8	10	13
9	0	11

5. What matrix statement can be used to replace the following statements?

```
10    DIM I(5,5)
20    FOR R = 1 TO 5
30      FOR C = 1 TO 5
40        IF R=C THEN I(R,C) = 1 ELSE I(R,C) = 0
50      NEXT C
60    NEXT R
```

6. Correct the error in the following statements. (Suppose appropriate DATA statements will be attached.)

```
10    DIM A(5,4),B(5,4),C(5,4)
20    MAT READ A,B
30    MAT C = 2*C
40    MAT C = A + B − C
50    MAT PRINT A,B,C,
```

7. For the matrices

A =

1	2	3
4	−5	3
2	−1	0

B =

7	1	3
1	0	2
5	−9	2

Write a program to show that

$$A \times B \neq B \times A$$

8. Write a program that will produce the following matrix, using MAT CON statement.

20	20	20	20
20	20	20	20
20	20	20	20

9. Given a matrix A,

A =

11	0.5	0
12	0.4	0.8
3	−4	1

Write a program to find its inverse, A1, and then show

$$A \times A1 = A1 \times A = I$$

10. Find the matrix A, so that

1	2
3	4

$\times$ A =

9	1
0	7

11. Write programs to solve the following sets of linear equations:

   (a) $7X + 3Y = 10$
             $2X + 4Y = 5$

   (b) $5X - 3Y + Z = 10$
             $15X - 3Y + 3Z = 15$
             $X - Y + Z = 1$

   (c) $X + 4Y = 10$
             $3X + 7Z = 7$
             $-Y - Z = 1$

   (d) $6X + 5Y = 10$
             $2X - Z = 3$
             $-12X + 10Y = -20$

   (e) $3X + 2Y - 2Z + W = 25$
             $2X + 3Y + Z - W = 10$
             $5X - 5Y + 3Z - 4W = -10$
             $8X + 2Y - Z + 2W = 55$

12. Siemens Gmbh manufactures three lines of computers; each has three models. The inventory at the beginning of the year reveals the following data:

	Model A	Model B	Model C
Siemens 4000	15	20	10
Siemens 6000	8	3	9
Siemens 7000	12	11	5

During the year, numbers of computers produced are indicated as following:

	Model A	Model B	Model C
Siemens 4000	10	15	12
Siemens 6000	10	8	11
Siemens 7000	10	15	15

Number of computers sold are represented in the following table:

	Model A	Model B	Model C
Siemens 4000	20	30	20
Siemens 6000	15	10	15
Siemens 7000	8	9	15

Write a program to print the information about the inventory at the end of the year. A proper heading and row labels should be added.

13. Dr. Hiller used to grade his students on a 30-point basis. His record book looks as follows:

	Test 1	Test 2	Test 3
Student 1	28	24	25
Student 2	19	12	25
Student 3	30	28	27
Student 4	10	12	5
Student 5	21	25	22

Finally, he was convinced to change his grading system to a 100-point basis. Write a BASIC program to convert his record book. (Hint: Scalar multiplication can be used.)

14. The management science department is making a survey about the faculty's preference for committee service. The survey questionnaire looks as follows:

	Very interested	Interested	Will accept if assigned	Not interested
Personnel				
Curriculum				
Budget				
Library				
Social				

The faculty is asked to enter a one (1) in the cell which represents his interest level; zeros should be placed in all other cells. Suppose 20 responses have been received, write a program to indicate the results of the survey

15. Jack, Jill, and Joe have emptied their coin banks. The coins they have are shown as follows. Write a BASIC program to determine how much money each child has.

	Pennies	Nickles	Dimes	Quarters
Jack	200	50	85	20
Jill	180	26	19	100
Joe	400	20	10	10

16. Three programmers at the computer center were jointly working on three projects in the last month. The hours they spent on each project are shown as follows:

	Week 1			Week 2			Week 3			Week 4		
	P1	P2	P3	P1	P2	P3	P1	P2	P3	P1	P2	P3
Brown	15	15	10	12	12	16	10	10	20	20	20	0
Carter	25	0	15	12	16	12	10	15	15	15	12	8
Kennedy	10	5	25	35	3	2	10	25	5	10	10	15

Suppose the wage rate for each programmer is

Brown	$6.8
Carter	$3.5
Kennedy	$10.5

Write a BASIC program which will calculate the labor cost of each project.

17. All-star basketball teams scoring data in last season looks as follows:

	Game 1	Game 2	Game 3	Game 4	Game 5
Jones	10	15	12	15	9
Anderson	8	9	10	9	12
Tallman	25	45	33	30	50
Bloom	10	5	1	5	15
Date	40	25	20	20	20

Write a program to calculate the average score per game and the average score for each player. Use only matrix statements to do the calculation.

18. Mrs. Kissinger is planning a wedding party for her daughter Amy. She would like to serve her guests with eggroll, sweetsauer, and wonton. The ingredients of the above types of food are:

	Flour	Meat	Pineapple	Bell pepper
Eggroll	0.3	0.5	0	1.0
Sweetsauer	0	5.0	5	3.0
Wonton	0.2	0.4	0	2.5

Suppose Mrs. Kissinger's cook Henry has purchased 60 ounces of flour, 350 ounces of meat, 250 ounces of pineapple, and 725 ounces of bell pepper, how many dishes of each type can Mrs. Kissinger prepare?

19. Residents in the Redland's community trade their cars on a yearly basis. Their purchasing preference can be represented by the following matrix, T:

Next Car / Current Car	Ford	Chevy	Dodge	Foreign
Ford	0.7	0.1	0.05	0.15
Chevy	0.2	0.5	0.1	0.2
Dodge	0.2	0.1	0.6	0.1
Foreign	0.1	0.2	0.1	0.6

The above matrix can be interpreted as follows: 70% of Ford drivers will stick with Ford; 10% of them will switch to Chevy; 5% of them will switch to Dodge; and 15% of them will buy a foreign car as their next car. The first, second, third, and fourth row of table T can be interpreted in the same manner. Suppose the Redland's community has the following cars at the beginning of this year

Ford	5000
Chevy	7000
Dodge	2000
Foreign	4000

How many cars of various makes will there be at the end of the third year? (Hint: If we denote the above vector as V, the solution will be V·T·T·T, of course, you need a program to do the calculation.)

20. This is an interesting project to review your knowledge of string manipulation and matrix manipulation. As an agent in the Secret Service, you need a sophisticated method to code and decode message. One widely used method is called the matrix method. Suppose the following message should be sent:

$$BA \ BA \ BLACK \ SHEEP$$

we will

(a) Group every three letters in the message:

$$BA \ BA \ BLA \ CK \ SHE \ EP$$

(b) Blanks are replaced by dashes:

$$BA- \ BA- \ BLA \ CK- \ SHE \ EP-$$

(c) Each character is converted into ASCII code, and every group makes a vector:

$$
B \begin{bmatrix} 66 \\ 65 \\ 45 \end{bmatrix}
\quad A
\quad
B \begin{bmatrix} 66 \\ 65 \\ 45 \end{bmatrix}
\quad A
\quad
B \begin{bmatrix} 66 \\ 76 \\ 65 \end{bmatrix}
\quad L \atop A
\quad
C \begin{bmatrix} 67 \\ 75 \\ 45 \end{bmatrix}
\quad K
\quad
S \begin{bmatrix} 83 \\ 72 \\ 69 \end{bmatrix}
\quad H \atop E
\quad
E \begin{bmatrix} 69 \\ 80 \\ 45 \end{bmatrix}
\quad P
$$

(d) Randomly define a 3 by 3 matrix, say

$$A = \begin{bmatrix} -1 & 4 & 0 \\ 2 & 0 & -3 \\ 7 & 8 & 9 \end{bmatrix}$$

(e) Each vector in Step c is multiplied by matrix A to make a set of new vectors

$$
\begin{matrix}
B \\ A \\ -
\end{matrix}
\begin{bmatrix} 194 \\ -3 \\ 1387 \end{bmatrix}
\begin{matrix}
B \\ A \\ -
\end{matrix}
\begin{bmatrix} 294 \\ -3 \\ 1387 \end{bmatrix}
\begin{matrix}
B \\ L \\ A
\end{matrix}
\begin{bmatrix} 238 \\ -63 \\ 1655 \end{bmatrix}
\begin{matrix}
C \\ K \\ -
\end{matrix}
\begin{bmatrix} 233 \\ -1 \\ 1474 \end{bmatrix}
\begin{matrix}
S \\ H \\ E
\end{matrix}
\begin{bmatrix} 205 \\ -41 \\ 1778 \end{bmatrix}
\begin{matrix}
E \\ P \\ -
\end{matrix}
\begin{bmatrix} 251 \\ 3 \\ 1528 \end{bmatrix}
$$

(f) Send the vectors in step e out.

The decoding procedure is the reverse of the coding procedure. Now write a program to

1. Code a message and send the vectors out.

2. Receive a set of 3 × 1 vectors and decode it.

You might

1. Use the following message to test your program:

    I WILL SEE YOU TONIGHT AT REDWOOD PARK

2. Allow your program to change matrix A from run to run (e.g., per MAT INPUT), so that the chance of being encrypted is minimum.

Chapter 12
Advanced BASIC Features

Objectives   You will learn:

To define a multiple line function.

To use a subprogram for BASIC-PLUS-2

Error handling routines.

To write an arithmetic time-test program.

String manipulation and matrix operations are two of the special features in the BASIC-PLUS programming language. In addition there are several advanced features of BASIC-PLUS that you will find are valuable in programming.

12.1 THE MULTIPLE LINE FUNCTION

We have learned the concept of functions in Chapter 9. We can define a simple function by setting the function name equal to a formula involving variables specified as arguments, for example,

$$10 \quad DEF \quad FNA(X) = 3*X**2 + 4*X - 1$$

The function definition takes up only one line. It is a straight calculation—no decision or iteration. BASIC-PLUS allows us to define multiple line functions. Decision structures and iteration structures can be part of the function body. Let's use the following example to show a multiple line function.

Example 12.1

Suppose the BASIC system you are using does not have the built-in function SGN. We can define a multiple line function FNS to act as a SGN:

```
10        REM A FUNCTION TO REPLACE THE BUILT-IN FUNCTION SGN
20        DEF FNS(X)
30            IF X>0 THEN FNS = 1
40            IF X=0 THEN FNS = 0
50            IF X<0 THEN FNS = -1
60        FNEND
65        PRINT 'A','FNS(A)'
70        FOR I = 1 TO 5
80            READ A
90            PRINT A, FNS(A)
100       NEXT I
110       DATA 43,-54,0,12,100
999       END
```

```
RUNNH
A              FNS(A)
 43             1
-54            -1
  0             0
 12             1
100             1

Ready
```

The function definition is the program segment from lines 20 to 60. Every multiple line function definition starts with a declaration of the function name, which is in the form of

> Line number   DEF   function name (dummy variables)

and ends with a end of function mark in the form of

> Line number   FNEND

The function name is any legal variable name preceeded by two letters—FN. Line 20 of the above program declared the function name as FNS, and the dummy variable is labelled as X. Just like single line functions, multiple line functions allow up to five dummy variables. However, because of the nature of multiple line functions, both numeric and alphanumeric variables are permitted. Thus,

$$10 \quad DEF \quad FNA(X,Y,A\$)$$

is a legal numeric function with two numeric arguments and one alphanumeric argument, and

$$20 \quad DEF \quad FNB\$(X,A\$,B\$)$$

is a legal string function with one numeric argument and two alphanumeric arguments. Notice that no equal sign or formula is followed. The value of function FNS must be assigned at least one place in the function body. The last assigned value is the final value of the function. The body of the function consists of three lines.[1] With a slight restriction, the body of a multiple line function can be any legal statement. Multiple line functions are called in the same way as single line functions. When FNS is referenced at line 90, the real argument, A, will replace the dummy argument when the function body is executed. As you can see, FNS acts exactly as the built-in function, SGN. We have mentioned earlier that there is a restraint on the function body. The function should have only one entrance and one exit. Both the following function definitions are illegal:

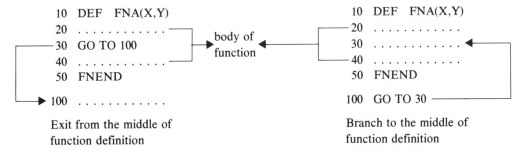

Exit from the middle of
function definition

Branch to the middle of
function definition

Branching beyond the boundaries of the function definition is not permissible.

Functions can call one another; that is, the function of being defined can call another function or itself. The following program illustrates this:

---

[1] It is more "structured" to have one nested IFTHENELSE statement to substitute for three IF statements, for example,

```
30   IF X > 0
            THEN FNS = 1
            ELSE IF X = 0   THEN FNS = 0
                            ELSE FNS = −1
```

Example 12.2

```
100     DEF FNA(X,Y)
110         IF X>Y THEN FNA = X
                ELSE FNA = Y
120     FNEND
130     DEF FNB(N1,N2,N3,N4)
140         IF FNA(N1,N2) > FNA(N3,N4) THEN FNB = FNA(N1,N2)
                    ELSE FNB = FNA(N3,N4)
150     FNEND
160     INPUT 'PLEASE ENTER FOUR NUMBERS';N1,N2,N3,N4
170     M = FNB(N1,N2,N3,N4)
180     PRINT 'THE LARGEST OF THE FOUR NUMBERS IS'; M
190     END
```

```
RUNNH
PLEASE ENTER FOUR NUMBERS? 1,5,0,-7
THE LARGEST OF THE FOUR NUMBERS IS 5

Ready
```

Function FNA determines the larger value of two numbers. Function FNB determines the largest of four numbers. We notice that in defining FNB (statements 130 to 150), FNA is used. We compared the two larger values of two pairs, (N1,N2) and (N3,N4). Note that the larger of these pairs is the value of function FNB.

Let's examine some more applications of the multiple line function.

Example 12.3

Suppose we want to define a function to convert a binary number into decimal. We know that the binary number 11001 is equivalent to decimal value 25. The procedure for conversion follows:

Step 1:	Separate digits	1	1	0	0	1	
Step 2:	Multiply the digit with corresponding position value	2^4	2^3	2^2	2^1	2^0	
Step 3:	Sum the products	$16 + 8 + 0 + 0 + 1 = 25$					

We input the binary number as a character string. It is necessary to do so. Otherwise, 101 will be interpreted as one hundred and one—not as one-zero-one in binary, which is equivalent to a 5 in decimal. We can separate the digits by using the string function

$$MID$$

Once a digit is separated, another string function

$$VAL$$

is used to convert the digit from its character representation to numerical representation. Powers of two are multiplied based on positional values; then, the products are accumulated.

The above procedure should be repeated as many times as the number of digits in the string. The total number of digits can be found by using the string function:

$$LEN$$

```
100      REM THIS IS A PROGRAM TO CONVERT BINARY NUMBER INTO DECIMAL
110      EXTEND
120      DEF FNDECIMAL(BINARY$)
130          NO.OF.DIGITS = LEN(BINARY$)
140          TOTAL = 0
150          FOR POSITION = 1 TO NO.OF.DIGITS
160              DIGIT$ = MID(BINARY$,POSITION,1)
170              NUMBER = VAL(DIGIT$)
180              TOTAL = TOTAL + NUMBER * 2 ** (NO.OF.DIGITS-POSITION)
190          NEXT POSITION
200          FNDECIMAL = TOTAL
210      FNEND
220      INPUT'PLEASE ENTER THE BINARY NUMBER';B$
230      D = FNDECIMAL(B$)
240      PRINT 'THE CORRESPONDING DECIMAL NUMBER IS';D
250      END


RUNNH
PLEASE ENTER THE BINARY NUMBER? 11001
THE CORRESPONDING DECIMAL NUMBER IS 25

Ready
```

12.2 SUBPROGRAM[2]

The advantage of the multiple line function over the single line function is apparent in the previous section. The following comparisons can be made between multiple line functions and subroutines:

1. While a subroutine can return more than one value, the multiple line function returns only one value.

2. Using a multiple line function we specify the actual arguments when the function is called. Whereas, using a subroutine, separate statements are needed to specify the actual arguments before the subroutine is called. The following example illustrates the different approaches of specifying arguments:

```
10   REM USING A FUNCTION TO           10   REM USING A SUBROUTINE TO
     FIND THE LARGER OF TWO                 FIND THE LARGER OF TWO
     NUMBERS                                NUMBERS
20   DEF FNA(X,Y)                       20   X = 3          arguments are specified
30       IF X>Y THEN FNA=X              30   Y = 5          before subroutine is
             ELSE FNA=Y                 40   GOSUB 60       called
40   FNEND                             50   STOP
50   M=FNA(3,5)                         60   REM SUBROUTINE
                                        70       IF X>Y THEN M=X
                                                    ELSE M=Y
                                        80   RETURN

     arguments are specified
     in function call
```

While functions and subroutines have their advantages and disadvantages, they have common shortcomings; namely,

1. All the variables in the function and subroutine are global. That means any change in the variables in the function and subroutine will be carried outside the function and subroutine. The concept of globality can be shown by the following simple example:

---

[2] This section is optional

Example 12.4

```
10      A$ = 'ADAM'
20      X = 1
30      Y = 2
40      GOSUB 100
50      PRINT A$;' ATE';M;'APPLES'
99      STOP
100     REM SUBROUTINE TO SUM X AND Y
110         A$ = 'EVE'
120         PRINT 'SUBROUTINE ';A$;' IS NOW EXECUTING'
130         M = X + Y
140     RETURN
999     END
```

```
RUNNH
SUBROUTINE EVE IS NOW EXECUTING
EVE ATE 3 APPLES
Stop at line 99

Ready
```

Before the subroutine was called, A$ was assigned the value ADAM. During the course of executing the subroutine, A$ was replaced by EVE. Hence, when the print statement at line 50 was encountered

EVE ATE 3 APPLES

was printed but not

ADAM ATE 3 APPLES

as we intended.

In many situations[3] we want to keep some variables restricted to a module. For example, A$ outside the subroutine and A$ in the subroutine should be treated differently so that the modules can be independent. Both subroutines and functions do not have the capability of being independent. Independence can only be achieved by using a subprogram, provided your system has that feature.

Another shortcoming of subroutines and functions is their use in arrays. While functions cannot handle subscripted variables at all, it is cumbersome to use a subroutine to handle subscripted variables. We can use a separate module to sort data in an array as the following program illustrates:

Example 12.5

```
10      DIM X(50)
20      DIM A(10),B(5)
30      MAT READ A,B
40      N = 10
50      MAT X = A
60      GOSUB 500
70      MAT A = X
80      MAT PRINT A,
90      N = 5
100     MAT X = B
110     GOSUB 500
120     MAT B = X
130     MAT PRINT B,
199     STOP
500     REM SUBROUTINE TO SORT ARRAY X WITH N ELEMENTS
510         FOR J = 1 TO N-1
520             FOR I = 1 TO N-J
530                 IF X(I)>X(I+1)
                        THEN T=X(I+1)\X(I+1)=X(I)\X(I)=T
```

---

[3] We usually use the variables I, J, K to indicate loop control variables or use them as subscripts. If the modules are not independent, the repetitive use of them will mix up the program.

```
540               NEXT I
550             NEXT J
599       RETURN
900       DATA 4,2,9,-2,0,6,5,10,1,6
910       DATA 90,30,10,40,50
999       END

Ready

RUNNH

-2              0             1             2             4
 5              6             6             9            10

10             30            40            50            90

Stop at line 199
```

Notice that by using a subroutine to sort an array, we needed to

1. Reserve a general array called X, so that in the subroutine only the general name is referenced; not a specific array.

2. Copy the contents of the array to be sorted into X, such as

$$50 \quad \text{MAT X} = \text{A}$$
$$100 \quad \text{MAT X} = \text{B}$$

hence, X must be defined large enough to accommodate any array to be sorted.

3. Copy the sorted data from X to the original array after we return from the subroutine.

$$70 \quad \text{MAT A} = \text{X}$$
$$120 \quad \text{MAT B} = \text{X}$$

The switching of values in an array is time-consuming and requires more primary memory. BASIC-PLUS-2 provides the feature of subprograms to overcome the shortcomings stated above. Subprograms also combine the advantages of functions and subroutines. The following example illustrates the use of a subprogram.

Example 12.6

The board of trustees of Form Engineering Co. has a policy that salaries of employees should not be less than $500 or higher than $5,000. Due to the job market, the data processing department finds it necessary to pay high salaries to attract key individuals. In order to keep within the budget, the DP department has hired several low-paid student programmers to do the coding. The monthly salary of 10 employees in the DP department looks as follows:

$1,000	$6,500
$1,200	$1,500
$ 250	$ 400
$2,500	$5,500
$ 330	$1,800

The following program will compare the expected range of salary with the actual range:

NEW SUBPRO

```
10  REM PROGRAM TO ILLUSTRATE SUBPROGRAM
20  DIM A(10)
30  L = 500
```

ıres

)
     .AD A
     .ANGE(A( ),10,R)
     THE EXPECTED RANGE is'; H−L
     'THE ACTUAL RANGE IS';R
     1000,1200,250,2500,330,6500,1500,400,5500,1800

NEW RANGE

```
100   REM THIS SUBPROGRAM CAN DETERMINE THE RANGE OF ANY ARRAY, X
          OF SIZE Y AND RETURN THE RANGE Z
110   SUB RANGE(X( ),Y,Z)
120       FOR J = 1 TO Y−1
130           FOR I = 1 TO Y−J
140               IF X(I) > X(I+1) THEN T=X(I) \ X(I)=X(I+1) \ X(I+1)=T
150           NEXT I
160       NEXT J
170       H = X(Y)
180       L = X(1)
190       Z = H − L
999   SUBEND
```

COMPILE

BUILD SUBPRO,RANGE

EXIT

TKB @SUBPRO

RUN SUBPRO

    THE EXPECTED RANGE IS 4500
    THE ACTUAL RANGE IS 6400

In a system which supports subprogram, the main program and subprogram must be compiled (translated) separately, just as if there were two independent programs. In a RSX-11 system, the following four commands are necessary to link the main program and subprogram together and to execute the entire program.

    BUILD SUBPRO,RANGE

    EXIT

    TKB @SUBPRO

    RUN SUBPRO

We read the data into array A, then the subprogram is called to sort the array and determine the range. The format of constructing a subprogram is:

```
Line number   SUB name (dummy argument list)
     Body of the subprogram
Line number   SUBEND
```

The subprogram definition starts with the key word, SUB. The name of a subprogram is any name from one to six characters. Unlike the functions, there is no prefix for the subprogram's name. Following the name, arguments of the program should be listed. Arguments are enclosed in a pair of parentheses and separated by commas.

Arguments listed in the SUB statement are those used as input and output to the subprogram. For example, the input to the subprogram RANGE described above is an unsorted array temporarily named as X, and the size of that array is temporarily named as Y. The output from the subprogram is the sorted version of array X and the range of that array temporarily named as Z.

The subprogram allows the subscripted variable to be the argument. The format to list an array as an argument is a subprogram is

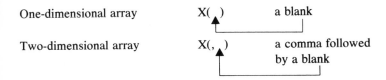

| One-dimensional array | X( ) | a blank |
| Two-dimensional array | X(,) | a comma followed by a blank |

All the arguments listed in SUB statements are dummy arguments. They can be variables, constants, or expressions. If an array is listed as an argument, that array should *not* be dimensioned in the subprogram because it is just a place holder. The actual array will take its place when the subprogram is called.

The body of the subprogram can be any statement except the one which causes a transfer passing the boundary of the subprogram. In addition to input and output variables, there are other variables in the subprogram (L and H in the above program). While the values of input and output variables can be carried outside the subprogram, the other variables are local. They do not have any effect on other part of the program. This situation can be depicted by the following diagram:

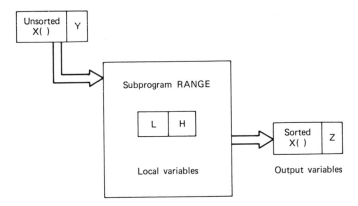

SUBEND marks the end of the subprogram, which works in the same way as a RETURN statement.

The subprogram can be called by using the CALL statement, its form is

> Line number CALL name (actual argument list)

The position and number of actual arguments must match the dummy argument list.

60 CALL RANGE(A( ),10,R)

When the CALL RANGE is invoked, A( ) will substitute X( ), 10 for Y, and R for Z. The control is then transferred to line 110. After the subprogram is completed, array A is sorted, and the range of A is stored in R, control returns to 70.

The values assigned to L and H before the subprogram call is not changed even though the same variables are used to represent the actual lowest and highest salary in the subprogram. Hence, at line 70, 4500 is printed which is the expected range.

A subprogram can be placed after the END statement. It is treated as an independent program. Other programs can also call this subprogram once it is defined.

12.3 OTHER ADVANCED BASIC-PLUS FEATURES

BASIC-PLUS provides several advanced features to enhance interactive processing. These features include error handling routines, time limit setting, and so on. We will use an integrated example to illustrate these features.

Example 12.7

In Chapter 9 we used a CAI program (see page 126). The program generates 10 subtraction questions and asks the player to answer questions one at a time. Scores of the test and comments about the performance are displayed at the end of the test. Pupils can use unlimited time to complete the test, provided the computer system permits it. This is not realistic in practice. Now, we want to set a limit of 20 seconds for answering each question. If the pupil fails to respond with 20 seconds, the question is considered to be wrong. Also, since it is common for the inexperienced pupil to type the letter "o" for zero, we need to print a message for him and ask him to correct the typing error. We do not want the data format error to terminate the program as occurred before. The program should look as follows:

```
100     REM THIS PROGRAM IS USED TO PRACTISE BASIC SUBTRACTION
110     REM THE RESPONSE SHOULD BE ENTERED WITHIN 20 SECONDS
120     REM OTHERWISE, IT IS CONSIDERED AS WRONG
130     RANDOM
140     EXTEND
150     ON ERROR GO TO 330  ◄─────────────────────────
160     INPUT 'WHAT IS YOUR NAME';N$
170     SCORE = 0
180     FOR I = 1 TO 10
190         MINUEND = INT((10+1)*RND)
200         SUBTRAHEND = INT((10+1)*RND)
210         IF SUBTRAHEND > MINUEND THEN 190
215         PRINT 'QUESTION';I
220         PRINT MINUEND; '-'; SUBTRAHEND; '=';
230         WAIT 20  ◄─────────────
240         INPUT DIFFERENCE
250         IF MINUEND - SUBTRAHEND = DIFFERENCE
                THEN ANSWER$ = 'CORRECT'
                ELSE ANSWER$ = 'WRONG'
260         PRINT ANSWER$
270         IF ANSWER$ = 'CORRECT'
                THEN SCORE = SCORE + 1
                ELSE PRINT 'THE CORRECT ANSWER IS';MINUEND-SUBTRAHEND
280     NEXT I
290     IF SCORE >= 8
                THEN COMMENT$ = 'YOU HAVE DONE A GOOD JOB'
                ELSE COMMENT$ = 'YOU NEED MORE PRACTICE'
300     PRINT SCORE; 'CORRECT OUT OF 10'
310     PRINT N$, COMMENT$
320     STOP
```

```
330        REM THIS IS A SUBROUTINE TO HANDLE ERRORS:──────┐
340        REM TIME OUT ERROR AND FORMAT ERROR              │
350           IF ERR = 15                                   │
                  THEN 360                                   │
                  ELSE IF ERR = 50 AND ERL = 240            │
                          THEN 410                           │
                          ELSE 450                           │
360           REM ----TIME OUT----                          │
370              PRINT 'YOU ARE TOO SLOW'                    │
380              PRINT 'THIS QUESTION IS CONSIDERED WRONG'   │◄──────
390              ANSWER$ = 'WRONG'                           │
400              RESUME 270                                  │
410           REM ----DATA FORMAT ERROR----                 │
420              PRINT 'YOU SHOULD ENTER A NUMBER'           │
430              PRINT 'TRY AGAIN!'                          │
440              RESUME 240                                  │
450           REM ----OTHER ERROR----                        │
460              PRINT 'OTHER ERROR OCCURS'                  │
470              PRINT 'THE ERROR OCCURS AT LINE';ERL        │
480              STOP                                        │
490        RETURN ─────────────────────────────────────────┘
500        END
```

```
RUNNH
WHAT IS YOUR NAME? JOHN
QUESTION 1
 5 - 1 =? 4
CORRECT
QUESTION 2
 6 - 0 =? YOU ARE TOO SLOW ◄──────── time out
THIS QUESTION IS CONSIDERED WRONG
THE CORRECT ANSWER IS 6
QUESTION 3
 6 - 4 =? 2
CORRECT
QUESTION 4
 9 - 8 =? 1
CORRECT
QUESTION 5
 9 - 9 =? O ◄──────────────────── a letter o
YOU SHOULD ENTER A NUMBER
TRY AGAIN!
? 0
CORRECT
QUESTION 6
 7 - 1 =? 4
WRONG
THE CORRECT ANSWER IS 6
QUESTION 7
 8 - 6 =? 2
CORRECT
QUESTION 8
 0 - 0 =? 0
CORRECT
QUESTION 9
 6 - 6 =? 0
CORRECT
QUESTION 10
 8 - 8 =? 0
CORRECT
 8 CORRECT OUT OF 10
JOHN            YOU HAVE DONE A GOOD JOB
Stop at line 320

Ready
```

Two improvements of this program over Example 9.12 are:

1. A time limit is set for responding to an INPUT statement.

2. An error handling routine is added to treat the time-out and format error.

In Chapter 5 we discussed three types of errors: syntax, run-time, and logical errors. The syntax error can be detected and corrected immediately. Logical errors cannot be detected by the computer. The run-time errors can be detected, and they may or may not be corrected by the computer.

In general, when a run-time error is detected, an error message will be printed, and the execution of the program is terminated. However, the run-time errors are classified into recoverable and nonrecoverable errors. (See appendix G.) If a nonrecoverable error is detected, such as

?FOR without NEXT at line 10

the only thing to do is to go back to program creating mode and insert the appropriate NEXT statement. The recoverable errors can be corrected in the program. This means that we can build certain statements in the program and tell the computer what to do if a recoverable error occurs. For example, if

10   LET X = A/B

may cause a division by 0 error. Since division by 0 is a recoverable error, we may want to tell the computer that in case that occurs, skip this instruction or divide A by another value. All of these should be coded in your program.

Time-out errors and data format errors are recoverable errors. To have a subroutine to recover the errors, the feature should be identified at the beginning of the program by using

150   ON ERROR GO TO 330

where 330 is the first line of the error recovery routine. The ON ERROR statement should be placed before any executable statements. Once a recoverable error is detected, the computer will suppress the error message and transfer control to the first line of the error handling routine. We will discuss the error handling routine a bit later.

The procedure of generating the test questions and determining the score (160–310) is the same as Example 9.12 except that one statement is inserted before the INPUT statement:

230   WAIT 20

WAIT is used to set a maximum of time (specified following the key word WAIT in seconds) for the computer to wait for input from the terminal. If the user fails to respond within the time limit, a time-out error occurs. Since we have used the error message, suppress statement

150   ON ERROR GO TO 330

the error message is suppressed, and control will be transferred to line 330. Line 330 is the error handling routine. Each recoverable error has a code. Once the error occurs, a predefined variable ERR will reveal the error code. Also, a predefined variable ERL will indicate the line which caused the error. A nested IFTHENELSE statement at line 350 is used to check the type of error. If error code is 15, control is passed to line 360. If

ERR = 50 AND ERL = 240

it is a data format error caused by line 240, transfer then passes to line 410.

In the time-put recovery routine, an appropriate message is printed, and the question is marked as WRONG; then the normal execution of the program is resumed by using the RESUME statement. The RESUME statement takes the following format

Line number   RESUME line #

The RESUME statement acts like a GO TO statement after the error is corrected. Lines 410 to 440 recover the INPUT data format error. For example, when the program is run, the response to question 3 is o instead of numeral 0. A format error occurs, and control is passed to 410 where the portion of the format recovery routine is executed.

Word List

Multiple-Line Function. A user-defined function which allows up to five dummy variables including numeric and alphanumeric variables.

ON ERROR Statement. A BASIC-PLUS statement used to transfer control to an error handling routine.

RESUME Statement. A BASIC-PLUS statement that transfers control following the correction of a recoverable error.

Recoverable Error. A program error that can be corrected through the use of special statements.

PROBLEMS

1. What will be printed by the following program segments:

(a)

```
10        FOR X = 1 TO 2
20            READ A,B,C
30            Y = FNM(A,B,C)
40            PRINT A,B,C,Y
50        NEXT X
99        STOP
100       REM -----A MULTIPLE LINE FUNCTION -----
110       DEF FNM(X1,X2,X3)
120           IF  X1 > X2
                       THEN IF X1 > X3
                               THEN FNM = X1
                               ELSE FNM = X3
                       ELSE IF X2 > X3
                               THEN FNM = X2
                               ELSE FNM = X3
130       FNEND
140       DATA 5,4,15,0,-3,1
```

(b)

```
10        EXTEND
20        FOR X = 1 TO 5
30            READ A
40            PRINT A, FNABS(A)
50        NEXT X
99        STOP
100       REM ----- A MULTIPLE LINE FUNCTION -----
110       DEF FNABS(Y)
120           IF Y >= 0
                       THEN FNABS = Y
                       ELSE FNABS = (-1)*Y
130       FNEND
140       DATA -5,0,4.5,8,-3
```

2. A function to compute N factorial, N.(N−1).(N−2) . . . . . .2.1, looks as follows:

```
100       DEF FNF(N)
110           IF N = 0 THEN 120 ELSE 150
120       REM -----THEN-----
130           FNF = 1
140           GO TO 210
150       REM -----ELSE-----
160           F = 1
170           FOR X = 1 TO N
180               F = F * X
190           NEXT X
195           FNF = F
200       REM -----END IF 110-----
210       FNEND
```

Use the multiple line function FNF to calculate binomial coefficient $_nC_r$, where

$$_nC_r = \frac{n!}{r!\,(n-r)!}$$

Test your program for $_5C_3$ and compare this program with Example 9.15

3. Write a BASIC program to evaluate function F(X) for X = −3, 0, 5, 7 and 12, where

$$F(X) = \begin{cases} \dfrac{X-1}{12} & \text{for } 1 <= X <= 6 \\[2mm] \dfrac{13-X}{12} & \text{for } 7 <= X <= 12 \\[2mm] 0 & \text{else} \end{cases}$$

4. Judy Tanaka is the student assistant of the business information systems department. Every week Judy has to fill out a time sheet. For example, last week's time sheet looks as follows:

Day	From	To
Mon	9:15 AM	12:45 PM
Tue	10:00 AM	12:00 PM
Wed	1:00 PM	5:00 PM
Thur	1:45 PM	4:30 PM
Fri	8:00 AM	10:30 AM

Write a BASIC program for Judy to calculate the total hours worked last week.

5. Payroll record of Landmark Inc. contains the following information:

1. Name.

2. Type of employment, coded as W, if on an hourly wage; coded as S, if salaried.

3. Monthly salary or hourly rate.

4. Hours worked.

5. Eligibility for overtime pay, coded as Y; if eligible, coded as N, if not.

In general, time and a half is applied for overtime (for salaried employees, the hourly rate is determined by salary divided by 160). Define a multiple line function to calculate the gross pay. Use the following data to test your function:

Name	Type of Employment	Monthly Salary/ Hourly rate	Hours Worked	Eligibility for Overtime Pay
Schutz T	W	$18.00	42	N
Shield D	S	$2,000.00	60	N
Smith E	W	$9.50	55	Y
Sneider J	S	$1,250.00	50	Y
Schimps E	W	$4.50	30	Y

6. The method to convert an integer decimal number into binary number involves only simple division by 2, keeping track of resulting quotients and a remainder list. For example, converting 37 to binary can be achieved by

		Quotient	Remainder
37/2	=	18	1
18/2	=	9	0
9/2	=	4	1
4/2	=	2	0
2/2	=	1	0
1/2	=	0	1

When the remainder list is inverted, the binary equivalent is provided. Thus,

$$37 = 1\ 0\ 0\ 1\ 0\ 1 \text{ in binary}$$

Write a multiple line function to convert the integer decimal number into binary. Then, test your function by converting the following numbers

$$4$$
$$128$$
$$1024$$
$$12345$$

7. The conversion for a fractional decimal number into a binary number is achieved by repetitive multiplication. Suppose we want to convert 0.875 into binary. The multiplication procedure is:

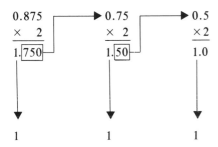

We kept track of the integer part of the product. The fractional part becomes the multiplicant of the following multiplication. The process stops when the product is 1. Thus,

$$0.875 = 0.111 \text{ in binary}$$

In many cases, there is no exact equivalent between a decimal fractional number and a binary fractional number; for example, the product will never equal 1. Hence, the degree of accuracy must be specified. Now, write a multiple line function to convert a fractional decimal number into a binary number. The two arguments of the function are:

1. The decimal number to be converted.

2. Number of binary places needed.

Test your program by converting the following numbers:

0.732

0.5412

0.125

0.4327

8. Combining question 6 and 7, write a BASIC program to convert *any* decimal number into binary.

9. Dr. Lee, director of Foreign Student Affairs, at Humerton University is interested in knowing the total number of Chinese and Polish students on the campus. As a rule of thumb, the Chinese name has only one syllable, and the Polish name ends with SKY or SKI. Write a BASIC program to search Chinese and Polish students from the following list:

Lee	Samulson
Baird	Allen
Einstein	Friedman
Kawaski	Hale
Kines	Li
Starsky	Hunch
Lenin	Danzig
Tschaikovsky	Lucey

Use a multiple line function to determine whether a name is a Chinese name or a Polish name.

Problems on Subprograms

10. Two roots of a quadratic function

$$aX^2 + bX + C = 0$$

are:

$$X1 = \frac{-b - \sqrt{b^2 - 4ac}}{2a}$$

$$X2 = \frac{-b + \sqrt{b^2 - 4ac}}{2a}$$

If $b^2 - 4ac < 0$, then the equation has imaginary roots, which consists of two parts:

Real number part $\qquad \dfrac{-b}{2a}$

Imaginary number part $\begin{cases} \dfrac{-\sqrt{|b^2 - 4ac|}}{2a} \; I \quad \text{for X1} \\[2ex] \dfrac{+\sqrt{|b^2 - 4ac|}}{2a} \; I \quad \text{for X2} \end{cases}$

Write a subprogram to calculate the roots of a quadratic equation. Your program should be able to handle imaginary roots case. Then, write a mainroutine to call the subprogram for solving the following quadratic equations:

$$X^2 - 2X - 3 = 0$$
$$4X^2 - 4X + 1 = 0$$
$$X^2 \qquad + 9 = 0$$
$$X^2 - 9X - 1 = 0$$

11. Merging of two sets of data can be achieved by completing the following steps:

(1) Store the two sets of data into two separate arrays and sort them in order,

| 3 | 5 | 8 | 10 | 11 | ◄─────── Array A
|---|---|---|----|----|

| 3 | 9 | ◄─────── Array B
|---|---|

(2) Compare each pair of elements in A and B and copy the smaller value to array C. The larger is then compared with the next element in the other array, for example,

Round of Comparison	Array A	Array B	Action
1st	3	4	3 ───────► C(1)
2nd	5	4	4 ───────► C(2)
3rd	5	9	5 ───────► C(3)
4th	8	9	8 ───────► C(4)
5th	10	9	9 ───────► C(5)

(3) Comparison procedure stops when one array is exhausted. The remaining data of the other array is then copied into C.

$$10 \longrightarrow C(6)$$
$$11 \longrightarrow C(7)$$

Write a BASIC program to merge two sets of data. Use one subprogram for sorting and other subprogram for merging.

12. The Empire Department Store initially issues 100 credit cards for its customers. The number on the credit card is a four-digit number plus a check digit. The four-digit number is generated randomly; no duplication is allowed. The check digit is generated by using the modulus 10 methods. Taking 4562 as an example, the procedure to generate the check digit is:

(1) Use a weighting of 2 for the low order digit; a weighting of 3 for the next higher digit, and so on until you reach the highest order digit in your numeric field

Example: in the number 4562
     (a) multiply $2 \times 2 = 4$
     (b) multiply $6 \times 3 = 18$
     (c) multiply $5 \times 4 = 20$
     (d) multiply $4 \times 5 = 20$

(2) Sum the products of the factors multiplied by the digits in numeric field; for example, $4 + 18 + 20 + 20 = 62$.

(3) Divide by the modulus (10) and note the remainder; for example, 62/10, remainder = 2.

(4) Subtract the remainder (2) from the modulus (10) and the result is the check digit; for example, $10 - 2 = 8$ (the check digit is 8).

(5) The check digit is the new low order value of the original number; for example, 45628

Write a BASIC program to generate 100 credit card numbers.

13. Fill in the following table for a comparison of subprogram, subroutine single line function and multiple line function

	Single Line function	Multiple Line function	Subroutine	Subprogram
Number of lines in definition				
Number of arguments allowed				
Approach of specifying arguments				
Number of values returns				
Capability of handling array				
Globability of other variables used in the function body				

Problems on Error Handling

14. An inexperienced person would have difficulty responding to a question caused by an INPUT statement in a BASIC program. Write a simple program to ask the player to input his/her name and age. Your program should be able to

    (a) Alert the player, if he fails to respond within 30 seconds.
    (b) Correct improper input—format error.

15. The following program allows the player to input his/her autobiography and store in an array MY.STORY$

```
100      EXTEND
110      DIM MY.STORY$(100)
120      PRINT 'PLEASE ENTER YOUR SENTENCE NOW'
130      PRINT 'HIT RETURN KEY WHEN THE SENTENCE IS COMPLETED'
140      PRINT 'THE SENTENCE SHOULD NOT BE LONGER THAN 255 CHARACTERS'
142      PRINT 'THERE SHOULD BE NO MORE THAN 100 SENTENCES'
145      PRINT 'WHEN YOU FINISH THE STORY, TYPE "THE END"'
150      FOR X = 1 UNTIL A$ = 'THE END' OR X = 100
160          INPUT A
170          MY.STORY$(X) = A$
180      NEXT X
190      FOR Y = 1 TO X-1
200          PRINT MY.STORY$(Y)
210      NEXT Y
220      END
```

    Modify the program, so that if the line entered is too long (error code 47) the program can still recover it.

16. Question 10 in Chapter 8 requires us to produce a twos power table. We notice that at the end of the table the error message, "Floating Point Error," will be printed when the value becomes too large. Write an error handling routine to eliminate the error and print a line such as

    THE LARGEST 2s POWER TO BE HANDLED IS 126

III
File Editing and
Processing in BASIC-PLUS

Chapter **13**
Using a Text
Editor to Prepare Files

Objectives   You will learn:

Reasons for using a Text Editor.

How to create a file by using a Text Editor.

How to modify a file.

More efficient methods to correct errors in your program.

13.1 REASONS FOR USING A TEXT EDITOR

Up to this point you have learned the major statements in the BASIC-PLUS language. You are able to write a BASIC program to solve problems provided you can develop the logic, but real life applications vary. Frequently, you have to write a complicated program, deal with large quantities of data, or spend several hours waiting for the results of your program's run. Section III of this text will provide you with techniques of handling real world applications of BASIC-PLUS programming. We will describe how to store data in separate file,[1] how to write programs to process those data stored separately, how to run a large program without the user being bound to the terminal, and more efficient ways to edit a large program. This chapter explains how to use a text editor to prepare and modify files. This is preparatory work for Chapter 14, File Processing, although this chapter is quite independent from the BASIC-PLUS language.

13.2 OVERVIEW OF TEXT EDITOR

Text Editor is a system program[2], just like the one which translates your BASIC-PLUS into machine language. Text Editor allows the user to read one or two files into editing buffer of the memory, modify the text, and write the revised version onto one or two output files. Associated with editing buffer is a *pointer* that refers to the line or character to be changed. A series of editing commands is necessary to input the text into buffer, direct the pointer to the right position, make the correction, and, finally, output the contents of the buffer to a new file. This procedure can be depicted by the following figure:

---

[1] A file is a collection of interrelated data. A set of instructions is a program file, a set of related data is a data file, and a set of commands indicating the procedure of running a job is called a job control file.
[2] Sometimes it is called utility program.

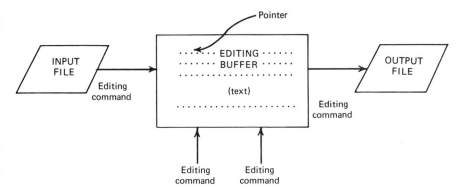

Figure 13-1. Overview of editing procedure.[3]

Now, let's examine the fundamental steps of using text editor.[4] They include:

1. Call text editor.

2. Specifying input and output files.

3. Enter editing commands.

4. Terminating editing session.

Step 1   Call text editor by typing

RUN $EDIT

RUN $EDIT tells the computer that we now want to edit a file instead of keying or executing a BASIC program. The computer will respond with a heading line and version number like

EDIT   V06C-03 RSTS V06-03 CSU Fullerton

Step 2   Specify input and output files. Once the EDIT program has been loaded into memory, the computer will prompt you with a number sign (#). This tells you that the computer is awaiting the files to be specified. The computer must be informed about input and output files as follows:

output file < input file

For example, if you want to modify a file, PROG1, you should type

#PROG1 < PROG1

If you want to create a new file, SALE.DAT,[5] we can simply type

#SALE.DAT

---

[3] In addition to the editing buffer, there is a *save buffer* which is used for temporary storage of information to be replaced in the editing buffer at sometime during editing.

[4] The editing commands in this chapter are those of the EDIT of the RSTS system. Refer to your system manual on this topic for exact specification of commands to be used. The other commonly used text editor, TECO, is explained in Appendix C.

[5] We have learned in Chapter 1 that a file name is a string up to six characters. Immediately after the name we can put a period and a three-character extension, which normally reveals the nature of the file. For example, PROG-1.BAS indicates a BASIC program file, SALE.DAT indicates a data file. If extension is not specified, default extension is BAS.

Step 3 Enter editing commands. Once the file specification has been entered, text editor prompts you with an asterisk (*). This tells you the specified files are set up and that text editor is awaiting a command. At this time you should continue entering editing commands until the editing task is completed. For simplicity, let's divide editing commands into five functions, namely:

1. To read text from the input file into editing buffer or write contents of editing buffer onto output file.

2. To move the pointer to the position we want to change.

3. To make a change on the character(s) on line(s) pointer refers to.

4. To print line(s) of the file on the terminal in order to verify the modification.

5. Miscellaneous functions.

1. Read and write commands are:

R   Read first section of text from input file into buffer, possibly all, if it is small.

N   Write buffer contents to output file and read next section of text from input file.

EX   Write contents of buffer and the remaining text from input file to output file, the editing with current file is terminated.

2. Pointer movement commands are:

There are two ways we can direct the buffer pointer to the right position. (1) Explicitly specify the number of lines and characters we want to advance or back up. (2) Implicitly search the proper character(s) where a change is to be made; this will guide the pointer directly after the last character that was searched for.

(a) Explicit pointer movement commands are:

nA   Advance pointer n lines. For example, 3A means move pointer to next three lines. −4A means back up pointer four lines, while /A means move pointer to the end of the buffer.

nJ   Jump over next n characters. For example, 4J means jump four characters forward, −10J means jump ten characters backwards, while 0J means move pointer to the beginning of the current line.

(b) Character search commands are:

nG/XXXX/   Search for the nth occurence of the character string XXXX, which is enclosed in a pair of slashes; For example, 3G/PRINT/, indicating search for the third PRINT. If the third PRINT is found pointer is moved to the position immediately after it, otherwise a question mark will appear, and the pointer is positioned at the end of the buffer.

nH/XXXX/   This command is almost the same as nG/XXXX/. The only difference is that if the character string is not found, current contents of editing buffer will be output to the output file and a new section of input file is read in before continuing the search.

3. Change commands are:

I   Insert lines before pointer position. After all the lines have been keyed in, line-feed key should be depressed. For example:

*I (CR)

LINE 1 (CR)

LINE 2 (CR)

(line-feed)

will insert LINE 1 and LINE 2 in the text.

I/XXXX/   This command will insert character string XXXX in the text. After the command is executed, pointer left immediately after last character in XXXX.

nK   Delete next n lines. For example, 3K indicates deleting next three lines, −5K means deleting previous five lines.

nD   Delete following n characters

nX   Replace following n lines with the new lines typed under nX command. For example,

*3X (CR)

NEW LINE 1 (CR)

NEW LINE 2 (CR)

(line-feed)

replaces the following three lines with NEW LINE 1 and NEW LINE 2.

nC/XXXX/   Replace following n characters with the character string XXXX. For example, 10C/BASIC/ replaces following 10 characters with 'BASIC'.

4. Print commands are:

V   Print the contents of current line.

nL   Print next n lines starting at pointer position. For example, 7L means printing following seven lines, −9L means printing previous nine lines, while /L means printing all of the lines between pointer position and end of the buffer.

5. Miscellaneous commands are:

S   Save current line in *save buffer* for purpose of macro execution.[6]

nEM   Execute first line of the save buffer as command n times (Example 13.5 illustrates usage of this command.)

---

[6] Macro is a series of predefined editing commands written on one line. Macro commands can be executed a number of times.

Step 4   Terminate editing session. After EX command is executed, the computer will prompt you with a number sign, which indicates another file specification is awaited. If you decide not to do further editing, control key and Z should be depressed simultaneously. When 'Ready' appears, you can return to BASIC programming mode.

13.3   CREATING A FILE

The best way to learn editor is through the use of examples, just as we learned BASIC statements. The next two sections will show you how to create a file and how to modify a file. Let's take a look at the following example:

Example 13.1

Below is the information about five employees at Humboldt Co.

	Hours Worked	Hourly Pay Rate	Number of Dependents	Insurance Code
Smith	25	$4.83	2	1
Taylor	52	$5.25	4	2
Schneider	33	$3.95	0	0
Brown	12	$9.55	0	1
Sawyer	37	$6.95	2	2

Now, let's create a data file 'PAYROL.DAT' to retain the employees' record. Each employee will have a record containing information about name, hours worked, hourly payrate, number of dependents, and insurance code. This can be done by keying the following underlined lines:

```
RUN $EDIT
EDIT    V06C-03A        RSTS V06C-03 CSU Fullerton

#PAYROL.DAT

*I
SMITH,25,4.83,2,1
TALOR,52,5.25,4,2
SCHNEIDER,33,3.95,0,0
BROWN,12,9.55,0,1
SAWYER,37,6.95,2,2
(line-feed)
*EX

#^Z

Ready
```

We first tell the computer that we want to run text editor to create a new file named 'PAYROL.DAT'. After naming the file, the computer tells you that it is ready to accept editing commands by printing the * sign. Since we are creating a file, the only command which may be used here is I (INSERT). After you hit the return key, you can start typing the employee's record, one for each line, separating the individual data item by a comma. Notice that nowhere are line numbers and the key word, DATA, indicated, since it is understood that the file contains data. It is not necessary to type that the line numbers are 'DATA'.[7] After all the lines have been keyed in, the carriage return and line-feed key should

---

[7] Use of data file is explained in Chapter 14.

be depressed to terminate the insertion mode. Text editor responds with another asterisk. The asterisk says that the computer is ready for further editing commands. At this time, you might want to type 'EX' to indicate that editing of this file is finished. Text editor will then close the new created 'PAYROL.DAT' file and respond with a number sign, #, and asks whether there are other files to be edited. If you decide not to do further editing work, you should depress control key and Z simultaneously. The computer replies with "Ready." Thereafter, if you check your directory by typing 'CAT', you will see 'PAYROL.DAT' is on the list.

In the previous example we separated employee's name, hours worked, and so on by a comma. However, we can conserve memory space and save typing effort by putting the entire record of an employee as a character string; for example, no commas are used to separate individual data items, provided values in each data item are of the same length. We will see this in the next example.

Example 13.2

Suppose Western Company's inventory data look as follows:

Product Name	Unit Price	On Hand	In Order
AAA123	$4.85	50	30
BBB213	$9.73	70	20
CCC333	$5.00	20	10
DDD195	$4.35	60	20
EEE332	$0.50	90	30

We can create a data file, INVENT.DAT, to store inventory information by doing the following:

```
RUN $EDIT
EDIT    VO6C-03A       RSTS VO6C-03 CSU Fullerton

$INVENT

*I
AAA1234.855030
BBB2139.737020          ⌐ to assure same length of
CCC3335.002010          | values in a data field,
DDD1954.356020          | leading zero and trailing zeros
EEE3320.509030          | should be typed.
(line—feed)             ⌐
*EX

$^Z

Ready
```

Notice, commas did not appear in the file. Chapter 14 will explain the technique for handling this type of file.

13.4 CHANGING A FILE

People are far from perfect. Files keyed in are likely to contain errors. Let's use several examples to show how to update a file and change a file.

Example 13.3

Suppose two new employees are hired by Humboldt Co. (See Example 13.1). Their payroll data looks as follows:

	Hours Worked	Hourly Pay Rate	Number of Dependents	Insurance Code
Miller	40	$5.25	0	1
Johnson	35	$6.95	2	2

One employee, Schneider, was fired from the company. Now we want to remove Schneider's record from 'PAYROL.DAT' file, and add Miller and Johnson's data to the file. These can be done as follows:

```
RUN $EDIT
EDIT    V06C-03A       RSTS V06C-03 CSU Fullerton

#NUPAYL.DAT < PAYROL.DAT

*R
*2A
*K
*/A
*I
MILLER,40,5.25,0,1
JOHNSON,35,6.95,2,2
(line—feed)
*B
*/L
SMITH,25,4.83,2,1
TALOR,52,5.25,4,2
BROWN,12,9.55,0,1
MILLER,40,5.25,0,1
JOHNSON,35,6.95,2,2
*EX

#^Z

Ready
```

We run the EDIT in the same way as described in Example 13.1 with one exception; instead of just entering the one file name, an input and output file must both be requested. If you decide that a new revised copy of the file should be called 'NUPAYL' in response to #, we type

$$\text{NUPAYL.DAT} < \text{PAYROL.DAT}$$

You should notice that the output file must be specified before the input file. If you enter the file specification in reversed format, the file containing the text to be edited (PAYROL.DAT) will be open for output and its contents will be destroyed immediately.

After file specification, EDIT opens the files, responds with an * and is ready to accept editing commands. Before we can work on the input text, it must be moved into the main buffer. This is done by typing 'R' command, meaning that EDIT should read one buffer full of text into buffer. If the contents of the input file is larger than a buffer, we type 'N' to read the next section of text after the previous one is edited.

The first change we want to make is to delete Schneider's record. Remember that when a section of text is read into buffer, the pointer is left at the beginning of the buffer. Type 2A to remove pointer to the third line (pass next two lines). A "K" command at this point will delete the third line, which is Schneider's record. We then move pointer to the end of the file by typing '/A'. An 'I' command can then be used to add lines. Underneath 'I' command, we key two new employees' records in. The line-feed key should be depressed after finishing line insertion. The updating task has been completed. Before you terminate the editing session, you might want to list the revised text at the terminal. Now, it is necessary to move pointer back to the beginning of the text. This is done by typing 'B'. Then, count the number of lines to be listed and type '6L' to list all the six lines. One can also use the slash option, meaning to print out all text in the buffer, thus, the editing command, '/L', is given.

The above example shows how to edit lines. The next example will illustrate how to change characters within the line.

Example 13.4

Suppose professor Carter has five students and their three test scores look as follows:

Name	Test 1	Test 2	Test 3
Jones	77	56	96
Card	88	78	94
Green	65	44	77
Kennedy	34	22	12
Lucey	95	99	95

A file named GRADE has been set up to retain student's grade record, but due to poor typing, GRADE file contains several errors:

1. Card's second test score is left out.

2. Kennedy is misspelled as Candy.

3. Lucey's first test score is mistyped as 9500 instead of 95 and looks as follows:

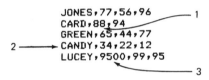

```
      JONES,77,56,96        —— 1
      CARD,88,94
      GREEN,65,44,77
2 ———→ CANDY,34,22,12
      LUCEY,9500,99,95
                           —— 3
```

(arrows point to place where changes are needed)

```
RUN $EDIT
EDIT    V06C-03A      RSTS V06C-03 CSU Fullerton

$GRADE.DAT < GRADE.DAT

*R
*A8JI/78,/0JV
CARD,88,78,94
*G/CANDY/-5J5C/KENNEDY/0JV
KENNEDY,34,22,12
*A8J2D0JV
LUCEY,95,99,95
*EX

$^Z

Ready
```

You might notice that the output file name is the same as the input file name. This is permissible, but after editing is finished, the original 'GRADE.DAT' file will be renamed to 'GRADE.BAK' meaning back-up file. After reading the text into buffer, move the pointer to the next line, 'A', and jump over eight characters to the position to insert information by typing '8J'. Then, we insert Card's second test score by typing I/78,/. Notice the text to be inserted is enclosed in a pair of slashes. After this is done, the pointer points to the newly inserted text. We move the pointer back to the beginning of the line by typing '0J' (zero-J). Now, a 'V' command can be entered to verify the change of current line. The computer then prints the new version of CARD's record for you. When it makes sense, commands may be put together on one line to correct an error,

$$A8JI/78,/0JV$$

The next change we want to make is to correct the error on 'CANDY'. Finding the right characters can be done by line advancing (A) and character jumping (J) as used above. This can be a very tedious process. If the character string is distinctive, it is more convenient to use the search command. G/CANDY/ will search for the character string 'CANDY'. After the command is executed, the pointer will be left after the last character that was searched. Now, we move the pointer five characters backwards by typing −5J. We may then use 5C/KENNEDY/ to change the next five characters from 'CANDY' to 'KENNEDY'. After the change is done, we move the pointer to the beginning of the line and verify the change by typing a '0J' followed by a 'V'. Thus, the entire command line to correct error 2 is

G/CANDY/−5J5C/KENNEDY/0JV

The last error needed to be corrected is deleting the two excess zeros from '9500'. This is done by moving pointer to the right position, 'A' and '8J'. The two zeros can be deleted by '2D'. The above commands, along with the verify command, are the entire command string needed for correcting error 3

A8J2D0JV

We now have completed all the changes that need to be made. We type 'EX' to close the files being worked on and control Z to terminate EDIT mode.

So far we have illustrated how to use a series of commands to make a *single* change. Now, we want to show how to use editing commands to change all occurences of a certain character string in the file. Remember that in addition to editing buffer there is a save buffer in memory. Save buffer can be used to hold a command line which will be executed several times. This command line is called a macro command. Let's show the convenience of macro execution.

Example 13.5

Suppose we want to change all 100 occurences of a variable name 'T1' in a BASIC program, MATH, to 'TEST1'. We could supply the following editing commands after text editor is called and input and output file are specified.

*RI

H/T1/−2C/TEST1/

(line-feed)

*BSK

*100EM

*EX

Change of each 'T1' can be done by a predefined series of editing commands, macro. We insert the command string at the top of editing buffer, 'H/T1/−2C/TEST1/'. This command string says to search the entire file for each occurence of the string 'T1'; when each one is found, change these two characters to 'TEST1'.

Remember that after text is read (R) into buffer, the pointer points to the top of the text. We then insert the macro command string at the top of the buffer by typing 'I', followed by the macro command string, H/T1/−2C/TEST1/.

After the insertion, pointer still stays at the place before the insertion command was given. The current status of the editing buffer looks like this:

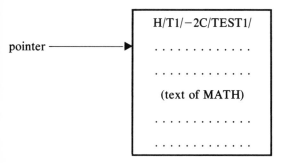

In order to put the newly created command string in save buffer to enable macro execution, we have to move the pointer to refer to this line. This is done by typing a 'B'. An 'S' will save this command line in save buffer; therefore a 'K' (kill a line) is followed. After command string 'BSK' is executed, save buffer and editing buffer look as follows:

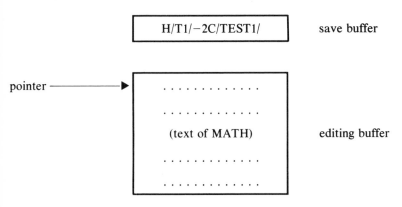

Now, the editing command '100EM' indicates the command string in save buffer should be executed 100 times. This has the same function as typing 'H/T1/−2C/TEST1/' 100 times. Notice that we are able to correct our BASIC program without retyping all of the lines.

File. A collection of interrelated records.

Job Control File. A set of commands that indicate procedures for running a job.

Macro Commands. A series of predefined editing commands.

Pointer. A reference point in memory that identifies locations to be edited.

Text Editor. A system program designed to modify and edit files.

1. Write editing commands to delete 11th and 12th line of a file, LINE.

2. Write editing commands to add one line between third and fourth line in file, SORT

3. Write editing commands to attach the following six lines at the end of file, CHAIRS:

ACCOUNTING,ANDERSON

MANAGEMENT,KING

MANAGEMENT SCIENCE,LAWRENCE

ECONOMICS,PICKERSGILL

FINANCE,MYKNARYK

MARKETING,LANGE

4. Write editing commands to replace fifth and sixth line of the file 'JOB' by

$RUN BASIC

5. Write editing commands to change a name, KOELN, into 'COLOGNE' in a text file, GERMANY

BERLIN,30000

FRANKFURT,43005

KOELN,23450

MUNICH,87000

6. Write editing commands to delete the underlined character in the following text file, NEUMAN

IT IS EVIDENT THATT THE MASCHINE MUST BE CAPABLE OF
STORING IN SOME MANNERER NOT ONLY THE DIGITAL INFORMATION
NEEDED IN A GIVEN COMPUTATION BUT ALSO INSTRUCTIONS
WHICH GOVERMENT THE ACTUAL ROUTINE TO BE PERFORMED
PERFORMED ON THE NUMERICAL DATA.

7. A file, BASIC, should look as follows:

THE BASIC LANGUAGE WAS DEVELOPED AT DARTMOUTH COLLEGE
IN 1965, CHIEFLY BY PROFESSORS KEMENY AND KURTZ. THEIR
INTENT WAS TO PROVIDE A LANGUAGE THAT WAS EASY FOR
STUDENTS TO LEARN.

Due to the poor typing skill of data entry operator, BASIC was mistyped as follows:

THE BASIC LENGUAGGE WAS DEVELOPED AT DART MOUTH CLOOGE
IN L965, CHEAPLY by PROFESSORS KEMENY. THEIR
INTENT WAS TO PROVIDE A LANGUAGE LANGUAGE TAHT WAS
EASY FOR THE STUDENT TO LEAN.

Use text editor to correct the errors.

8. Some time-sharing systems provide the capability to implement the FORTRAN programming language. Use text editor to prepare a FORTRAN program file, which looks as follows:

PROGRAM DEMO

READ(5,10) A

WRITE(7,20) A

10   FORMAT(I6)

20   FORMAT(F9.2)

END

9. Following are information on five students in Dr. Carter's class. Use text editor to create a data file named STUDEN to store the information,

Name	Major	Year level	GPA
Adams,B	Business	Frosh	3.5
Benson,W	Fishery	Junior	2.98
Conway,A	Math	Soph	4.0
Denny,M	History	Junior	3.9
Edden,F	English	Soph	3.03

10. The MBI company manufactures four products. Below is their production cost budget. Create a data file, COST, to retain the information

Product	Materials	Labor	Fixed Cost
X-12	$25,000	$12,000	$40,000
A-01	$60,000	$72,000	$88,000
N-99	$23,000	$43,000	$10,000
H-55	$78,000	$12,000	$25,000

11. Suppose production plan of A-01 is canceled, and a new product Y-00 is introduced. Material, labor, and fixed cost of product Y-00 are $43,000, $23,000, and $50,000, respectively. Write editing commands to update COST file in problem 10.

12. In some system we can always omit the key word 'LET' in an assignment statement; instead of keying

$$10 \quad \text{LET } X = 5$$

we can just type

$$10 \quad X = 5$$

to conserve memory space. Write editing commands to omit all the 100 occurences of 'LET' in a BASIC program, NOLET. (Hint: Use macro execution feature.)

Chapter 14
File Processing

Objectives You will learn:

Reasons for using a file.

Differences between sequential access files and random access files.

Differences between display files and binary files.

Various types of files in BASIC-PLUS.

Ways to create, use, and update a formatted ASCII file.

Ways to create, use, and update a virtual array.

Ways to handle a large matrix.

14.1 INTRODUCTION

We have learned to enter large amounts of data by using READ/DATA statements. Several situations may arise to prove that the current method is inadequate;

The amount of data is vast. The computer memory cannot accommodate too many DATA statements or too large a matrix. This is frequently the situation in real life data processing.

The result of one program may be used as input for another program.

More than one program shares a common set of data.

For example, if we have to process payroll information for 5,000 employees, main memory probably cannot accommodate all the DATA statements. In addition, the output of a payroll program, which indicates gross pay, withholding, deductions, and net pay for each employee, may be used as input data for preparing a ledger report for the accounting department. Another example: Admissions and records has a program to prepare the dean's honor list and the registrar has another program to process a student's course requests. Both programs need students' information. In fact one common set of data is enough.

14.1.1 Data Files

In both these cases, data should be separated from the program and placed on an external device (e.g., a data file should be used). A data file consists of related records. Records can be subdivided into fields. For example, a data file contains records for all students in a class. Each record is composed of four fields: name, first, second, and third test scores

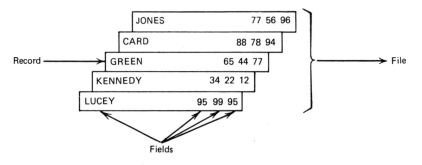

Records can be placed in a file in sequential order. Starting with the first record in the file, the program reads the record from an external device into main memory and processes it sequentially. For example, if we want to process Green's record, the computer has to scan the records one by one until the desired information is located.

| JONES,77,56,96 | CARD,88,78,94 | GREEN,65,44,77 | KENNEDY,34,22,12 | LUCEY,95,99,95 |

This means Jones' and Card's records should be read in first.

Another method allows us to access any record or any field without processing the preceding records. The system mechanism has the capacity of calculating the actual location of the desired record. Differences between sequential files and random access files are analogous to the differences between cassette tapes and records. In order to get your favorite hit song, you need to advance the tape to the right segment. To locate a specific song on the record, you just position the stylus on the platter at the proper position.

14.1.3 Display vs. Binary Files

In terms of data representation on a file, a numerical data item can be expressed in ASCII code form or in binary form. For example, the integer 1234 can be stored in a PDP 11 computer as

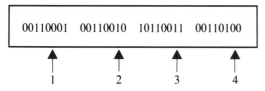

The number 1234 takes up 4 bytes.[1] Each byte represents the ASCII code of a digit. Integer 1234 can also be stored in the computer as a binary number and looks as follows:

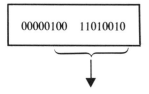

Binary equivalent of decimal number 1234

Representing 1234 in binary form just takes up 2 bytes (one word).

If all numerical items are expressed in ASCII code form, the contents of the file can be displayed on the terminal by calling the system program, PIP. The following command will list the contents of a display file, PAYROL.DAT, on the terminal:

PIP PAYROL.DAT

---

[1] One byte of PDP 11 computer has 8 bits. Two bytes make up a word. One byte is used to represent one character, and one word can be used to represent a binary number.

Contents of a binary file cannot be displayed on the terminal by using the system program, PIP. A BASIC program must be written for this purpose. A display file can be created by using the text editor (discussed in Chapter 13), but a binary file must be created by using a user-written BASIC program.

14.1.4 File Processing in BASIC-PLUS

BASIC-PLUS has three methods of handling a data file;

—Formatted ASCII (sequential file).

—Virtual array (random access file).

—Record I/O.

Using formatted ASCII, records should be processed sequentially. The numerical data are represented in ASCII format. Virtual arrays can be randomly accessed (nonsequentially), and the numerical data are represented in their binary form. We will discuss formatted ASCII files and virtual arrays in this chapter. Record I/O has both the advantages of ASCII files and random access files. Due to its complexity, record I/O will be explained in Appendix D.

14.2 GENERATING REPORTS FROM FIRST TYPE SEQUENTIAL FILE

In Chapter 13 we explained how to use the text editor to create a data file[2] Text editor creates a formatted ASCII file which must be processed sequentially. Although this is not the most efficient way to store information, it is easy to learn and widely used. Now, let's take a look at an example of a sequential file.

Example 14.1

Suppose a sequential file, GRADE.DAT, contains names and three test scores of five students in professor Carter's class (see page 209). We want to write a BASIC program to prepare a report to list each student's name, three test scores, and the average of the three test scores. This can be done by the following program:

```
5        REM THIS PROGRAM WILL GENERATE REPORT FROM A SEQUENTIAL FILE
10       OPEN 'GRADE.DAT' FOR INPUT AS FILE 1
20       PRINT 'NAME','TEST 1', 'TEST 2', 'TEST 3', 'AVERAGE'
25       PRINT
28       F$ = '\         \    ##          ##          ##          ##.#'
30       FOR X = 1 TO 5
40           INPUT #1, N$,T1,T2,T3
50           A = (T1+T2+T3)/3
70           PRINT USING F$, N$,T1,T2,T3,A
80       NEXT X
90       CLOSE 1
99       END
```

---

[2] A formatted ASCII file can be created by the user's own program, but correcting errors is very tedious. Therefore, employing the text editor to create sequential file is highly recommended.

However we will show how to use BASIC program to create sequential files in case that you don't want to use text editor or your computer system does not have a text editor.

```
RUNNH
NAME            TEST 1         TEST 2         TEST 3       AVERAGE

JONES            77             56             96          76.3
CARD             88             78             94          86.7
GREEN            65             44             77          62.0
KENNEDY          34             22             12          22.7
LUCEY            95             99             95          96.3

Ready
```

Notice that the name of the program, GRADE.BAS, is almost the same as the name of data file used for this program, GRADE.DAT. It is a good programming practice to give the same name to the program and its associated data file. Program files and data files are identified by their extension, for example, BAS and DAT.

Files must be opened before processing starts and closed after processing is finished. Line 10 instructs the computer to search for an existing data file, GRADE.DAT. If it is found, a communication link between program in the memory and data on the disk will be established. A channel number is given to indicate the association (1 in this case). Later, we can always use #1 in the program to reference the data file, GRADE.DAT. This relationship can be shown as follows:

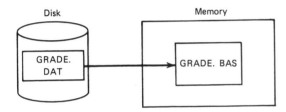

If the data file, GRADE.DAT, doesn't exist, an error message

?can't find file or account

will appear on the terminal. The general format for OPEN . . . . FOR INPUT statement is

Line number   OPEN ''file name''   FOR INPUT AS FILE channel number

File names must be enclosed in quotation marks. Channel numbers can be any integer between 1 and 12. It is important to remember that line 10 merely informs the computer that we want to use the file, GRADE.DAT. No actual input is performed.

Lines 20 and 25 print the heading line. Line 28 sets format for the following report lines. We want to process records for five students. Thus, the processing procedure, line 40 to line 70, is enclosed in a FOR/NEXT loop (line 30 and line 80). We started processing the records by reading data from a file on the disk.

40   INPUT #1, N$,T1,T2,T3

Statement 40 directs the computer to read the appropriate information from the file, GRADE.DAT. The first time this statement is encountered, the computer reads the file, GRADE.DAT, starting at its beginning. Location N$ is assigned the value JONES; T1, the value 77; T2, the value 56; and T3, the value 96.

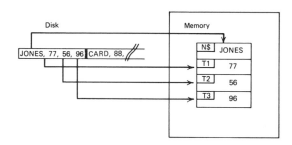

The input statement used here is similar to the input statement introduced in Chapter 3 except that INPUT # cause the computer to take values from a file instead of a terminal. The general format for an INPUT FILE statement looks as follows:

> Line number   INPUT # channel number, variable list

The INPUT statement causes the computer to read data from the file associated with the channel number indicated into a location specified on the variable list. We use commas to separate variables. The correct order of variables is essential. They must be arranged in the same sequence as the data in the file.

After values have been read into memory locations, line 50 will calculate the average of T1, T2, and T3. The result is stored in location A. Line 70 prints the information.

When the loop (lines 30 to 80) has been executed five times, processing of the file is completed. The file should be closed. This is accomplished by the statement

90   CLOSE 1

All files open must be closed. Otherwise, unexpected damage to the file might occur. The general format for CLOSE statement is

> Line number   CLOSE   channel number

If there is more than one file to be closed, channel numbers are separated by commas; for example, 90   CLOSE 1,2,3.

14.3 GENERATING A REPORT FROM THE SECOND TYPE OF SEQUENTIAL FILE

In the previous example, individual data items of a record are separated by commas. A second type of sequential file arranges the entire record as a character string. Now let's discuss how to prepare a report by using this type of sequential file.

Example 14.2

Suppose Western Company's inventory data appears as follows:

Product Name	Unit Pirce	On Hand	In order
AAA123	$4.85	50	30
BBB213	$9.73	70	20
CCC333	$5.00	20	10
DDD195	$4.35	60	20
EEE332	$0.50	99	30

A data file, INVENT.DAT, has been created (described on page 207).

AAA1234.855030	BBB2139.737020	CCC333 ┆ EEE3320.509930

We notice that there are no commas between fields. A record is stored as an entire character string. The following program will prepare an inventory report for Western Company.

```
10      REM THIS PROGRAM CALCULATES TOTAL COST OF INVENTORY
20      OPEN 'INVENT.DAT' FOR INPUT AS FILE 1
30      F$ = '      \            \        $#.##        ##        $###.##'
40      G$ = '          TOTAL COST OF INVENTORY           $#,###.##'
50      PRINT TAB(15);'W E S T E R N    C O M P A N Y'
60      PRINT
70      PRINT TAB(22);'INVENTORY REPORT'
80      PRINT
90      PRINT '        PRODUCT        UNIT PRICE      QUANTITY         COST'
100     PRINT
110     T = 0
120     FOR X = 1 TO 5
130         INPUT LINE #1, A$
140         N$ = LEFT(A$,6)
150         P$ = MID(A$,7,4) \ P = VAL(P$)
160         Q$ = MID(A$,11,2) \ Q = VAL(Q$)
170         C = P*Q
180         T = T+C
190         PRINT USING F$, N$,P,Q,C
200     NEXT X
210     PRINT
220     PRINT USING G$, T
230     CLOSE 1
999     END
```

```
RUNNH
            W E S T E R N    C O M P A N Y

                 INVENTORY REPORT

        PRODUCT        UNIT PRICE      QUANTITY         COST

        AAA123          $4.85            50          $242.50
        BBB213          $9.73            70          $681.10
        CCC333          $5.00            20          $100.00
        DDD195          $4.35            60          $261.00
        EEE332          $0.50            99          $ 49.50

        TOTAL COST OF INVENTORY                     $1,334.10

Ready
```

Data file, INVENT.DAT, is opened at line 20. INVENT.DAT is associated with channel 1 thereafter. We set the printing format for the record lines and summary line at lines 30 and 40. Lines 50 through 100 print the title, subtitle, and column heading. Then, we initialized the counter for the total inventory cost, T, with a value 0. The loop, lines 120 through 200, is used to process each of the five inventory items.

130 INPUT LINE #1, A$

Statement 130 informs the computer to read one entire line of data as a character string from the file, INVENT.DAT, into a memory location A$. The general format for the INPUT LINE instruction is

Line number   INPUT LINE # channel number, string variable

Any imbedded blank and punctuation will be treated as parts of the record, rather than an item separator. After the entire line of a record is read in, we need to separate it into data items.

$$140 \quad N\$ = LEFT(A\$,6)$$

Statement 140 informs the computer to extract the leftmost six characters of A$ and store this substring in N$, which is the product name.

$$150 \quad P\$ = MID(A\$,7,4) \setminus P = VAL(P\$)$$

Statement 150 is a multiple statement. First, we extract a substring, P$, starting with the seventh character in A$, obtaining a substring of four characters. This substring contains the unit price. Although P$ only consists of digits, remember that strings cannot be used for calculations. Digit strings must be converted into numbers, which is accomplished by the second part of line 150;

$$P = VAL(P\$)$$

Line 160 does the same thing for the quantity on hand. After lines 130 through 160 have been executed for the first time, the data file and memory locations appear as follows:

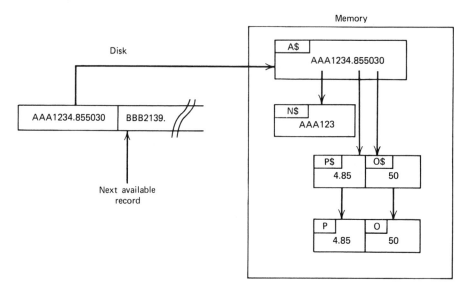

Notice that the last two characters of A$, which contains information about the quantity of the order are not used. Line 170 multiplies the quantity by price, and the result is stored in C. Line 180 adds the cost of current item to a total counter, T. Line 190 prints N$ (name of product), P(rice), Q(uantity), and C(ost) on the terminal, according to the printing format F$. The loop should be executed five times for five inventory items. Remember that every time line 130 is encountered, an entire line of data will be read into the memory location, A$. After all five inventory items have been processed, wrap-up operations should be performed, which includes printing the summary lines and closing the file (line 210 to 230).

Now, you might question the efficiency of this type of sequential file. While it does require extra effort to extract data items, storage is conserved and data entry is simplified—a worthwhile tradeoff!

14.4 UPDATING SEQUENTIAL FILES

A common problem when working with files is updating the file. Quite often we need to add information to the file, change information on the file, and delete information from the file. Let's explain one way of adding information to the file first.

Example 14.3

In Example 14.1, we used GRADE.DAT file to prepare a report about student's names, three test scores, and their averages. Now, let's store the average along with the other information on the file. Since sequential files cannot be changed without rewriting the entire file, all we can do is create a new file that encompasses the previous data as well as new data. This can be done by the following program:

```
100     REM THIS PROGRAM ADDS INFORMATION TO A SEQUENTIAL FILE
110     ON ERROR GO TO 190
120     OPEN 'GRADE.DAT' FOR INPUT AS FILE 1
130     OPEN 'GRADE1.DAT' FOR OUTPUT AS FILE 2
135     REM FOLLOWING IS LOOP TO READ RECORD FROM GRADE FILE
            AND WRITE RECORD ONTO GRADE1 FILE
140         INPUT #1, N$,T1,T2,T3
150         A = (T1+T2+T3)/3
160         A1 = INT(A*10+0.5)/10
170         PRINT #2, N$;',';T1;',';T2;',';T3;',';A1
180         GO TO 140
185     REM END OF LOOP
190     IF ERR <> 11 THEN PRINT 'OTHER ERROR OCCURS'
200     CLOSE 1,2
999     END
```

Line 120 instructs the computer to reopen the old file, GRADE.DAT.[3] GRADE.DAT is a standard sequential file; fields are separated by commas. Line 130 opens a new file,

---

[3] If GRADE.DAT file is not created by using a text editor, the following program can be used to create it.

```
100     REM THIS PROGRAM CREATES A STANDARD SEQUENTIAL FILE
110     OPEN 'GRADE.DAT' FOR OUTPUT AS FILE 1
120     PRINT 'ENTER NAME AND THREE TEST SCORES OF EACH STUDENT'
130     PRINT 'AT END OF DATA ENTRY, ENTER DUMMY AS NAME'
140     REM FOLLOWING IS THE LOOP FOR DATA ENTRY
150         INPUT 'NAME';N$
155         IF N$ = 'DUMMY' THEN 220
160         INPUT 'TEST 1';T1
170         INPUT 'TEST 2';T2
180         INPUT 'TEST 3';T3
190         PRINT #1, N$;',';T1;',';T2;',';T3
200         GO TO 150
210     REM END OF LOOP
220     CLOSE 1
999     END
```

```
RUNNH
ENTER NAME AND THREE TEST SCORES OF EACH STUDENT
AT END OF DATA ENTRY, ENTER DUMMY AS NAME
NAME? JONES
TEST 1? 77
TEST 2? 56
TEST 3? 96
NAME? CARD
TEST 1? 88
TEST 2? 78
TEST 3? 94
NAME? GREEN
TEST 1? 65
TEST 2? 44
TEST 3? 77
NAME? KENNEDY
TEST 1? 34
TEST 2? 22
TEST 3? 12
NAME? LUCEY
TEST 1? 95
TEST 2? 99
TEST 3? 95
NAME? DUMMY

Ready
```

GRADE1.DAT, which is associated with channel number 2. If GRADE1.DAT already exists, this instruction will erase the contents of GRADE1.DAT and make it available for outputting information. The format of OPEN FILE FOR OUTPUT is similar to OPEN FILE FOR INPUT statement.

> Line number   OPEN   ' file name ' FOR OUTPUT AS channel number

The loop, lines 140 to 180, takes information from GRADE.DAT (line 140), calculates and rounds the average (line 150, 160), and writes information onto the file.

170   PRINT #2, N$;',';T1;',';T2;',';T3;',';A1

Statement 170 informs the computer to print nine items on the file associated with channel 2; five variables and four commas are used to separate values of variables of a record. The general format of the PRINT file statement is

> Line number   PRINT # channel number, printing item list

The print file statement is similar to the ordinary print statement except that we must tell the computer which file to write on. The way to print items is the same as on the terminal. Here we use the ; to separate items listed on the PRINT statement. Thus, a compact image is assured. Printing commas is necessary, otherwise, names, three test scores, and averages will bunch together—a second type of sequential file.

Notice, we did not use a FOR/NEXT statement to construct the loop. Quite often we do not know how much data are stored on a file. If we attempt to read past the end of the file,[4] the computer will generate an

?end of file on device

error message, which is similar to the OUT OF DATA error message in the READ/DATA statement. We remember that, in Chapter 12, the error message can be suppressed, and the error can be recovered by transferring control to the error handling routine. Thus, we include

110   ON ERROR GO TO 190

at the beginning of the program. When the loop is executed for the sixth time, an error occurs. Control will be transferred to

190   IF ERR <> 11 THEN PRINT 'OTHER ERROR OCCURS'

Then, the computer checks to see if the error code is 11, which is an end of file error. If this is true, we close the file; otherwise, a message will be printed on the terminal. The computer cycled through the loop five times. The sixth time line 140 is encountered, an error occured. Line 100 directed the computer to check the error code at 190 and to perform the wrap-up operation at line 200. This is the technique BASIC-PLUS uses to detect an end-of-file condition. After the program is run, the old file remains unchanged, and a new file, GRADE1.DAT, retaining the information about student names, test scores, and averages, is created. No output on the terminal is generated from this program.

Now, let's use another example to update a sequential file.

---

[4] When we use text editor to create a data file, EDIT program automatically places an end of file mark, control Z symbol at the end of the file.

Example 14.4

Suppose a data file, KONTO.DAT, records information about six savings accounts. We would like to enter deposits and withdrawals from a terminal to update balances. This can be done with the following program:

```
100      OPEN'KONTO.DAT' FOR INPUT AS FILE 1
110      OPEN 'KONTO1.DAT' FOR OUTPUT AS FILE 2
115      REM ----- MAIN LOOP TO UPDATE RECORDS -----
120      FOR X = 1 TO 6
130          INPUT #1, N$,B
140          D1 = 0 \ C1 = 0
150          PRINT \ PRINT
160          PRINT 'CURRENT BALANCE OF ';N$;"'S ACCOUNT IS ";B
165      REM PROCESS DEPOSIT
170          PRINT "ENTER ";N$;"'S DEPOSIT ('0' IF NO MORE)"
180          INPUT D
190          IF D <> 0 THEN D1 = D1 + D \ GO TO 180
195      REM PROCESS WITHDRAWAL
200          PRINT "ENTER ";N$;"'S CHECK AMOUNT ('0' IF NO MORE)"
210          INPUT C
220          IF C <> 0 THEN C1 = C1 + C \ GO TO 210
225      REM CALCULATE NEW BALANCE AND WRITE RECORD
230          B1 = B + D1 - C1
240          PRINT "NEW BALANCE OF ";N$;"'S ACCOUNT IS";B1
250          PRINT #2, N$;',';B1
260      NEXT X
265      REM ----- END OF MAIN LOOP -----
270          PRINT \ PRINT 'END OF PROCESSING'
280          CLOSE 1,2
290          KILL 'KONTO.DAT'
300          NAME 'KONTO1.DAT' AS 'KONTO.DAT'
999      END
```

```
RUNNH

CURRENT BALANCE OF ADAMS'S ACCOUNT IS   500
ENTER ADAMS'S DEPOSIT ('0' IF NO MORE)
? 1000
? 100
? 0
ENTER ADAMS'S CHECK AMOUNT ('0' IF NO MORE)
? 500
? 0
NEW BALANCE OF ADAMS'S ACCOUNT IS 1100

CURRENT BALANCE OF BROWN'S ACCOUNT IS   150
ENTER BROWN'S DEPOSIT ('0' IF NO MORE)
? 44
? 0
ENTER BROWN'S CHECK AMOUNT ('0' IF NO MORE)
? 50
? 0
NEW BALANCE OF BROWN'S ACCOUNT IS 144

CURRENT BALANCE OF CARLSON'S ACCOUNT IS   26000
ENTER CARLSON'S DEPOSIT ('0' IF NO MORE)
? 1200
? 0
ENTER CARLSON'S CHECK AMOUNT ('0' IF NO MORE)
? 0
NEW BALANCE OF CARLSON'S ACCOUNT IS 27200

CURRENT BALANCE OF DICKSON'S ACCOUNT IS   885.5
ENTER DICKSON'S DEPOSIT ('0' IF NO MORE)
? 45.5
? 0
ENTER DICKSON'S CHECK AMOUNT ('0' IF NO MORE)
? 60
? 0
NEW BALANCE OF DICKSON'S ACCOUNT IS 871
```

```
CURRENT BALANCE OF EDWARD'S ACCOUNT IS   200
ENTER EDWARD'S DEPOSIT ('0' IF NO MORE)
? 0
ENTER EDWARD'S CHECK AMOUNT ('0' IF NO MORE)
? 10
? 0
NEW BALANCE OF EDWARD'S ACCOUNT IS 190


CURRENT BALANCE OF FANNY'S ACCOUNT IS   10
ENTER FANNY'S DEPOSIT ('0' IF NO MORE)
? 0
ENTER FANNY'S CHECK AMOUNT ('0' IF NO MORE)
? 0
NEW BALANCE OF FANNY'S ACCOUNT IS 10

END OF PROCESSING

Ready
```

We open the old file, KONTO.DAT, and the new data file, KONTO1.DAT, at lines 100 and 110. The loop, lines 120 through 260, is used to process each account. We began by reading a record from the old data file at line 130. Line 140 cleared the total deposit, D1, and total withdrawal, C1. After the current balance is printed on the terminal, line 170 prints a message to inform the user to enter deposits. The user is instructed to enter 0, if there is no deposit. Every time line 180 is encountered, the computer will print a question mark on the terminal. The deposited amount should be keyed in.

$$190 \quad \text{IF } D <> 0 \text{ THEN } D1 = D1 + D \setminus GO\ TO\ 180$$

Statement 190 checks whether $D = 0$. As long as D is not 0, the amount will be added to the total account, D1, and line 180 will be executed again. Once $D = 0$, control is transferred to 200. Lines 200 through 220 do the same thing for withdrawals. Line 230 calculates the new balance, B1. Line 240 prints the updated information on the terminal and line 250 writes it on the new file. The whole procedure of input/output can be visualized as follows:

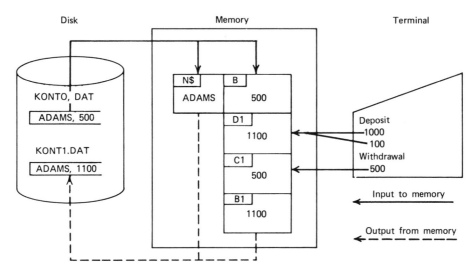

After we finish processing all five records, a message is printed on the terminal (line 270), and files are closed (line 280).

To this point we have learned that in order to update a sequential file, a new file should be created. Once the new file is created, the old file becomes obsolete. We might want to remove it from the disk. The KILL statement in the form of

> Line number   KILL 'file name'

can be used to erase the old file.

After the old file, KONTO.DAT, is killed we might want to give that name to the new file, so that the name can be unique. We need not use a different name every time the file is updated. The NAME . . . . AS statement takes the form as follows:

```
Line number   NAME 'old file name'   AS 'new file name'
```

After line 300 is executed, the name of the new file is changed from KONTO1.DAT to KONTO.DAT. Thus, we still have one file, KONTO.DAT, but its contents are updated.

14.5 CREATING A VIRTUAL FILE

The second method of storing large amounts of data is to use a virtual array. A virtual array can be viewed as a matrix on disk. Each element can be referenced directly. Numerical data are expressed in binary form. While sequential files can be created by the systems program, EDIT, and listed by the systems program, PIP, virtual arrays must be created and displayed under the user's BASIC program.

Example 14.5

Suppose we want to set up a virtual array to retain information about 40 presidents of the United States of America, using each name, starting year of term, and termination year. We want to store the presidents' data in chronological order. The following program will serve this purpose:

```
10        REM THIS PROGRAM IS USED TO CREATE A VIRTUAL FILE
20        REM TO RETAIN THE INFORMATION ABOUT AMERICAN PRESIDENTS
30        OPEN 'PRESDT.DAT' FOR OUTPUT AS FILE 1
40        DIM #1, N$(40)=32,S(40),T(40)
50        FOR X = 1 TO 40
60            N$(X) ="" \ S(X) = 0 \ T(X) = 0
70        NEXT X
80        FOR X = 1 TO 40
90            PRINT "PLEASE ENTER INFORMATION FOR THE";X;"TH PRESIDENT"
100           INPUT "PRESIDENT'S NAME";N$(X)
110           INPUT "STARTING YEAR";S(X)
120           INPUT "TERMINATION YEAR";T(X)
130       NEXT X
140       CLOSE 1
150       END
Ready

RUNNH
PLEASE ENTER INFORMATION FOR THE 1 TH PRESIDENT
PRESIDENT'S NAME? WASHINGTON
STARTING YEAR? 1776
TERMINATION YEAR? 1784
PLEASE ENTER INFORMATION FOR THE 2 TH PRESIDENT
PRESIDENT'S NAME? ADAMS J
STARTING YEAR? 1784
TERMINATION YEAR? 1800
............................
............................
............................
PLEASE ENTER INFORMATION FOR THE 38 TH PRESIDENT
PRESIDENT'S NAME? FORD
STARTING YEAR? 1974
TERMINATION YEAR? 1977
PLEASE ENTER INFORMATION FOR THE 39 TH PRESIDENT
PRESIDENT'S NAME? CARTER
STARTING YEAR? 1977
TERMINATION YEAR? 1981
PLEASE ENTER INFORMATION FOR THE 40 TH PRESIDENT
PRESIDENT'S NAME? REAGAN
STARTING YEAR? 1981
TERMINATION YEAR? 1985

Ready
```

A virtual file can be opened in the same way as a sequential file. The file, PRESDT.DAT, is associated with channel 1 at line 30. The dimension of the virtual array should be defined before we use it. The general format to declare the dimension of a virtual array is

Line number   DIM # channel number, matrix list

$$40 \quad DIM \; \#1, \; N\$(40)=32,S(40),T(40)$$

Statement 40 informs the computer to allocate an array of character strings, N$, and two arrays of numerical elements, S and T. Each array contains 40 elements. The three arrays make up the virtual file, PRESDT.DAT. S array is used to store the starting year, and T the termination year. N$ is the array to store the name of the president. Each element in N$ has a maximum length of 32 characters.[5]

Unlike a regular matrix in memory, the computer will not clear the virtual array automatically. It is advisable to empty the file before putting new information on it.

$$60 \quad N\$(X) = '''' \setminus S(X) = 0 \setminus T(X) = 0$$

blanks out the string variable N$(X), zero numerical variables S(X) and T(X). Since all 40 elements should be cleared, we put this instruction in a loop (line 50 through 70). Now we can start entering data. When lines 100, 110, and 120 are encountered, the president's name, starting year, and termination year should be keyed in from a terminal. The computer takes the information, stores in memory, and then writes it on the right element of the array on the file. For example, when the loop is executed for the sixteenth time the computer will put LINCOLN in N$(16), 1861 in S(16), and 1865 in T(16). The transfer of information from memory to the virtual array is done by the computer automatically, and no PRINT file statement is necessary. The loop was executed 40 times. We closed the virtual file in the same way as a sequential file.

14.6 LISTING A VIRTUAL FILE

We cannot use the system program PIP to examine the contents of a virtual file since numerical data are expressed in binary form. A BASIC program must be written. For example, in order to list 'PRESDT.DAT' file, which looks as follows on the disk:

N$(1)	WASHINGTON
N$(40)	REAGAN
S(1)	1776
S(40)	1981
T(1)	1784
T(40)	1985

---

[5] Strings are allocated with a maximum length in a virtual array. There are nine possible lengths. The programmer can choose one of the following numbers

$$2,4,8,16,32,64,128,256,512$$

Length of the string is defined by placing an equal sign, =, after string matrix notation, for example, A$(10)=64. If the length is not given, 16 will be assumed.

The following program should be used:

Example 14.6

```
10      REM THIS PROGRAM LISTS A VIRTUAL ARRAY
20      OPEN 'PRESDT.DAT' FOR INPUT AS FILE 1
30      DIM #1, N$(40)=32,S(40),T(40)
40      PRINT 'TERM','NAME','STARTING YEAR','TERMINATION YEAR'
50      FOR X = 1 TO 40
60          PRINT X,N$(X),S(X),T(X)
70      NEXT X
80      CLOSE 1
99      END
```

We open the virtual array for input in the same way as a sequential file. At line 30, the structure of the virtual array is declared exactly in the same fashion as it was created. After printing the heading, the loop (lines 50 through 70) prints the records one by one.

$$60 \quad PRINT \ X,N\$(X),S(X),T(X)$$

Statement 60 informs the computer to bring the relevant elements from disk into memory and print it on the terminal. When we reference any element in the virtual array, back and forth swapping of the element's value is automatically done by the computer; no INPUT file statement is necessary for virtual array.

As result of running the above program, the following list is generated:

```
TERM            NAME        STARTING YEAR TERMINATION YEAR
1               WASHINGTON   1776          1784
2               ADAMS J      1784          1800
3               JEFFERSON    1801          1809
4               MADISON      1809          1817

....................
....................
....................

35              KENNEDY      1961          1963
36              JOHNSON L    1963          1969
37              NIXON        1969          1974
38              FORD         1974          1977
39              CARTER       1977          1981
40              REAGAN       1981          1985

Ready
```

14.7 USING A VIRTUAL ARRAY

After the virtual array has been created, it can be accessed randomly. We can reference any item in any record without having read the preceeding records. Thus, access to a virtual array is easier than to a sequential file.

Example 14.7

We have created and listed a virtual array, PRESDT.DAT, in the previous two sections. The following program allows the user to acquire information about a president for a specific term. Since we arranged the president's data in chronological order, we need to enter the ordinal number to specify the term.

```
10      REM THIS PROGRAM ACCESSES A VIRTUAL ARRAY
20      OPEN 'PRESDT.DAT' FOR INPUT AS FILE 1
30      DIM #1, N$(40)=32,S(40),T(40)
40      INPUT 'WHICH PRESIDENT ARE YOU LOOKING FOR';I
50      PRINT "******INFORMATION ABOUT";I;"TH PRESIDENT******"
60      PRINT 'NAME';TAB(25);N$(I)
70      PRINT "STARTING YEAR";TAB(25);S(I)
80      PRINT "TERMINATION YEAR";TAB(25);T(I)
90      CLOSE 1
99      END


RUNNH
WHICH PRESIDENT ARE YOU LOOKING FOR? 16
******INFORMATION ABOUT 16 TH PRESIDENT******
NAME                    LINCOLN
STARTING YEAR           1861
TERMINATION YEAR        1865

Ready
```

If we respond to line 40 with 16 (I=16), when line 60 is encountered, contents of N$(16) will be transferred to memory and printed on the terminal. Line 70 will print S(16) and line 80 T(16). Notice that we didn't need to read in the preceeding 15 records. However, this is not true in sequential files. If data file, PRESDT.DAT, is a sequential file, the following program should be used to make an inquiry.

Example 14.8

```
10      REM THIS PROGRAM ACCESSES A SEQUENTIAL FILE
20      OPEN 'PRESDT.DAT' FOR INPUT AS FILE 1
40      INPUT 'WHICH PRESIDENT YOU ARE LOOKING FOR',I
45      FOR X = 1 TO I-1
46          INPUT #1, N$,S,T
47      NEXT X
48      INPUT #1, N$, S, T
50      PRINT "INFORMATION ABOUT";I;"TH PRESIDENT******"
60      PRINT 'NAME';TAB(25);N$
70      PRINT "STARTING YEAR:";TAB(25);S
80      PRINT "TERMINATION YEAR:";TAB(25);T
90      CLOSE 1
99      END
```

We omitted line 30, since the structure of the sequential file need not be defined. Instead of directly referencing the Ith record, we have to read the preceding I-1 records, which is done by the loop—lines 45, 46, and 47

$$48 \quad \text{INPUT \#1, N\$,S,T}$$

first reads the Ith record.

14.8 UPDATING A VIRTUAL ARRAY

Now, we will describe a situation where a virtual array can be updated randomly. In general, when we wish to change an item on a file, we have to write the new item in the original item's place. While sequential files requires us to rewrite the entire file, virtual arrays allow us to make a selective change without changing any other element in the array.

Example 14.9

Suppose we want to write a program to update the inventory file of a dress department in the ABC company to reflect a sale (transaction). Inventory quantities of various styles and sizes are stored in two-dimensional table form on a virtual file, DRESS.DAT, which appears as follows:

	size		
	1	**2**	**3**
1	10	50	30
2	60	100	20
3	40	55	29
4	45	50	60

style

The following program will achieve this goal:

```
10       REM THIS PROGRAM UPDATES A VIRTUAL ARRAY
20       OPEN 'DRESS.DAT' AS FILE 1
30       DIM #1, D(4,3)
40       INPUT 'DRESS STYLE';I
50       INPUT 'DRESS SIZE';J
60       D(I,J) = D(I,J) - 1
70       CLOSE 1
99       END


RUNNH
DRESS STYLE? 3
DRESS SIZE? 1

Ready
```

We opened the DRESS.DAT file without specifying whether it is FOR INPUT or FOR OUTPUT. Actually, data file, DRESS.DAT, was opened both for input and output. An OPEN statement without input or output destination takes the format as follows:

Line number OPEN 'file name' AS FILE channel number

The OPEN statement causes the computer to search for an existing file. If this fails, a new file will be created. In updating the program, the virtual array should be declared as it was set up. We notice that double subscript virtual arrays can be used in addition to single subscript arrays. The size of this table is defined by

30   DIM #1, D(4,3)

Line 30 informs the computer that the virtual array associated with channel 1 is four rows and three columns. After style code, I, and size code, J, are keyed in (lines 40 and 50), the computer will reduce the value of the item on the Ith row and Jth column of the table by 1. This statement is exactly the same as dealing with a regular table, except that the computer had to bring information back and forth between memory and disk. After one transaction has been recorded, Dress file appears as follows:

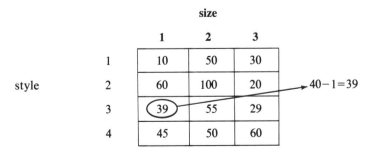

	size		
	1	**2**	**3**
1	10	50	30
2	60	100	20
3	39	55	29
4	45	50	60

style

40−1=39

14.9 OTHER APPLICATIONS OF VIRTUAL ARRAYS

Chapter 11 discusses matrix manipulation in detail. But in many situations we will find the main memory[6] is not capable of accommodating a large matrix. For example, if you key in

10   DIM B(300,300)

after you depress return key, the computer may tell you

?Matrix or array too big at line 10

In this case, matrix B should be defined as a virtual array on disk instead of a matrix in main memory. Let's have an example to show how could a virtual array be used to substitute a large matrix.

Example 14.10

Suppose we want to use a BASIC program to reserve seats in a large auditorium, which has 300 rows, 300 seats each row. The first part of the following program ensures that all seats are empty. Then, when a specific seat is requested, a mark is placed on the relevant cell in the matrix.

```
10        REM THIS PROGRAM HANDLES TICKECT RESERVATION
15        REM ----- INITIALIZE ALL THE SEATS WITH 0 -----
20            OPEN 'SEATS.DAT' AS FILE 1
30            DIM #1, S(300,300)
40            MAT S = ZER
100       REM ----- RESERVE SEATS -----
110           INPUT 'WHAT ROW, SEAT';I,J
120           IF S(I,J) = 0 THEN 130 ELSE 140
130       REM     THEN
132               PRINT 'SEAT IS RESERVED'
134               S(I,J) = 1
136               GO TO 150
140       REM     ELSE
142               PRINT 'SEAT IS NOT EMPTY, ANOTHER CHOICE?'
144               GO TO 110
150       REM ----- END IF 120
155           INPUT 'ANOTHER RESERVATION, YES OR NO'; A$
160           IF A$ = 'YES' THEN 110
170       REM ----- WRAP UP -----
175           CLOSE 1
999       END


RUNNH
WHAT ROW, SEAT? 4,10
SEAT IS RESERVED
ANOTHER RESERVATION, YES OR NO? YES
WHAT ROW, SEAT? 19,25
SEAT IS RESERVED
ANOTHER RESERVATION, YES OR NO? YES
WHAT ROW, SEAT? 4,10
SEAT IS NOT EMPTY, ANOTHER CHOICE?
WHAT ROW, SEAT? 5,10
SEAT IS RESERVED
ANOTHER RESERVATION, YES OR NO? NO

Ready
```

Virtual arrays not only overcome the limitation of memory capacity but also make the matrix permanent. However, the processing time of virtual arrays is substantially longer than that for matrices, since the elements must be swapped.

---

[6] Maximum size of memory matrix varies from computer to computer.

Binary Files. Numbers stored in binary form rather than in the ASCII code form.

Random Access Files. Interrelated records stored such that access can be effected without a complete search of the file.

Sequential Files. Interrelated records stored in a logical, sequential order.

Virtual Files. Interrelated records stored on disk that are accessible on a random basis.

1. What is a file? Why should a data file be used?

2. What are the differences between a sequential file and a random access file? Under which circumstances would you use a random access file?

3. What are the differences between a display file and a binary file?

4. How can we check the end-of-file condition in a formatted ASCII file?

5. Under which circumstances would you use first-type sequential file, and under which circumstances would you put all data items in a record as an entire string?

6. How can you check the contents of a sequential file to test whether information was written into it correctly? How can you do this to a virtual array?

7. A sequential file named AIR consists of 1,000 records. Each record has five numerical data items, which appear as follows:

   123,4.86,3.985,3.0,12

   23,4.5,333,4.76,2.13

   . . . .

   Write a BASIC program to extract the first and third items from each record of AIR and write them in a new file, WATER.

8. Gallup conducts a poll about a nuclear power plant. Each interviewee responded with a number from 1 to 3 as follows:

   (1) Pro nuclear power plant.

   (2) Against nuclear power plant.

   (3) No opinion.

   All the 10,000 responses are stored in a file named, KILLER. Write a BASIC program to tally the poll result.

9. Assuming two sequential files recording students' GPA of two departments exist. They are ART.DAT and FOREST.DAT. The ART.DAT file looks like this:

   11234,ADAMS,3.12

   11298,BELL,2.56

   12345,BROWN,1.11

   . . . .

File FOREST.DAT looks as follows:

11245,MOORE,4.00

12000,DICKSON,3.88

13000,LIN,2.51

. . . .

In each file, first data field is student's ID; second field, student's name; and third field, GPA. Suppose in each file, student's IDs have been sorted in ascending order. Write a program which merges the two files and creates a new file. (IDs in the new file should also be in ascending order.)

10. Cost information of five products of CALSHU Co. are stored in a file, COST, which appears as follows:

SHOES,1000,12,300,25

BOOT,2500,25,120,40

SANDAL,2000,25,200,50

CLOG,300,3,400,15

SLIPPER,500,5,1000,12

The first data item in the record is product name; second, a fixed cost; third, a variable cost; fourth, units sold; fifth, sale price. If CALSHU Co. considers a product with 20% profit as high profit item, write a program to list all the high profit items.

11. The Dating Service Company maintains a virtual array of information about their members, which appears as follow:

Name	Sex	Age	Height	Interest	Education	Salary	Area	Mate
Ford	M	23	5′11″	Sports	16	25000	LA	Card
Davis	F	19	5′4″	Music	12	8000	OR	Morrin
. . . .								
Tally	F	18	6′4″	Sports	12	7000	LA	NIL

The data file, DATING.DAT, has a capacity of 10,000 records. At present, 5,000 records fill in the file. Write a program to do the following: Every time a new member is accepted, his/her data should be attached to the file. Then, search the file to find his/her most compatible match, who is still available, and write her/his name in the MATE column. (Set up your own criterion to determine the match. If there is more than one, take the first one. If no match is found, write NIL in the MATE element). Then, the mate's record should also be updated. For example, if the following person is newly accepted as a member

Name	Sex	Age	Height	Interest	Education	Salary	Area
Giant	M	20	7'2"	Sports	14	9000	LA

This information should be placed in the 5001th row of the virtual array. After the search, his mate will be TALLY, and Miss TALLY's mate will be changed from NIL to GIANT.

Chapter 15
Batch Processing Mode

Objectives

You will learn:

The concept of batch processing under a time-sharing system.

How to set up a job control file.

How to request the job run.

How to examine the status of your job.

How to obtain the output from batch processing.

15.1 INTRODUCTION TO BATCH PROCESSING MODE

We have learned the techniques for preparing a data file and processing data files in the previous two chapters. Running a large program takes several hours. We certainly do not want to be bound to the terminal during a long run because it wastes your time and deprives others of using the terminal. Fortunately, many computer systems have a SPOOLING capability, which allows batch processing mode. While your program is still running *time-shared* with other jobs, it can be run without the attendance of the programmer. In addition to this advantage, batch processing normally sends the output to a *line printer* which produces faster and better print.

Running a job under batch processing mode involves four phases. They include:

1. Create a BASIC program and data file, if necessary.

2. Use a text editor to set up a job control file.

3. Request a job run by calling the system program, QUE.

4. Obtain the output.

Now, we want to examine all four phases in detail. Chapters 1 through 14 have shown us how to write BASIC programs and create data files. Let's use the following example to illustrate batch processing:

Example 15.1

Suppose we want to write a program to generate a virtual array of 10,000 random numbers; the BASIC program should look as follows:

Program RANDOM.BAS

```
10      REM THIS PROGRAM GENERATES A TABLE OF 10000 RANDOM NUMBERS
20      OPEN 'RANDOM.DAT' FOR OUTPUT AS FILE 1
30      DIM #1, A(10000)
50      FOR X = 1 TO 10000
60          A(X) = RND
70      NEXT X
80      CLOSE 1
99      END
```

SAVE

After the program, RANDOM.BAS, is created; be sure to SAVE it.

15.2 JOB CONTROL FILE TO RUN A BASIC PROGRAM WITHOUT INTERACTIVE INPUT STATEMENT

In order to run a program under batch processing mode, a job control file must be set up which reveals the information about these specific jobs—running a BASIC program; RANDOM.BAS, in this case.

A job control file consists of records of BATCH command, one per line. The general format of a BATCH command looks as follows:

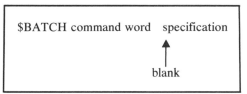

A dollar sign, $, is the first character in a BATCH command record. Immediately following the $ is the BATCH command word. There are about 15 BATCH command words.[1] Each BATCH command word performs a specific function after a blank a list of specifications can be indicated. Let's use the text editor to prepare the neecessary job control file for running the program, RANDOM. This can be done as follows:

```
RUN $EDIT
EDIT    V06C-03A       RSTS V06C-03 CSU Fullerton

#RANDOM.CTL

*I
$JOB
$BASIC RANDOM.BAS/SOURCE
$EOJ

*EX

#^Z

Ready
```

The job control file is called RANDOM.CTL. For the purpose of consistency, we gave the job control file the same name as the BASIC program and use the extension CTL to indicate that this is a job control file. RANDOM.CTL contains the following three records:

$JOB

$BASIC RANDOM.BAS/SOURCE

$EOJ

$JOB is always the first command in a job control file, which marks the beginning of a job. We can place certain specifications after $JOB. The next record in the job control file is

$BASIC RANDOM.BAS/SOURCE

---

[1] Refer to system manual for exact specification of BATCH command words to be used.

which informs the batch processor that the language translator required is BASIC[2] Right after the BATCH command word, BASIC, and a blank, we specified the program's name, RANDOM.BAS, which is a source program.[3] Thus, a slash, \, and the word, SOURCE, follows $BASIC command is equivalent to the system commands OLD and RUN together. $BASIC RANDOM.BAS/SOURCE informs the computer to bring up your old program, RANDOM, from the disk, translate it into maching language, and execute it.

The last record in the job control file is

$EOJ

which marks the end of a job. Both $JOB and $EOJ are necessary for every job control file. Before we explain the next action to be taken for batch processing, we would like to show more examples of job control files.

Example 15.2

Suppose we want to have a program listing printed in addition to the execution of the program. The job control file should appear as follows:

$JOB

$BASIC RANDOM.BAS/SOURCE

LIST

$EOJ

Notice that one more record, LIST, was inserted into the job control file which informs the batch processor to print a listing of the BASIC program and acts as though you typed the BASIC system command word, LIST, on the terminal. Following the BASIC command, any legal BASIC system command can be indicated. While every *BATCH command* must start with a dollar sign, $, no dollar sign is necessary for a *BASIC system command*.

15.3 JOB CONTROL FILE FOR RUNNING A BASIC PROGRAM WITH INTERACTIVE INPUT STATEMENT

In the previous section, we learned how to set up a job control file to run a BASIC program, RANDOM.BAS, which generated 10,000 random numbers. We also explained how to print a listing of this program through batch processing. Note that there was no INPUT statement in this program. This is not always true for other programs. For instance, if we want to leave the total number of random numbers as a variable, the program should appear as follows:

Example 15.3   Program ZUFALL

```
10      REM THIS PROGRAM GENERATES A MAXIMUM OF 10,000 RANDOM NUMBERS
20      OPEN 'RANDOM.DAT' FOR OUTPUT AS FILE 1
30      DIM #1, A(10000)
40      MAT A = ZER      !CLEAR THE VIRTUAL ARRAY
50      INPUT 'HOW NAMY RANDOM NUMBERS  DO YOU WANT';N
60      IF N>10000 THEN PRINT 'MAXIMUM IS 10,000' \ STOP
70      FOR X = 1 TO N
80          A(X) = RND
90      NEXT X
100     CLOSE 1
999     END
```

---

[2]In addition to BASIC, your time-sharing system may have other language compilers, such as FORTRAN, PASCAL.

[3]A source program is a program written in high level language or assembly language which needs to be compiled into an object program (machine language program) before the computer can understand it.

If you run program ZUFALL on the terminal, when line 50 is encountered, you will need to key in the number of random numbers you want (e.g., 5,000). In the case of batch processing (e.g., running your program *off* terminal), there is no interactive dialogue. You need to put all of the responses to all INPUT statement (your input data) in a job control file at one time. Thus, the job control file should use the following format:

ZUFALL.CTL

$JOB

$BASIC ZUFALL.BAS/SOURCE

LIST

$DATA

5000

$EOD

$EOJ

Job control file ZUFALL.CTL is almost the same as RANDOM.CTL except that we added three more records to it:

$DATA

5000

$EOD

$DATA is a BATCH command word, which indicates the following lines are INPUT data to the BASIC program specified above. The INPUT data appear on the job control file in the same sequence as they appear in the BASIC program. $EOD is the BATCH command word to mark the end of the data set. Now, let's use another example of a job control file for a BASIC program with INPUT statements.

Example 15.4

Suppose we want to run a program in batch processing mode. This program will list the principals of any initial deposit for the next 100 years. We INPUT the name of the account holder, initial deposit interest, in the program, SAVING, which looks as follows:

```
10      REM THIS PROGRAM LISTS THE NEW PRINCIPAL FOR 100 YEARS
20      INPUT 'NAME OF ACCOUNT OWNER';N$
30      INPUT 'INITIAL DEPOSIT';P
40      INPUT 'INTEREST RATE';I
50      PRINT FOR X = 1 TO 3
60      PRINT TAB(15); 'ACCOUNT OF ';N$
65      PRINT
70      PRINT 'YEAR                        BALANCE'
75      PRINT
80      F$ = '###                     $###,###.##'
100     FOR X = 1 TO 100
110         P = P*(1+I)
120     PRINT USING F$,X,P
130     NEXT X
199     END
```

In order to run the BASIC program, SAVING, in batch processing mode, the following job control file should be created:

SAVING.CTL

$JOB

$BASIC SAVING.BAS/SOURCE

LIST

$DATA

BOB DEAR

1000

0.06

$EOD

$EOJ

Notice that we listed the INPUT data in the job control file in the same order as it appeared in the program. Keep in mind that we put records in the job control file just as if we keyed in data and system commands on the terminal.

15.4 REQUEST FOR BATCH PROCESSING

To request running a batch job, the system program, QUE, should be used. The QUE program will check the validity of your request and place your request in the "system queue" along with other jobs. When your turn arrives, the BATCH processor will execute your job. This can be compared to handing your card deck to the operator in a *real* batch system. In order to issue a request for running the random number program illustrated in Section 15., calling the QUE program and file specification requires the following format:

```
RUN $QUE
QUE      V06C-03ABCDEFGH RSTS V06C-03 CSU Fullerton
#Q BA:=RANDOM.CTL
#E

Ready
```

System program QUE was called by keying

RUN $QUE

After a heading line

QUE   V06C-03ABCDEF   RSTS   V06C-03   CSU Fullerton

appeared, the computer will prompt you with a number sign, #. This tells you that QUE is awaiting a QUE command. At this time, you should enter any of the following commands:

Q: Queue a job

L: List status of the queue

E: Exit from the QUE program

M: Modify previous job request

K: Kill a job request

H: Hold a job request

For simplicity, we just use the first three types of QUE commands. The first QUE command should be

#Q BA:=job control file name

The Q command issues a request for batch processing. The colon after BA and equal sign before name of job control file should not be left out. After the return key is pressed, the QUE program will check for syntax errors, search for the job control file specified on the lefthand side of the equal sign, and place this job in the waiting line. If no error is detected, another number sign will appear. You must type an E to get out of the QUE program. In case you make any mistakes in keying the QUE command (for instance if you forgot the equal sign), an error message,

?Illegal input file - BA:RANDOM.CTL(90,199)

will be sent to the terminal. All you need to do now is to retype the Q command.

15.5 CHECK YOUR JOB STATUS

After you have made a request for running your job, you might want to know whether or not your job has been processed or where your job is in the queue. This can be done by:

```
RUN $QUE
QUE      V06C-03ABCDEFGH RSTS V06C-03 CSU Fullerton
#L BA:
BA QUEUE LISTING        14-Jul-80        05:14 PM
UNIT    JOB           S / P      FILES

  O     DEMO   [90,199]/SE:1943
                        S /128/TY:EMB
                              SY :[90,199]DEMO   .CTL

  *     RANDOM[90,199]/SE:1944
                        O /128/TY:EMB
                              SY :[90,199]RANDOM.CTL

#E

Ready
```

Note that the underscored lines are entered by the user. We run the system program QUE again. Instead of typing a Q command, we type a L(ist) command;

#L   BA:

to display the current status of the batch processor. This command causes the QUE program to print the two header lines and then to list all jobs on the queue. At the time we took a snapshot of the queue, there were two jobs. For simplicity, you just need to examine the first word of each line. Thus, we understand a job called DEMO is sending for processing (S), and our job RANDOM was waiting for processing (o).

Now, we are sure that our job is in the waiting line, and you can log-off and leave the terminal.

15.6 OBTAIN YOUR OUTPUT

From time to time you might want to check the progress of your job. What you need to do is repeat the following three lines:[4]

---

[4] In order to check the status of the queue, we don't really need to log into the system. We just need to get onto a terminal and key in the following line:

QU/L BA:

Then, the current status of the queue will be printed on the terminal you are using.

```
RUN $QUE
#L BA:
#E
```

Once your job is no longer in the queue, this tells you whether or not execution of your program was successful. The output can be obtained from two sources:

1. A regular printout from the computer center.[5]

2. A log file in your account.

Both outputs are exactly the same. As a product of batch processing, a log file will be created. One copy is printed through the line printer. You can go to the computer center and obtain your printout. You can also take a look at the log file stored under your account by keying

PIP job name.LOG

For instance, the log file, RANDOM, can be displayed on the terminal by keying

PIP RANDOM.LOG

A log file shows the sequence of batch processing during the course of the job execution. Let's look at the log file, RANDOM.LOG. Remember that the BATCH processor will analyse the BATCH command in the job control file one by one and take the corresponding action if there is no error in that command.[6]

Job control file RANDOM.CTL consists of three records:

```
$JOB
```

```
$BASIC RANDOM.BAS/SOURCE
```

```
$EOJ
```

BATCH program encountered the first command, $JOB, which marked the beginning of a job. What BATCH processor did was to log you in a *pseudo* terminal. You can see the normal log-in procedure on the log file, which is exactly the same as if you were logged on a real terminal. Entries at the left margin indicate the time that line was printed. For example, the BATCH processor started to execute this job at 5 o'clock, 08 minutes, and 25 seconds. The second line on the log file reveals this information;

05:08:25 PM   HELLO

After the log-in procedure, a Ready appeared. BATCH processor started to analyse and execute the next BATCH command:

$BATCH RANDOM.BAS/SOURCE

At first the old program, RANDOM.BAS, was swapped into main memory, and the computer started executing it at

05:08:35 PM

---

[5] While some computer centers sort the printouts by last name, some may sort the printouts by your account number.

[6] If any error in BATCH command is detected, scanning of the remaining BATCH commands will continue, but the job will not be executed.

The run of RANDOM.BAS was completed at

05:08:48 PM   Ready (second Ready on the log file)

```
PIP RANDOM.LOG
------------$JOB
05:08:25 PM  HELLO

05:08:27 PM  RSTS V06C-03 CSU Fullerton  Job 9  KB1  14-Jul-80  05:08 PM
05:08:27 PM  #90/199
05:08:28 PM  Password:
05:08:30 PM  1 other user is logged in under this account


05:08:30 PM            Summer weekend hours for the Computer Center
05:08:30 PM                      are from 10:00am to 6:00pm.




05:08:31 PM  Ready


------------$BASIC RANDOM.BAS/SOURCE
05:08:32 PM  OLD RANDOM.BAS

05:08:34 PM  Ready


05:08:35 PM  RUN
05:08:36 PM  RANDOM  05:08 PM          14-Jul-80

05:08:48 PM  Ready

------------$EOJ
05:08:48 PM  BYE
05:08:50 PM  Confirm? YES
05:08:51 PM  Saved all disk files; 3112 blocks in use
05:08:51 PM  Job 9 User 90,199 logged off KB1 at 14-Jul-80 05:08 PM
05:08:51 PM  1 other user still logged in under this account
05:08:51 PM  System RSTS V06C-03 CSU Fullerton
05:08:51 PM  Run time was 7.8 seconds
05:08:51 PM  Elapsed time was 0 minutes
05:08:51 PM  Good afternoon
```

Since the BASIC program, RANDOM, was used to generate a virtual array of 10,000 random numbers, no output on the terminal was created. No output was printed on the log file.

The third BATCH command, $EOJ, performed a log-off from the pseudo terminal. We can see the BASIC system command BYE, confirm, and the account status on the log file.

Now, let's take a look at the output of the program, SAVING. Remember that there were three INPUT statements in SAVING; namely,

20   INPUT 'NAME OF ACCOUNT OWNER';N$

30   INPUT 'INITIAL DEPOSIT';P

40   INPUT 'INTEREST RATE';I

In order to run this program off the terminal, we put the INPUT data in the job control file. After this job is executed, the output file looks as follows:

```
PIP SAVING.LOG
------------$JOB
02:47:59 PM  HELLO

02:48:02 PM  RSTS V06C-03 CSU Fullerton  Job 9  KB1  10-Apr-79  02:48 PM
02:48:04 PM  #90/199
02:48:06 PM  Password:
02:48:07 PM  1 other user is logged in under this account
02:48:08 PM  One hour time limit 7am to 9pm, every day.




02:48:09 PM  Ready


------------$BASIC SAVING/SOURCE
02:48:10 PM  OLD SAVING.BAS

02:48:14 PM  Ready

02:48:14 PM  LIST
02:48:15 PM  SAVING  02:48 PM        10-Apr-79
02:48:15 PM  10      REM THIS PROGRAM LISTS THE NEW PRINCIPAL FOR 100 YEARS
02:48:15 PM  20      INPUT 'NAME OF ACCOUNT OWNER';N$
02:48:15 PM  30      INPUT 'INITIAL DEPOSIT';P
02:48:15 PM  40      INPUT 'INTEREST RATE';I
02:48:15 PM  50      PRINT : PRINT : PRINT
02:48:15 PM  60      PRINT TAB(15); 'ACCOUNT OF ';N$
02:48:15 PM  65      PRINT
02:48:15 PM  70      PRINT 'YEAR                            BALANCE'
02:48:15 PM  75      PRINT
02:48:15 PM  80      F$ = '###                    $###,###.##'
02:48:15 PM  100     FOR X = 1 TO 100
02:48:15 PM  110     P = P*(1+I)
02:48:15 PM  120     PRINT USING F$,X,P
02:48:15 PM  130     NEXT X
02:48:15 PM  199     END

02:48:15 PM  Ready


02:48:17 PM  RUN
02:48:18 PM  SAVING  02:48 PM        10-Apr-79
------------$DATA
02:48:18 PM  NAME OF ACCOUNT OWNER? BOB DEAR
02:48:19 PM  INITIAL DEPOSIT? 1000
02:48:20 PM  INTEREST RATE? 0.06


02:48:21 PM                      ACCOUNT OF BOB DEAR

02:48:21 PM  YEAR                            BALANCE

02:48:21 PM   1                          $***1,060.00
02:48:22 PM   2                          $***1,123.60
02:48:22 PM   3                          $***1,191.02
02:48:22 PM   4                          $***1,262.48
02:48:22 PM   5                          $***1,338.23
02:48:34 PM  95                          $253,545.00
02:48:34 PM  96                          $268,758.00
02:48:34 PM  97                          $284,883.00
02:48:35 PM  98                          $301,976.00
02:48:35 PM  99                          $320,095.00
02:48:35 PM  100                         $339,300.00

02:48:35 PM  Ready

------------$EOD
------------$EOJ
02:48:35 PM  BYE
02:48:40 PM  Confirm: YES
02:48:44 PM  Saved all disk files; 2764 blocks in use, 236 free
02:48:44 PM  Job 9 User 90,199 logged off KB1 at 10-Apr-79 02:48 PM
02:48:44 PM  1 other user still logged in under this account
02:48:44 PM  System RSTS V06C-03 CSU Fullerton
02:48:44 PM  Run time was 10.6 seconds
02:48:44 PM  Elapsed time was 1 minute
02:48:44 PM  Good afternoon
```

Notice that the lines preceded by a string of dashes ------------- are BATCH commands in the job control file. After the third record, LIST, was analyzed and executed, a listing of the BASIC source program, SAVING, was printed. Then, the computer started running the program at 2:48:17. $DATA brought the data set to respond to the inquiries. When line 20 was encountered, the descriptive words

NAME OF ACCOUNT OWNER?

were printed. The first data line in the job control file was used to answer this question; then 1000 for INITIAL DEPOSIT and 0.06 for INTEREST RATE. The program proceeded just like the normal terminal dialogue. When the loop, line 100 through 130 was executed, a list of new principals for the next 100 years was printed.

Word List

Batch Processing. Processing a large file as a batch or group of records without interaction.

Job Control File. A set of BATCH commands necessary for running a batch job.

Log File. A file created as a product of batch processing which shows the sequence of the batch run.

QUE Program. A system program which places jobs in the system que awaiting execution.

PROBLEMS

1. Explain the reason for using the batch processing mode under a time-sharing system.

2. Set up a job control file to execute a BASIC program BALL.

3. Set up a job control file, OSCAR.CTL, which will execute and list the BASIC program OSCAR.

4. If in a community the number of both sexes are equal, then the probability that in a group of N people there are at least R females will be

$$\sum_{X=0}^{R} \frac{N!}{X! \cdot (N-X)!} \cdot (1/2)^N$$

Given N and R, the Following BASIC program will find the probability for you.

Program   WOMAN

```
100        EXTEND
110        INPUT 'NUMBER OF PEOPLE IN A GROUP';N
120        INPUT 'NUMBER OF FEMALES YOU ARE INTERESTED';R
130        REM ----- LOOP TO CALCULATE PROBABILITY -----
140            P1 = (1/2)**N
150            Y=N \ GOSUB 200 \ NFAC=YFAC
160            FOR X = R TO N
170                Y=X \ GOSUB 200 \ XFAC=YFAC
180                Y=N-X \ GOSUB 200 \ NMINUSXFAC=YFAC
190                PROBABILITY = PROBABILITY + NFAC/(XFAC*NMINUSXFAC)
191            NEXT X
192        PRINT 'PROBABILITY THAT THERE ARE AT LEAST';R;'FEMALES AMONG';
193        PRINT N;'PEOPLE IS';PROBABILITY*P1
194        STOP
200        REM ----- SUBROUTINE TO CALCULATE FACTORIALS -----
210            F = 1
220            IF Y = 0 THEN 299
230            FOR NUMBER = 1 TO Y
240                F = F * NUMBER
250            NEXT NUMBER
299            YFAC = F
310        RETURN
999        END
```

Suppose you are interested in the probability that there are less than 12 females in a group of 30 people. Set up a job control file, so that the program WOMAN can be executed under batch processing mode.

5. Write a QUE command to request running a job PRO13.CTL.

6. After your job, ETHICS, has been submitted for batch processing, explain how can you examine the current status of ETHICS.

7. The TIME.DAT file contains information of 10,000 subscribers. How can you utilize the SPOOLING capability to dump(print) the contents of this sequential file?

8. Professor S wants to make a report for his large BASIC class. His record book carries the information about each student's name, three test scores, grades for 10 lab assignments, and a final project. Professor S also keeps track of each student's attendance. One column of his record book shows the number of times a student has been marked as absent. The maximum score for each test was 100, the lab assignment 10, and the final project 200. He determines the letter grade in the following way:

92% or over	A
80%-92%	B
70%-80%	C
Below 70%	F

In borderline situations (e.g., 2% lower than the next highest grade), he takes attendance into consideration. In order to be moved to an A grade, the student shouldn't have any absences; to a B grade, no more than one absence; to C grade, no more than two absences.

Suppose data of 500 students are stored in an ASCII sequential file, FINAL.DAT, write a BASIC-PLUS program and use the batch processing mode to generate a grade report from file FINAL.DAT.

9. Humboldt State University uses the following form to evaluate teaching effectiveness of their professors:

COURSE CODE ☐☐☐☐☐☐ YEAR ☐☐ NUMBER OF STUDENTS ☐☐☐

(1-6)   (7-8)   (9-11)

EVALUATION OF TEACHING EFFECTIVENESS
HSU SCHOOL OF BUSINESS & ECONOMICS

Place your coded response to each of the following questions in the <u>box</u> provided.

YEAR	CODE	YEAR RESPONSE CODE
Freshman	1	
Sophomore	2	☐ (12)
Junior	3	
Senior	4	
Graduate	5	
Other	6	

QUARTER	CODE	QUARTER RESPONSE CODE
Fall	1	
Winter	2	☐ (13)
Spring	3	
Summer	4	

EXPECTED GRADE IN THIS CLASS	CODE	GRADE RESPONSE CODE
A	7	
B	6	
C	5	☐ (14)
D	4	
F	3	
CR	2	
NC	1	
INC	0	

IS THIS COURSE REQUIRED OR AN ELECTIVE?	CODE	REQUIRED/ELECTIVE CODE
Required	1	☐ (15)
Elective	2	

IS THIS COURSE WITHIN YOUR		MAJOR/MINOR RESPONSE CODE
Major	1	
Minor	2	☐ (16)
Other	3	

	STRONGLY AGREE	AGREE	NEUTRAL	DISAGREE	STRONGLY DISAGREE	RESPONSE
HAS COMMAND OF THE SUBJECT	1	2	3	4	5	☐ (17)
EXPRESSES HIMSELF OR HERSELF CLEARLY	1	2	3	4	5	☐ (18)
ENCOURAGES STUDENT QUESTIONS & DISCUSSION	1	2	3	4	5	☐ (19)
IS INTERESTED IN STUDENTS AS PERSONS	1	2	3	4	5	☐ (20)
IS ENTHUSIASTIC ABOUT TEACHING	1	2	3	4	5	☐ (21)
MAKES THE COURSE MATERIAL MEANINGFUL	1	2	3	4	5	☐ (22)
PRESENTS MATERIAL IN AN ORGANIZED MANNER	1	2	3	4	5	☐ (23)
GIVES ASSIGNMENTS THAT AID LEARNING	1	2	3	4	5	☐ (24)
IS FAIR AND IMPARTIAL IN GRADING	1	2	3	4	5	☐ (25)
IS READILY AVAILABLE FOR CONSULTATION	1	2	3	4	5	☐ (26)

PLEASE RATE THE <u>OVERALL</u> TEACHING EFFECTIVENESS OF THIS INSTRUCTOR IN THIS CLASS:

1 EXCELLENT: 2 ABOVE AVERAGE: 3 AVERAGE: 4 BELOW AVERAGE: 5 POOR: ☐ (27)

IN COLLEGE I HAVE HAD APPROXIMATELY _____ INSTRUCTORS,   NUMBER   ☐☐☐ (28-9-30)

AND THIS INSTRUCTOR RANKS NUMBER _____ . #1 RANKS HIGHEST.   RANK   ☐☐☐ (31-2-33)

PLEASE COMPLETE THE BACK SIDE OF THIS FORM   INSTRUCTOR
(DO NOT COMPLETE 34-35 BOXES)   NUMERIC CODE   ☐☐ (34-35)

4,000 forms have been filled out by the student in last quarter. Responses of the forms are stored in a formatted ASCII file, TEVAL.DAT. Each response was represented in the file as a 35 character long string, which looks as follows:

170020780252362212221221212030010	17002078025235

Take the necessary action to generate a statistical report for each evaluation item (items 17 to 27) Report of each item should look like the following:

Has command of the subject		
Distribution table		
Rating	**Absolute frequency**	**Relative frequency**
1	XXXX	X.XX
2	XXXX	X.XX
3	XXXX	X.XX
4	XXXX	X.XX
5	XXXX	X.XX
Total	XXXX	X.XX

Median =   X

Mode   =   X

Mean   =   X.XX

Standard deviation =   X.XX

Note: Your program should include the feature to check data error.

Appendix A
BASIC-PLUS Error Messages

Illegal file name	The file name specified is not acceptable. It contains unacceptable characters, or the file name specification format has been violated.
Cannot find file or account	Although the syntax or format of the file specification was correct, the file specified was not found. Check for spelling errors.
Protection violation	The user has attempted to read or write operation on a file which excludes him because of a particular protection code. If the user has attempted a cross-account reference, there is no recommended action. If the file is in his account, he may use the NAME AS command to change the protection code.
End of file on device	The user has exhausted the data in the file but is continuing to attempt to read, or else is attempting to load a BASIC-PLUS source which contains no END statement.
Name or account now exists	An attempt was made to rename or save a file which already exists. Try REPLACE or create a new file name.
Matrix or array too big	In-core array size too large. Redimension.
Line too long	Attempt to input a line longer than 255 characters (which includes any line terminator).
Floating point factor	Attempt to use a computed floating point number outside the range $1E-38 < n < 1E38$ excluding zero. If no transfer to an error handling routine is made, zero is returned as the floating point value.
Data format error	A READ or INPUT statement detected data in an illegal format; that is, violated rules for forming real, integer, or string constants.
Integer error	Attempt to use a computed integer outside the range $-32768 < n < 32767$.
Subscript out of range	Attempt to reference an array element beyond the number of elements created for the array when it was dimensioned.
Out of data	A READ instruction is attempted, but all items in the DATA list have been read.
On statement out of range	The index value in an ON-GOTO or ON-GOSUB statement is less than one or greater than the number of line numbers in the list.

Not enough data in record	An INPUT statement did not find enough data in one line to satisfy all the specified variables.
Division by zero	Attempt by the user program to divide some quantity by zero. If no transfer is made to an error handler routine, a zero is returned as the result.
Illegal expression	Double operators, missing operators, mismatched parentheses, or some similar error has been found in an expression.
Illegal mode mixing	String and numeric operations cannot be mixed.
Inconsistent sub-scripted user	A subscripted variable is being used with a different number of dimensions from the number with which it was originally dimensioned.
Literal string needed	A variable name was used where a number or character string was necessary.
Modifier error	Attempt to use one of the statement modifiers (FOR, WHILE, UNTIL, IF or UNLESS) incorrectly.
Number is needed	A character string or variable name was used where a number was required.
Statement not found	Reference is made within the program to a line number which is not within the program.
Stop	STOP statement was executed. The user can usually continue program execution by typing CONT and the RETURN key.
String is needed	A number or variable name was used where a character string was necessary.
What?	Command or immediate mode statement could not be processed. Illegal verb or improper format error most likely.
Bad line number pair	Line numbers specified in a LIST or DELETE command were formatted incorrectly.
Bad number in PRINT-USING	Format specified in the PRINT-USING string cannot be used to print one or more values.
End of statement not seen	Statement contains too many elements to be processed correctly.
File exists-RENAME/REPLACE	A file of the name specified in a SAVE command already exists. In order to save the current program under the name specified, use REPLACE or RENAME followed by SAVE.
FOR without NEXT	A FOR statement was encountered in the user program without a corresponding NEXT statement to terminate the loop.
Illegal conditional clause	Incorrectly formatted conditional expression.

Illegal expression	Double operators, missing operators, mismatched parentheses, or some similar error has been found in an expression.
Illegal IF statement	Incorrectly formatted IF statement.
Illegal line number(s)	Line number reference outside the range $1 < n < 32767$.
Illegal mode mixing	String and numeric operations cannot be mixed.
Illegal statement	Attempt was made to execute a statement that did not compile without errors.
Illegal verb	The BASIC verb portion of the statement cannot be recognized.
NEXT without FOR	A NEXT statement was encountered in the user program without a previous FOR statement having been seen.
ON statement needs GOTO	A statement beginning with ON does not contain a GOTO or GOSUB clause.
Please say HELLO	Message printed by the LOGIN system program. User not logged into the system has typed something other than a legal, logged-out command to the system.
PRINT-USING format error	An error was made in the construction of the string used to supply the output format in a PRINT-USING statement.
RETURN without GOSUB	RETURN statement encountered in user program without a previous GOSUB statement having been executed.

Note: Error messages and systems commands used by permission of Digital Equipment Corporation.

Appendix B
System Commands for the RSTS System.

Command	Explanation
BYE	Indicates that a user wishes to leave the terminal.
CAT	Returns the user's file directory.
CONT	Allows the user to continue execution of the program currently in core, following the execution of a STOP statement or the typing of a CTRL/C.
DELETE	Allows the user to remove one or more lines from the program currently in core. Following the word DELETE, the user types the line number of the single line to be deleted or two line numbers separated by a hyphen, indicating the first and last lines of the section of code to be removed.
LIST	Allows the user to obtain a printed listing at the user terminal of the program currently in core, or one or more lines of that program. The word LIST by itself will cause the listing of the entire user program. LIST followed by one line number will list that line; and LIST followed by two line numbers separated by a hyphen will list the lines between and including the lines indicated.
LISTNH	Same as LIST, but does not print header containing the program name and current date.
NEW	Clears the user's area in core and allows the user to input a new program from the terminal. A program name can be indicated following the word NEW or when the system requests it.
OLD	Clears the user's area in core and allows the user to recall a saved program. The user can indicate a program name following the word OLD or when the system requests it.
RENAME	Causes the name of the program currently in core to be changed to the name specified after the word RENAME.
REPLACE	Same as SAVE, but allows the user to substitute a new program with the same name for an old program, erasing the old program.
RUN	Allows the user to begin execution of the program currently in core. The word RUN can be followed

by a file name in which case the file is loaded
from the system disk, compiled, and run.

RUNNH

Same as RUN, but does not print header containing
the program name and current date.

SAVE

Causes the program currently in core to be saved on
the system disc under its current file name with
the extension .BAS. When the word SAVE is followed by a file name, the program in core is
saved under the name given.

UNSAVE

The word UNSAVE is followed by the file name and
extension of the file to be removed. If no extension is specified, .BAS. is assumed.

SPECIAL TERMINAL KEYBOARD CONTROL CHARACTERS

The following control characters are found on timesharing terminal keyboards. They may be
used to perform the described functions:

Command	Explanation
RETURN key	Enters a typed line to the system; results in a carriage return/line feed operation at the user terminal.
LINE FEED key	Used to continue the current logical line on an additional physical line (i.e., BASIC continuation). Performs a carriage return/line feed operation. (Maximum 255 characters)
RUBOUT KEY	Deletes the last character typed on that physical line. Erased characters are indicated on hardcopy terminals between backslashes.
CTRL/C	Causes the system to return to BASIC command mode to allow issuing additional commands or editing.
CTRL/U	Deletes the current typed line.
CTRL/S	Stall. Delays output to the terminal until control Q is transmitted. This command is especially useful for viewing CRT output.

Appendix C
Text Editor TECO

TECO is the most powerful text editor used by most of the PDP 11 computers. TECO is both versatile and complex. The beginner only needs to learn the basic set of the TECO commands which is sufficient for any editing application, although it is sometimes less convenient.

The fundamental concept of TECO is the same as EDIT. The input file is read into the buffer. Insertions, deletions, and changes can be made by moving the position pointer and specifying the change command. The edited text is then written onto the output file. The following illustration shows this situation:

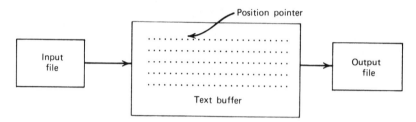

Calling the text editor TECO can be achieved by typing

RUN $TECO

under the RSTS system. After TECO is called in, an asterisk, *, is printed which indicates that TECO is awaiting the editing commands. The TECO command should then be specified subsequentially. TECO commands can be classified into the following six categories:

1. File specification commands:

Command	Function
ER<file name>$	ER command designates the input file, every TECO command has to be terminated by an escape[1], which echoes as a dollar sign.
EW<file name>$	EW specifies the output file.
EX$	move the remainder of the current input file, close the output file.

Each command line should be terminated by two escapes. More than one command can be specified on one line. For example,

*ERMYFILE$$
*EWURFILE$$

specifies MYFILE as the input file and URFILE as the output file. The two command lines can be placed together as one command line:

---

[1] The escape key is labelled as ESC on some terminals and ALT on others.

*ERMYFILE$EWURFILE$$

When a new file is created, no input file specification should be made. When we desire to examine a file without making permanent changes, no output file needs to be specified. The EX$ command should be included at the end of each editing session. For example, the following command line will copy the content of MYFILE onto URFILE:

*ERMYFILE$EWURFILE$EX$$

2. Input and output commands:

Y	Clear the text buffer and then read the next page[2] of the input file into the buffer.
P	Write the contents of the text buffer onto the next page of the output file; then, clear the buffer and read the next page of the input file into the buffer.
nP	Execute P command n times. n must be a positive integer.

3. Pointer positioning commands:

J		Move the pointer to the beginning of the text buffer.
nL	n>0	Move the position pointer to the beginning of the nth line, following the current position pointer.
	n=0	Move the position pointer to the beginning of the line on which it is currently positioned.
	n<0	Move the position pointer backward n lines.
nC	n>0	Advance the pointer n characters forward
	n<0	Backward the pointer n characters.

4. Print command:

nT	n>0	Print n lines. If n = 1, the content of the text buffer from the current position of pointer through the end of the line is printed.
	n=0	The content of the text buffer from the beginning of the line on which the pointer is located up to the pointer is printed.
	n<0	The n lines preceeding the pointer are printed.
	n=H	The entire content of the text buffer is printed.
V		The entire current line is printed.

---

[2] TECO considers text to be any string of ASCII codes. Text is broken down into pages, lines, and characters. A page consists of all ASCII characters between tow form feeds, a line consists of all ASCII characters between two line feed characters.

5. Text modification commands:

nK	n>0	n lines following the position pointer are deleted.
	n=0	The content of the text buffer from the beginning of the line on which the pointer is located up to the pointer is deleted.

nK $\begin{cases} n<0 \\ n=H \end{cases}$

n<0 — n lines preceeding the pointer are deleted.

n=H — The entire text buffer is deleted.

nD $\begin{cases} n>0 \\ n<0 \end{cases}$

n>0 — Delete n characters following the pointer.

n<0 — Delete n characters preceeding the pointer.

I<text>$[3]   Insert the text at the place where the pointer is located.

6. Search commands:

S<text>$ Search for the first occurence of the text specified. If the text is found, the pointer is positioned after the last character in the text. If it is not found, the pointer is positioned at the beginning of the buffer and an error message is printed.

N<text>$ Performs the same function as S command except that if the text is not found in the current page, next page is read-in and the search is continued.

The following examples illustrate how to use the TECO.

---

[3] Keep in mind that a dollar sign, $, indicates an escape key.

Example 1   Creating a New File[4]—LETTER

```
RUN $TECO
*EWLETTER$$  ◄──────────────────── specifying 'LETTER' as output file
*HKIMR. JOHN SMITH  ◄───────────── clearing the entire buffer and
1250 FREEDOM AVE.                  insert text
FULLERTON, CALIFORNIA

DEAR MR. SMITH:

I WAS PLEASED TO RECEIVE YOUR INQUIRY ABOUT
OUR DEPARTMENT IN MANAGEMENT INFORMATION
SYSTEMS.

ENCLOSED IS A BOOKLET ABOUT CALIFORNIA
STATE UNIVERSITY, FULLERTON AND A BROSCHURE
OF OUR MIS PROGRAM, WHICH SHOULD ANSWER
ALL OF YOUR QUESTIONS.

SINCERELY,


DR. LAWRENCE JONES, CHAIR
$$  ◄────────────────────────────── terminating text insertion
*JSNIA$I 92634$$  ◄───────────────── moving pointer back to the beginning of change
FULLERTON, CALIFORNIA^                buffer and insert zip code
*STMENT$-10C10DIPROGRAM$$ ◄─────
OUR DEPARTMENT^ IN MANAGEMENT INFORMATION
*3L14C7DICATALOGUE$$  ◄───────────── change 'BOOKLET' to 'CATALOGUE'
*SBROS$-CD$$ ◄───────────────────── delete 'S' from 'BROSCHURE'
STATE UNIVERSITY, FULLERTON AND A BROS^CHURE
*SERELY$0KIVERY TRULY YOURS$$ ◄──── change 'SINCERELY' to 'VERY TRULY YOURS'
SINCERELY^,
*HT$$  ◄──────────────────────────── list text buffer
MR. JOHN SMITH
1250 FREEDOM AVE.
FULLERTON, CALIFORNIA 92634

DEAR MR. SMITH:

I WAS PLEASED TO RECEIVE YOUR INQUIRY ABOUT
OUR PROGRAM IN MANAGEMENT INFORMATION
SYSTEMS.

ENCLOSED IS A CATALOGUE ABOUT CALIFORNIA
STATE UNIVERSITY, FULLERTON AND A BROCHURE
OF OUR MIS PROGRAM, WHICH SHOULD ANSWER
ALL OF YOUR QUESTIONS.

VERY TRULY YOURS,


DR. LAWRENCE JONES, CHAIR
*EX$$  ◄──────────────────────────── exit from TECO

Ready
```

---

[4] Lines underscored are typed by the user.

Example 2   Modifying the Old File—LETTER

```
RUN $TECO
*ERLETTER$EWKB:$$          ←——————— SPECIFY "LETTER" as input file and
*Y5KIMS, JUDY ALLEN                    designate the output to keyboard
2009 WOODS DR.             ←——————— read text in and replace the address
ARLINGTON, TEXAS 75010

DEAR MS. ALLEN:
$$
*HT$$
MS. JUDY ALLEN
2009 WOODS DR.
ARLINGTON, TEXAS 75010

DEAR MS. ALLEN:

I WAS PLEASED TO RECEIVE YOUR INQUIRY ABOUT
OUR PROGRAM IN MANAGEMENT INFORMATION
SYSTEMS.

ENCLOSED IS A CATALOGUE ABOUT CALIFORNIA
STATE UNIVERSITY, FULLERTON AND A BROCHURE
OF OUR MIS PROGRAM, WHICH SHOULD ANSWER
ALL OF YOUR QUESTIONS.

VERY TRULY YOURS,



DR. LAWRENCE JONES, CHAIR
*EX$$                     ←——————————————— exit from TECO
MS. JUDY ALLEN
2009 WOODS DR.
ARLINGTON, TEXAS 75010

DEAR MS. ALLEN:

I WAS PLEASED TO RECEIVE YOUR INQUIRY ABOUT
OUR PROGRAM IN MANAGEMENT INFORMATION
SYSTEMS.
                                           current content of
ENCLOSED IS A CATALOGUE ABOUT CALIFORNIA   the text buffer is listed
STATE UNIVERSITY, FULLERTON AND A BROCHURE ←——— at the end of editing
OF OUR MIS PROGRAM, WHICH SHOULD ANSWER
ALL OF YOUR QUESTIONS.

VERY TRULY YOURS,



DR. LAWRENCE JONES, CHAIR

Ready
```

All those underlined were keyed by the user.

Appendix D
Record I/O

Record I/O is the most sophisticated method of file handling in BASIC-PLUS. It allows random access of data and intermixing of string and numeric elements, the weakness of formatted ASCII and virtual array, respectively. The following statements are used to handle Record I/O files:

1. Statement to open the file:

> Line number   OPEN 'file name' for   INPUT / OUTPUT   AS FILE channel number

FOR INPUT specifies an existing file as input file; FOR OUTPUT specifies creation of a new file. Channel number should be an integer between 1 and 12.

2. Statement to close a file:

> Line number   CLOSE channel number

While the CLOSE statement for ASCII file and virtual array causes the final record of the file to be written before closing file, Record I/O does not. Be sure to write the last record onto a Record I/O file before closing the file.

3. Statement to read record from the file:

> Line number   GET # channel number,   RECORD expression

GET statement reads one record into the I/O buffer, which was associated with the channel by the OPEN statement. If the RECORD option is not specified, the GET statement places the next sequential record from the file in the I/O buffer.

4. Statement to write to a file:

> Line number   PUT # channel number,   RECORD expression

PUT statement writes content of the I/O buffer, which was associated with the channel by the OPEN statement, on the file. If the RECORD option is not specified, the PUT statement writes content of I/O buffer on the next sequential record of the file.

5. Statement to define fields of a record:

> Line number, FIELD # channel number,   expression AS string var

The phrase *expression AS string var* can be repeated and separated by commas, if there is more than one field in the record. FIELD statement allows us to divide the I/O buffer into string locations, whose order should match the layout of the fields on record. For example, if each record in a RECORD I/O file consists of two fields, Name (20 characters) and address (30 characters), the following statements will read the first name and first address into N$ and A$ in I/O buffer associated with channel number 3:

    10   OPEN 'FILE1' FOR OUTPUT AS FILE 3

    20   FIELD #3, 20 AS N$, 30 AS A$

    30   GET #3, RECORD 1

6. Statement to place a string in a field of I/O buffer:

> Line number LSET string var = string

> Line number RSET string var = string

Both LSET and RSET statement are used to change the values of a field in the I/O buffer. LSET will assign a string to the string var designated at the left side of equal sign; the string is left justified. RSET performs the same function as LSET, except that the string is right justified. For example, if we add

40   LSET N$ = 'CHEN'

Field N$ of I/O buffer associated with channel 3 will be replaced by CHEN. The unused spaces will be padded by blanks.

7. Statement to convert the storage format of a numeric field: All the numeric data are stored on a RECORD I/O file floating-point form, which takes up 4 bytes. Hence, a back and forth conversion is necessary when numeric data are manipulated in the memory. After a numeric item was read into the I/O buffer, the following statement should be used to map the four-character string to a floating-point number on which the arithmetic operations can first be performed.

> Line number var = CVT$F(string var)

Before a numeric item can be placed in the I/O buffer for the purpose of output, it must be converted from floating-point storage form to a four-character string. The following statement is necessary:

> Line number string var = CVTF$(var)

The following examples illustrate procedure of using Record I/O:

Example 1: Creating a Record I/O File

```
100       REM ***************************************************
110       REM *                                               *
120       REM * PROGRAM TO CREATE A RECORD I/O FILE           *
130       REM * RECORDS IN THE FILE ARE DESIGNED AS           *
132       REM *   FIELD NAME      LENGTH      CONTENT          *
134       REM *   IONAME$          20          NAME            *
135       REM *   IODEPARTMENT$     3          DEPARTMENT CODE *
136       REM *   IOHOUR$           4          HOURS WORKED    *
137       REM *   IORATE$           4          RATE            *
138       REM *   IOGROSS$          4          GROSS PAY       *
139       REM *   IOWIHHOLDING$     4          WITHHOLDING     *
140       REM *   IONET$            4          NET PAY         *
142       REM *                                               *
144       REM *   FIRST 4 FIELDS IN THE RECORD WILL BE FILLED *
146       REM *   THROUGH TERMINAL INPUT                      *
147       REM *   THE LAST 3 FIELDS WILL BE BLANKED OUT IN    *
148       REM *   THIS PROGRAM AND RESERVED FOR LATER USAGE   *
149       REM *                                               *
150       REM ***************************************************
155       EXTEND
160       OPEN 'WAGE' FOR OUTPUT AS FILE 1
170       FIELD #1, 20 AS IONAME$, 3 AS IODEPARTMENT$, 4 AS IOHOUR$,
                    4 AS IORATE$, 4 AS IOGROSS$, 4 AS IOWITHHOLDING$,
                    4 AS IONET$
180       PRINT 'ENTER DATA FOR THE FIRST 4 FIELDS OF A PAYROLL RECORD'
190       PRINT 'AT END TYPE DUMMY FOR NAME'
200       REM ----- LOOP TO ENTER DATA -----
210          INPUT 'NAME';NAME1$
220          FOR X = 1 UNTIL NAME1$ = 'DUMMY'
230             INPUT 'DEPARTMENT';DEPARTMENT$
240             INPUT 'HOURS WORKED';HOUR
250             INPUT 'HOURLY RATE';RATE
260             LSET IONAME$ = NAME1$
270             LSET IODEPARTMENT$ = DEPARTMENT$
280             LSET IOHOUR$ = CVTF$(HOUR)
290             LSET IORATE$ = CVTF$(RATE)
300             LSET IOGROSS$ = SPACE$(4)
310             LSET IOWITHHOLDING$ = SPACE$(4)
320             LSET IONET$ = SPACE$(4)
330             PUT #1, RECORD X
340             INPUT 'NAME';NAME1$
350          NEXT X
370       PRINT \ PRINT 'END OF DATA ENTRY'
380       PRINT 'TOTAL NUMBER OF RECORDS IS'; X-1
999       END
```

Example 2: Modifying and Displaying a Record I/O File

```
100     REM *********************************************************
110     REM *                                                       *
120     REM * THIS PROGRAM WILL LIST A RECORD I/O FILE AND          *
130     REM * MAKE CORRECTION ON THE RECORDS                        *
140     REM *                                                       *
150     REM *********************************************************
200     EXTEND
205     ON ERROR GO TO 300
210     OPEN 'WAGE' AS FILE 1
220     FIELD #1, 20 AS IONAME$, 3 AS IODEPARTMENT$, 4 AS IOHOUR$,
                4 AS IORATE$, 4 AS IOGROSS$, 4 AS IOWITHHOLDING$,
                4 AS IONET$
230     F1$ = 'REC NO.  NAME          DEPARTMENT    HOURS    RATE'
240     F2$ = '  ##       \             \  \         ##     ##.##'
250     PRINT \ PRINT F1$        !PRINT HEADER
260     REM ------- LOOP TO DISPLAY WAGE FILE -------
280         FOR X = 1 TO 1000
282             GET #1
284             NAME1$ = IONAME$
286             DEPARTMENT$ = IODEPARTMENT$
288             HOUR = CVT$F(IOHOUR$)
290             RATE = CVT$F(IORATE$)
292             PRINT USING F2$, X,NAME1$,DEPARTMENT$,HOUR,RATE
295         NEXT X
300     IF ERR <> 11 THEN PRINT 'OTHER ERROR OCCURS'
310     CLOSE #1
500     REM ------- CORRECTION ERRORS IN THE FILE ------
510     OPEN 'WAGE' AS FILE 1
520     FIELD #1, 20 AS IONAME$, 3 AS IODEPARTMENT$, 4 AS IOHOUR$,
                4 AS IORATE$, 4 AS IOGROSS$, 4 AS IOWITHHOLDING$,
                4 AS IONET$
525     PRINT
530     INPUT 'DO YOU WANT TO MAKE ANY CHANGE OF THE FILE';A$
540     IF A$ <> 'YES' THEN 700
550     FOR Y = 1 UNTIL A$ <> 'YES'
560         INPUT 'WHICH RECORD YOU WANT TO CHANGE',X
570         GET #1, RECORD X
580         PRINT 'INPUT CORRECT DATA FOR RECORD';X
582         INPUT 'NAME';NAME1$
584         INPUT 'DEPARTMENT';DEPARTMENT$
586         INPUT 'HOURS';HOUR
588         INPUT 'RATE';RATE
590         LSET IONAME$ = NAME1$
592         LSET IODEPARTMENT$ = DEPARTMENT$
594         LSET IOHOUR$ = CVTF$(HOUR)
596         LSET IORATE$ = CVTF$(RATE)
598         PUT #1, RECORD X
600         INPUT 'ANOTHER CHANGE, YES OR NO';A$
620     NEXT Y
700     CLOSE 1
999     END
```

```
RUNNH

REC NO.  NAME          DEPARTMENT    HOURS    RATE
    1    BRYAN B.         401          35     6.25
    2    VINOKUR P.       401          40     7.00
    3    WARREN A.        401          45     6.15
    4    SELLERS F.       401          30     9.25
    5    RALSTON          555          15    10.60
    6    SCHUBERT         555          20     5.50
    7    HIGHTOWER T.     506          35     6.90
    8    WARD B.          605          10     3.50

DO YOU WANT TO MAKE ANY CHANGE OF THE FILE? YES
WHICH RECORD YOU WANT TO CHANGE            ? 7
INPUT CORRECT DATA FOR RECORD 7
NAME? HIGHTOWER T.
DEPARTMENT? 605
HOURS? 35
RATE? 6.9
ANOTHER CHANGE, YES OR NO? NO

Ready
```

Example 3: Updating and Writing Report from a Record I/O File

```
100      REM *********************************************************
110      REM *                                                       *
120      REM *   THIS PROGRAM WILL CALCULATE THE GROSS PAY, WITHHOLDING *
130      REM *   AND NET PAY FOR EACH EMPLOYEE AND STORE THE PAY INFO *
140      REM *   IN WAGE FILE. FOR THE SAKE OF SIMPLICITY, OVERTIME PAY *
150      REM *   IS TIME-AND-HALF AND THE WITHHOLDING IS 30% OF THE GROSS *
160      REM *                                                       *
170      REM *   LATER A REPORT WILL BE GENERATED TO SHOW THE PAY INFO *
190      REM *                                                       *
199      REM *********************************************************
200      EXTEND
205      ON ERROR GO TO 400
210      OPEN 'WAGE' AS FILE 1
220      FIELD #1, 20 AS IONAME$, 3 AS IODEPARTMENT$, 4 AS IOHOUR$,
                  4 AS IORATE$, 4 AS IOGROSS$, 4 AS IOWITHHOLDING$,
                  4 AS IONET$
230      REM ----- INITIALIZE THE TOTAL COUNTERS -----
245          TOTAL.HOUR = 0
246          TOTAL.GROSS = 0
247          TOTAL.WITHHOLDING = 0
248          TOTAL.NET = 0
250      REM ----- SET PRINTING FORMAT AND HEADERS -----
252          F1$ = 'NAME            DEPT   HOURS RATE   GROSS     WITHHOLD. NET'
254          F2$ = '\               \  \ \     ##  ##.## ###.##    ###.##   ###.##'
256          F3$ = 'TOTAL               ###        #,###.## #,###.## #,###.##'
280      PRINT TAB(15);'S U N N Y    C O M P A N Y'
282      PRINT \PRINT
284      PRINT F1$ \ PRINT
300      REM ----- MAIN LOOP TO PROCESS RECORDS ------
310          FOR X = 1 TO 1000
320              GET #1, RECORD X
330              GOSUB 500          !MAP NUMERIC FIELDS
340              GOSUB 600          !MAKE PAY CALCULATION
350              GOSUB 685          !WRITE RECORDS
399          NEXT X
400      REM ----- END OF FILE -----
410          IF ERR = 11 THEN RESUME 450
                      ELSE PRINT 'OTHER ERROR OCCURS'\
                           CLOSE 1\
                           STOP
450          GOSUB 700              !DISPLAY TOTAL
470          CLOSE 1
499          STOP
500      REM ----- SUBROUTINE TO MAP NUMERIC FIELDS -----
510          HOUR = CVT$F(IOHOUR$)
520          RATE = CVT$F(IORATE$)
525      RETURN
600      REM ----- SUBROUTINE TO MAKE CALCULATION -----
610          IF HOUR <= 40 THEN GROSS = HOUR * RATE
                      ELSE GROSS = 40*RATE + (HOUR-40)*RATE*1.5
620          WITHHOLDING = GROSS *0.3
630          NET = GROSS - WITHHOLDING
640          TOTAL.HOUR = TOTAL.HOUR + HOUR
650          TOTAL.GROSS = TOTAL.GROSS + GROSS
660          TOTAL.WITHHOLDING = TOTAL.WITHHOLDING + WITHHOLDING
670          TOTAL.NET = TOTAL.NET + NET
680      RETURN
685      REM ----- SUBROUTINE TO WRITE RECORDS -----
687          PRINT USING F2$, IONAME$, IODEPARTMENT$,HOUR,RATE,GROSS,
                           WITHHOLDING,NET
689          IOGROSS$ = CVTF$(GROSS)
691          IOWITHHOLDING$ = CVTF$(WITHHOLDING)
695          IONET$ = CVTF$(NET)
697          PUT #1, RECORD X
699      RETURN
700      REM ----- SUBROUTINE TO PRINT TOTAL -----
705          PRINT
710          PRINT USING F3$, TOTAL.HOUR,TOTAL.GROSS, TOTAL.WITHHOLDING,
                  TOTAL.NET
720      RETURN
999      END
```

```
RUNNH
             S U N N Y    C O M P A N Y


NAME          DEPT   HOURS RATE   GROSS     WITHHOLD. NET

BRYAN B.       401    35    6.25  218.75     65.63    153.13
VINOKUR P.     401    40    7.00  280.00     84.00    196.00
WARREN A.      401    45    6.15  292.13     87.64    204.49
SELLERS F.     401    30    9.25  277.50     83.25    194.25
RALSTON        555    15   10.60  159.00     47.70    111.30
SCHUBERT       555    20    5.50  110.00     33.00     77.00
HIGHTOWER T.   605    35    6.90  241.50     72.45    169.05
WARD B.        605    10    3.50   35.00     10.50     24.50

TOTAL                230         1,613.88   484.16  1,129.71
Stop at line 499

Ready
```

Appendix E
File Handling with BASIC-PLUS-2

BASIC-PLUS-2 also handles three types of files, namely:

1. ASCII sequential file.

2. Virtual array.

3. Record I/O.

The statements for handling virtual arrays in BASIC-PLUS-2 are the same as BASIC-PLUS. For ASCII sequential files, BASIC-PLUS-2 has more powerful features than BASIC-PLUS. The following are ASCII file handling statements in BASIC-PLUS-2:

1. Statement to open the file:

> Line number OPEN file name FOR $\frac{\text{INPUT}}{\text{OUTPUT}}$ AS FILE channel number

FOR INPUT specifies an existing file as input file; FOR OUTPUT specifies creation of a new file. The channel number should be any integer between 1 and 12.

2. Statement to close the file:

> Line number CLOSE channel number

If no channel number is specified, BASIC-PLUS-2 closes all the open files. More than one file can be closed by using one CLOSE statement, the channel numbers are separated by commas.

3. Statement to read data from the file:

> Line number INPUT channel number, variable list

> Line number INPUT LINE # channel number, variable

INPUT LINE reads the entire line of data into the variable location specified. The entire line of data is treated as a character string.

> Line number LINPUT   # channel number, variable

Like INPUT LINE, the linput statement also reads the entire line of data except that the line feed and carriage return characters are not included.

4. Statement to write to a file:

> Line number PRINT # channel number, print list

Print list contains items you want to print. They can be constants, variables, or expressions.

5. Statement to reset the file pointer

> Line number RESTORE # channel number

The RESTORE # statement resets the specified file to its beginning from the current position of the file.

6. Statement to check for the end of ASCII file

> Line number IFEND # channel number THEN statement

If the file pointer is at the end, the statement following the keyword THEN will be executed. If the statement is a GOTO statement, two abbreviation forms can be used:

100   IFEND #3 THEN 1000   or

100   IFEND #3 GO TO 1000

> Line number IFMORE # channel number THEN statement

IFMORE statement tests whether the file pointer is at the end of the file specified. IF *not* at the end, BASIC-PLUS-2 executes the statement following the key word THEN. (If it is a GOTO statement, the same abbreviation forms as IFEND statement can be used.)

7. Statement for changing the margin of a file:

> Line number MARGIN # channel number, expression

The margin statement allows you to modify the margin setting of an ASCII file or the margin setting of the your terminal, if the channel number is not specified. Consider the following example:

```
10   MARGIN 5
20   FOR X = 1 TO 10
30       PRINT '*';
40   NEXT X

RUNNH
*****
*****                    ◄─────────────── the terminal width is set to 5,
                                          so that 10 asterisks were printed
                                          on two lines
```

Appendix F
Reserved Words in BASIC-PLUS

The following is a list of all reserved words in BASIC-PLUS that may not be used as variable names. This includes prefixing the names with FN (a function name) or postfixing either a "%" or "$" to the names. Any use of these variables will result in anything from syntax errors to programs that compile correctly but give improper results. One other reason not to use these names or names very similar is that code becomes very confusing with their use.

ABS	AND	APPEND	AS	ASCII
ASSIGN	ATN	ATTACH	BUFSIZ	BYE
CAT	CATALOGUE	CCONT	CHAIN	CHANGE
CHR	CLOSE	CLUSTERSIZE	COMP	COMPILE
CON	CONT	COS	COUNT	CUT
DATA	DATE	DEASSIGN	DEF	DELETE
DET	DIFF	DIM	ELSE	END
EQV	ERL	ERR	ERROR	EXP
EXTEND	FIELD	FILE	FILESIZE	FIZ
FNEND	FOR	GET	GOSUB	GOTO
HELLO	IDN	IF	IMP	INPUT
INPUTLINE	INSTR	INT	KEY	KILL
LEFT	LEN	LENGTH	LET	LINE
LIST	LISTNH	LOG	LOG10	LOGIN
LSET	MAGTAPE	MAT	MID	MODE
NAME	NEW	NEXT	NOEXTEND	NOT
NUM	NUM1	NUM2	OLD	ON
OPEN	OR	PEEK	PI	PLACE
POS	PRINT	PROD	PUT	QUO
RAD	RANDOM	RANDOMIZE	READ	REASSIGN
RECORD	RECOUNT	REM	RENAME	REPLACE
RESTORE	RESUME	RETURN	RIGHT	RND
RSET	RUN	RUNNH	SAVE	SCALE
SGN	SIN	SLEEP	SPACE	SQR
STATUS	STEP	STOP	STRING	SUM
SWAP	SYS	TAB	TAN	TAPE
THEN	TIME	TO	UNLESS	UNLOCK
UNSAVE	UNTIL	VAL	WAIT	WHILE
XLATE	XQR	ZER		

Appendix G

Selected User Recoverable Error Messages[1]

Message Printed	ERR	Meaning
?Illegal file name	2	The filename specified is not acceptable. It contains unacceptable characters or the filename specification format has been violated.
?Can't find file or account	5	The file or account number specified was not found on the device specified. Check for spelling error!
?I/O channel not open	9	Attempt to perform I/O on one of the twelve channels which has not been previously opened in the program.
?End of file on device	11	Attempt to perform input beyond the end of a data file; or a BASIC source file is called into memory and is found to contain no END statement.
?Keyboard WAIT exhausted	15	Time requested by WAIT statement has been exhausted with no input received from the specified keyboard.
?Line too long	47	Attempt to input a line longer than 255 characters (which includes any line terminator). Buffer overflows.
%Floating point error	48	Attempt to use a computed floating point number outside the range $1E\text{-}38 < n < 1E38$ excluding zero. If no transfer to an error handling routine is made, zero is returned as the floating value.
%Argument too large in EXP	49	Acceptable arguments are within the approximate range $-89 < arg < +88$. The value returned is zero.
%Data format error	50	A READ or INPUT statement detected data in an illegal format.
%Integer error	51	Attempt to use a computed integer outside the range $-32768 < n < 32767$.
?Illegal number	52	Integer overflow or underflow or floating point overflow. The range for integers is -32768 to $+32767$.
%Illegal argument in LOG	53	Negative or zero argument to LOG function. Value returned is the argument as passed to the function.

[1] Used with the ON ERROR statement. For a complete listing, refer to the BASIC-PLUS language manual.

%Imaginary square roots	54	Attempt to take square root of a number less than zero. The value returned is the square root of the absolute value of the argument.
?Subscript out of range	55	Attempt to reference an array element beyond the number of elements created for the array when it was dimensioned.
?Can't invert matrix	56	Attempt to invert a singular or nearly singular matrix.
?Out of data	57	The DATA list was exhausted and a READ requested additional data.
?ON statement out of range	58	The index value is an ON-GOTO or ON-GOSUB statement is less than one or greater than the number of line numbers in the list.
?Integer overflow, FOR loop	60	The integer index in a FOR loop attempted to go beyond 32766 or below −32767.
%Division by 0	61	Attempt by the user program to divide some quantity by zero. If no transfer is made to an error handler routine, a 0 is returned as the result.

Appendix H
How to Use the RSTS System[1]

Section 1 Information about your account.

Before you can have access to the RSTS system, you need to request an account number from your instructor.

Name _____

Class _____

Account No. _____

Password _____

Section 2 LOG-IN procedure.

1. Turn on keyboard, if off (knob on upper left corner of CRT).

2. Set the five switches at the top:

    2.1. Set "Full-Half" to Full.

    2.2. Set "Local-Remote" to Remote.

    2.3. Set "High-Low" to Low (If it is at high, type 'SET SPEED 300') hit return key and then set switch to Low).

    2.4. Set "Wide-Narrow" to Narrow.

    2.5. Set "Printer" to Off.

3. Push cap key on left side of keyboard down to 'Lock'.

4. Type 'HELLO' and hit return key.

5. After the header and # sign, type in your account number and hit return key.

6. After PASSWORD, enter your password (your password will not be printed), and then hit the return key.

7. If the LOG-IN is successful, a second header will appear followed by READY. READY indicates that the system is ready to accept any command. Now you can create a new program, recall an old program or run a library program.

Section 3 How to run a BASIC program on RSTS.

1. Request to become connected.
   Take LOG-IN PROCEDURE (see Section 1).

2. Input new program or recall old program.

---

[1] Variation in the system may exist depending on the system program and/or the type of terminal that is used.

2.1. If you are creating a new program, type 'NEW', enter new file name of up to six characters, hit return key, wait for the response, 'READY', then key in your instructions one by one.

2.2 If you are recalling your old program, type 'OLD', enter the name of your program, hit the return key, wait for 'READY,' and then change your old program.

3. When you have your program corrected, print out the program listing and run the program by taking the following steps:

3.1. Push the Extel printer power switch 'ON'.

3.2. Push the CRT printer switch 'ON'.

3.3. Type system command 'LIST', hit return key.

3.4. Type system command 'RUN' and hit return key when your program listing has finished.

3.5. Turn the printer switch 'OFF' when your run has finished.

4. Retain your program for later use:

4.1. If it is a new program, type system command 'SAVE'.

4.2. If it is an old program and some instructions have been changed, type system command 'REPLACE'.

4.3. Otherwise, you need not do anything.

5. Exit from the system.

Take Log-OFF procedure (see section 4).

6. Turn in your work. Put your name and class on upper right corner. Fold the paper to letter size.

Section 4   LOG-OFF procedure.

The user should properly log off before leaving terminal.

1. Type 'BYE' and hit return key.

2. The system responds 'CONFIRM:'. *One* of the following replies should be given:

?	Cause an explanation of possible responses to be printed.
N	Terminate the LOG-OFF procedure and the system replies READY.
Y	Proceed with LOG-OFF procedure. The system checks to see that the user has not exceeded the disk quota for this account number. If the user has used more than his share of disk storage, an appropriate message is printed and he is not allowed to leave the

	system until he is within his disk quota.
F	Fast LOG-OFF. Same as Y except that the system messages are not printed.
I	Cause individual files to be inspected so that users may delete them if desired. Responses to individual inspection are 'K' to delete the file, and return key to save the file.

Index